Truth, Grace, and Security

Truth, Grace, and Security

BRUNO CORDUAN

Translated into English by
WOLFGANG CORDUAN

RESOURCE *Publications* · Eugene, Oregon

TRUTH, GRACE, AND SECURITY

Originally published as *Vom Tagelöhnersohn zum Diplomaten: Mein Leben unter der Führung Gottes*© 2009 Edition Schönbuch 71088 Holzerlingen, Germany.

Copyright © 2012 Bruno Corduan. All rights reserved. Except for brief quotations in critical publications or reviews, no part of this book may be reproduced in any manner without prior written permission from the publisher. Write: Permissions, Wipf and Stock Publishers, 199 W. 8th Ave., Suite 3, Eugene, OR 97401.

Resource Publications
An Imprint of Wipf and Stock Publishers
199 W. 8th Ave., Suite 3
Eugene, OR 97401

www.wipfandstock.com

ISBN 13: 978-1-61097-700-5

Manufactured in the U.S.A.

All scripture quotations, unless otherwise indicated, are taken from *New American Standard Bible*. electronic edition. La Habra, CA: The Lockman Foundation, 1986.

Scripture quotations marked (ESV) are taken from: *The Holy Bible: English Standard Version*. Wheaton: Standard Bible Society, 2001.

Scripture quotations marked (KJV) are taken from: *The Holy Bible: King James Version*. Electronic Edition of the 1900 Authorized Version. Bellingham, WA: Logos Research Systems, Inc., 2009.

Scripture quotations marked (NASB95) are taken from: *New American Standard Bible: 1995 Update*. LaHabra, CA: The Lockman Foundation, 1995.

Scripture quotations marked (NIV) are taken from: *The New International Version*. Grand Rapids, MI: Zondervan, 2011.

Scripture quotations marked (NLT) are taken from: Tyndale House Publishers. *Holy Bible: New Living Translation*. 3rd ed. Carol Stream, IL: Tyndale House Publishers, 2007.

Scripture quotations marked (GNT) are taken from: American Bible Society. *The Holy Bible: The Good News Translation*. 2nd ed. New York: American Bible Society, 1992.

Contents

PART 1: A LIFE GUIDED BY JESUS: THE SON OF A DAY LABORER BECOMES A DIPLOMAT

Introduction to Part 1   3
1. Childhood and Early Youth   7
2. Life with My Own Family   38
3. On Foreign Soil   46
4. Coming Home   54
5. My Service among the People of God   61
6. The Evening of Our Years in Pilgerheim Weltersbach   65
7. Working Together on the Church Board   67
8. Closing Remarks   69

PART 2: PRESENTATION OF BASIC CONCEPTS DERIVED FROM THE BIBLE

Introduction to Part 2   73
9. Living by God's Ordinances   79
10. God's Covenant with Humanity   85
11. God, the Trinity   93
12. The Visible Beginning of the Plan of Salvation   100
13. Living for the Honor of Jesus in the World   109
14. Keeping an Eye on the Goal   125
15. The Equipment of Jesus' Disciples for Service   133
16. Baptism   140
17. Scientific Critique of the Bible   150

Contents

- 18 The Work of the Holy Spirit 155
- 19 Grace Is Greater than Reward 165
- 20 The True Pontifex Maximus; or, Jesus, the Bridge to God 172
- 21 Receiving Blessings and Being a Blessing 181
- 22 The Return of Jesus Christ 188
- 23 Before the Judgment Seat of Christ 196

PART 1

A Life Guided by Jesus
The Son of a Day Laborer Becomes a Diplomat

Introduction to Part 1

THE BIBLE IS A much-read book.[1] It is also a book about which much has been written. Seemingly uncountable pages of print seek to inform us not only about the nature of the Bible and its content, but also about its proper interpretation and its influence on us in our daily lives. Needless to say, what this mountain of literature asserts about these subjects goes into many different, often contradictory, directions. This variety has many causes. We can certainly account for much of it on the basis of different confessions advanced by churches and denominations, but the public media—newspapers, magazine articles, radio talk shows, and television programs—also play an important role.

Chances are good that you may find yourself reading or hearing assertions, supposedly based on the Bible, that may seem totally novel to you, and you may have a hard time understanding what some alleged authority is saying. The fault may not be yours; the reason may very well be the indisputable fact that not everything you read or hear is theologically or historically sound. If you cannot follow someone's exposition, it could be because what they are saying is purely the product of their imagination and personal creativity.

Are publishers and editors not responsible for the truth of what they put out, if not legally, then at least on the basis of a code of ethics? Except in the crassest cases of obvious libel, publishers or journalists are not obligated to set forth proofs for their reports or presentations, nor do they have to apologize for any obvious misinformation, and what they write about religion and theology is no exception. Furthermore, even if they should issue a correction, most likely it will not receive the same degree of exposure as their original erroneous reports. Consequently, many misconceptions about the Christian faith are just left floating in an intellectual

---

1. Unless otherwise indicated all Scripture references will be from the *New American Standard Bible* (NASB).

ether, and people are encouraged to feel free to believe or not to believe, as they see fit. Like it or not, on the whole there seems to be a lack of accountability in news reports in terms of controversial matters in general, and in religion and issues of faith in particular.

Focusing now specifically on the Christian faith, we are all aware that differing versions of the Christian doctrines, as they are advocated by many churches and congregations, frequently clash with each other. For instance, consider the question of what God's expectations are concerning the actions of human beings. Some folks believe that our ministers have spent a long time and effort studying to qualify for their positions, making them experts on what the Bible teaches. If they lay out for us certain standards of how we should live, and if we abide by them, that must surely be sufficient. Others point out that a personal commitment is essential; the New Testament asks us to turn our lives over to Jesus Christ in personal faith. There certainly is no unanimity.

One could reason that fulfilling all the obligations conveyed to us by the experts implies a personal commitment to Christ. As in other world religions, Christianity, as it is proclaimed from many pulpits, focuses on the demand for us to perform various acts of piety at some minimal level of commitment. Just as in other religions, we are asked to demonstrate our devotion by means of not only making routine observances but perhaps also by maintaining strict disciplines, giving offerings, and—particularly in Christendom— attending as many meetings, worship services, Bible studies, seminars, workshops, and conferences as possible. By these means, believers are assured that they can pacify an angry God—insofar as they are even permitted to think of God as offended by sin. As I will describe in my biography, even as a young boy who often could only study the Scriptures surreptitiously, it became quite clear to me that my own piety could not possibly be sufficient for me. I could not attain to a righteousness that could satisfy a God from whom I was separated by my sin, even if he (perhaps paradoxically) says about himself "I am gracious." But, I learned that this is a God who, rather than waiting for us to do the impossible and fulfill our quota of righteousness, freely offers righteousness as a gift to everyone who accepts the sacrifice of his own Son on our behalf as sufficient.

Here is my main thesis for this book: *when we are talking about Jesus, the Christ of God, we are not referring to a religion, but to a person.* That means that we need to focus on who he is and what he has done, not on our own actions. As a corollary it follows that if I could conceivably achieve a level of righteousness that is acceptable to God by means of my own piety, then the death of Jesus would have been unnecessary, a vain act by a confused God.

In the first part of this book I have sketched out my life, which from early childhood on has been directed and guided by Jesus, the Son of God, the Second Person of the Trinity. I have often been astounded, and even today I still marvel, at the ways in which my life has been better than it might have been because I trusted the Son of God. Since I have led a normal middle-class life I have often been asked if I am a pious or religious person. In response I have always sought to express the conviction that my personal piety is of no consequence; it could never be sufficient to open heaven's gate for me. The crucial issue is that all my life I have placed my life in the hands of Jesus, and he has been my constant guide and companion. In the following pages, I shall recount some of the events of my life and how Jesus has led and guided me throughout.

A typical Bible study or sermon begins with an exposition, followed by an illustration. In this book, I am reversing the process. Once you have seen what God has done in my life, you may want to know more about the fundamental truths as they have emerged from my study of the Bible. Thus, in the second part I will lay them out more systematically. You may find that, because I try to remain as true to the Bible as I possibly can, my conclusions may differ significantly from the messages you may have heard from the pulpits or read in the books of those who put their own ideas ahead of what God has revealed. I am not putting forward anything new, but I am calling us back to what the Bible teaches. Today, as perhaps throughout much of the history of the church, a theology that is both scriptural and a magnification of the grace of God is often pushed into a corner. Those who do so may even describe themselves as conservative or evangelical, but they may have been caught up in substituting morality and religiosity for the gospel as given to us in the Bible. Theoretically, there should be nothing novel in what you read here because the Bible has not changed. But speaking practically, the same truths need to be taught repeatedly to each new generation. It is precisely the drive towards novelty and the adaptation of the biblical message to the standards of the world that frequently obscures the clear teachings of the Bible.

Ultimately you, the reader, need to come to your own conclusions once you have engaged the Bible itself.

1

Childhood and Early Youth

MY HOME

I WAS BORN IN Germany in 1926 as the son of the day laborer Max Corduan. Our family, which only a few generations ago bore the name of "von Lettow," had been involved in an inheritance dispute. A special court for aristocracy awarded the family the name "Corduan" and assigned to us special property rights. This ruling was satisfactory. My grandfather was the owner of a large farm with much livestock and land, and thus he was relatively well-to-do. Additionally, he was also a master shoemaker and had another source of income in the field of shoe manufacturing. My grandfather intended that my father should receive an education that would make it possible for him to be a teacher.

All this changed, as one is wont to say, overnight. My grandfather's property was totally destroyed in a fire. This event was the financial ruin of the family because in those days, in contrast to current practice, he did not carry any fire insurance. There no longer was any money for my father to study to become a teacher. The family was now reduced to nothing but maintaining a livelihood. What type of work my father did prior to his being called up for military duty in 1913, I do not rightly know. After World War I, due to the high unemployment rate of that time, my father worked in quite a variety of jobs. Throughout, in spite of the current conditions, my father placed a high value on proper and appropriate conduct in keeping with one's social standing. When I was born he worked on an estate. The owner would have liked to have made him the caretaker of the entire property, but somehow that did not work out. Later on the water company responsible for the regulation of the river Wipper turned over to him the supervision of the maintenance of the Wipper. He was, therefore, in today's language, the manager.

In 1934 our family moved from the village of Alt-Schlawe into the town of Schlawe. This move was especially important to us four children. It gave us an opportunity to acquire a good education because in the little village of Alt-Schlawe there was only a three-room elementary school. I was eight years old at the time, and the change pleased me tremendously. I really enjoyed the fact that I was now receiving an education at an actual eight-grade boy's school.[2]

In the new school, there were three of us who tried hard to become the top student, designated by the Latin term, *Primus*. Our teacher, a committed follower of Adolf Hitler who, following the German system, remained with our class from grade to grade, had divided the class into three groups. He made each of the three of us the leader of one of the groups, thereby implementing what he called the "*Führer* principle."

My mother, too, was happy with the change. But then quite suddenly she began feeling very weak, and, after some medical tests, the diagnosis was that she had diabetes. In those days the efficacy of insulin was not fully accepted. She only received injections for a short while. The other medications prescribed by the doctors were ineffective. Finally she fell into a coma and was hospitalized.

My grandmother came to stay with us for a little while. She went to the hospital to see how my mother was doing. I was playing out of doors with my siblings when she returned. To my immense horror she told us that my mother had passed away. I have no independent recollection of what happened next. I was told about it later. As the family was trying to come to grips with this sorrowful news they received another shock:

---

2. An eighth-grade basic education was essentially the lowest level of education acceptable in Germany. We can contrast this level with "high school" (*Gymnasium*), which normally takes twelve years, resulting in the *Abitur*. Usually the *Abitur* constitutes the minimum requirement for subsequent study at a university. This is an important fact to keep in mind in the light of events to follow.—Trans.

Bruno was missing. After several hours of searching I had not been found. Finally someone looked under the living room table, which had been covered with a long tablecloth, and there I was. From the moment that I received the news of my mother's death, I had only one thought namely, "Where is my mommy now?" That question gripped me and did not let go of me for many years because from my mother I had learned: "Death is not death, but life" (John 5:24).

Since my father was a lay preacher, he had a small library. I would often secretly search through it and study his books in order to find the answer to the question that continued haunting me: "Where is my mommy now?" Through a special grace I was given a clear answer: my mommy was now with Jesus. That solution brought me peace. On the other hand I simultaneously recognized the necessity of belonging to Jesus myself. I did so in the best way I knew how: by resolving to let Jesus be my Lord and turning my life over to him—quietly, and without any outward ceremony, since I knew of none and wouldn't have been able to perform one if I did. (Now I know that there is none but that this is a personal transaction between the Lord and the sinner coming to him.) Unfortunately I had no one in whom I could or wanted to confide. Then, when I had just turned nine, I wanted to make my conversion publicly known, but neither my father nor my stepmother took me seriously. Instead they instructed me to pursue a lifestyle based on my works rather than on a direct relationship with my Lord. They admonished me to conform my life from there on out to God's laws and various rules of piety. I was disappointed, but not frustrated. My life with Jesus had started, and he has always been true to me, just as I have always desired to be true to him. It was not always easy, but he has always sustained me.

SCHOOL YEARS DURING THE HITLER REGIME

Our family lived in the Fellowship House of the "Christian Faith Community." This evangelical fellowship, which considered itself as a part of the state church, belonged to the Association of Pentecostal Assemblies in Mühlheim an der Ruhr, which had been founded and administered by the frequently misunderstood, and always controversial, Pastor Paul. Aside from Sunday school and the common additional worship services, I also eagerly attended the children's services of the Protestant State Church. When I reached the appropriate age, I also attended meetings of the YMCA, of which my older brother was already a member.

Naturally, my classmates were fully aware of where I lived, and that I considered myself a child of God. I made no attempt to conceal this fact, and during our religious studies class, as long as that remained as a part of the curriculum, I participated fully in our teacher's presentations. My classmates called me the Pentecostal ox, and after the religious studies class, they would kneel before me in mock obeisance. This did not particularly bother me because I was the top student in all subjects.

HITLER YOUTH

My age group was the first to come under the new law requiring participation in *Jungvolk* (the Nazi youth organization) upon completion of the tenth year of life. My father advised those in charge that in trying to raise four children he did not have the financial ability to acquire the required outfits; in other words, he would not purchase a uniform for me. My health had become quite fragile, causing me to be bedridden for weeks on end. According to the doctors my complaints were symptomatic of cystic fibrosis. When both my brother Benno and I were sent to a rehabilitation clinic on the island Norderney for a time of rest and recuperation, the NSV (*Nationalsozialistische Volkswohlfahrt*, the Nazi-welfare organization) provided both of us with a complete Hitler Youth uniform with nothing missing. The reason for this generosity was revealed to us later by the regional head of the NSV, Herr Sylvester.

Herr Sylvester made an appointment with my father and during the conversation touched on many different topics. After all, my father had been awarded two medals during World War I. Because of his job, he worked closely with the *Reichsarbeitsdienst* (Reich's job service). He also participated actively in the Association of Large Families (for, after my father remarried, we became a family with six children). All those matters provided plenty of topics for conversation. Finally, Herr Sylvester came to the real reason for his visit. He called my father a worthy contemporary and said that, furthermore, our large family was very important to the city. The NSV had already honored the family by sending his sons, Benno and Bruno, to a children's home for rest and recuperation on two occasions. Furthermore, they had provided both boys with the best Hitler Youth uniforms, so that our family would not be left behind other families. One thing, however, was lacking, namely, that my father should join the NSDAP (*Nationalsozialistische Deutsche Arbeiter Partei*, the Nazi Party). Even today I am amused by my father's reply. He stated, "In one of his recent addresses the Führer pointed out that all Germans are National Socialists, but that the best are members of the party. I ask for your understanding, because, you see, I do not consider myself worthy to be called one of the best Germans." Noticeably, after this conversation with the NSV regional head, there was always an underlying tension whenever we dealt with party members, and for me, personally, that tension became quite drastic and palpable at times, as you will see below.

As already mentioned above, I had no choice but to be a member of the Hitler Youth. I looked for, and found, an opportunity to avoid the common Hitler Youth indoctrination. I requested to serve in the *Motor-HJ* (the motorized Hitler Youth). With time I became a leader. Together with my brother, I was very active, and we learned a lot about motor vehicles. At age fifteen, I acquired the license to operate motorcycles, and soon I became known as a good motorcyclist. The NSKK (*Nationalsozialstisches Kraftfahrer Korps*, the Nazi Motor Vehicle Corps) recognized me as a good trainer. At age seventeen, the city, upon request by the NSKK, issued me a license that gave me the right to train motorcycle operators and to administer examinations for motorcycle licenses. We organized, in conjunction with the NSKK, a number of motorcycle meets, which our city really enjoyed and appreciated. The party leadership now left me alone, and the Hitler Youth leadership recognized my service. Indeed, I received the request to expand my activities to the regional level, and I was even issued a red band designating me as *Motor HJ* leader.

However, I also remained active in the church and the YMCA. One time we presented a play based on the parable of the wedding feast, in which I played the leading role. My point is that I did not hide my Christian affiliation. On the surface all appeared to be as it was supposed to be. However, somehow I had the feeling that the leaders of the party and the head of the Hitler Youth were not willing to let things rest. It troubled them that they could not bring me to see things their way. So, they used whatever means they had available to put pressure on me.

The day came when my peers from school were to be initiated into the NSDAP. The event was a festive occasion and took place in a large auditorium. And, of course, I was ordered to be present as well. However, my name was the only one that was never called. I was publicly branded as one who was not worthy to be a party member. Everyone also knew that I belonged to a religious "sect" and that I attended and actively participated in the meetings of the YMCA. I had been publicly humiliated.

What that meant back in those days is difficult to fathom today. Shortly after this event, the party formed a goon squad to lie in wait for me when I returned from the YMCA meeting. Their purpose was to give me a severe thrashing, possibly to put me within an inch of my life. These kinds of vigilante attacks had become common in Germany and were praised by the government under the rationale that the Nazi ideology was flowing in the blood of the German people and that they were learning to act on it themselves without directions from above. A leader of the SA (*Sturmabteilung*, a paramilitary arm of the Nazi Party), a good acquaintance of mine, alerted me of the impending attack. His message to me was both a warning and a threat: I could avoid the thrashing if I no longer attended those meetings. Still, certain of my security in Jesus, I did not change my routine, but went to the next YMCA meeting. And I was not assaulted. The very SA leader who was supposed to prevent my attendance at the YMCA meetings, and who had given me the ultimatum, used his own people to prevent the goon squad from attacking me. To this day, I find this almost incomprehensible.

Around the same time, I volunteered to attend a special course in first aid. Once again, I found myself carrying a leading role, which made it possible for me to express my God-given talents. Previously, during a camping trip I had already come to the attention of several high level leaders of the *Reichsjugendführung* (the Reich's Youth Guidance Service). Now I was taking part in a special course under their oversight. The consequence was that I was recommended for admission to the Langemark scholarship (*Langemarkstudium*). This was a scholarship issued by a foundation formed after the First World War by the parents of two student regiments who had been decimated at the battle of Langemark. Its intent was to give disadvantaged but highly gifted young people the opportunity to attend a university and earn an advanced degree. This recommendation came without consultation with or even the knowledge of the local party leadership. And remember, I only had an eighth-grade education.

BEGINNING A CAREER

At the time of graduation from public school I was encouraged to continue my education at the trade school in the town of Stolp. Having obtained the appropriate recommendations in writing, I traveled to Stolp for the entrance exam, which I passed with high marks. However, the tuition for this school was thirty deutsche marks per month. Most of that amount was waived, leaving but five marks for me to pay. Unfortunately my parents could not see their way clear to providing even this small amount. Isn't it interesting that my having missed this particular training program did not impact my later career negatively? My Lord in his faithfulness always provided in ways that, in retrospect, appear nothing short of miraculous. The city administration of Schlawe (my hometown) offered me an entry-level position for upper grade regional public service. After the completion of my probationary period I passed the examination at the Pomeranian School for Community Affairs in Stettin. My supervisors in the city administration were amazed at my success because prior to that time only one young man, whose formal education far exceeded mine, had been able to pass the exam. By this time, it was already the autumn of 1943. Normally, after passing this examination, I should have been offered the position of a tenured civil servant. However, the Ministry of the Interior had not yet approved the new ordinance for regional trainees. So, I was offered a contract as a hired public servant.[3]

CALL-UP FOR MILITARY SERVICE

A common question, heavily debated among young men in those days, was whether, for conscience's sake, they should or even must refuse

---

3. There is an important distinction hidden within this terminology. The actual German word for a "tenured civil servant" is *Beamter*, for which there is no equivalent in English. This is the word for a permanently appointed, rather than contracted, government worker. This institution preceded the Nazi era and continues to this day. The *Beamten* collectively form the permanent operational backbone of the government. They have a hierarchy of ranks that are similar to ranks in the military, and, thus, to rise in rank implies a permanent increase in stature and authority, not just an advance in pay grade. Almost reminiscent of a nobility, or again, similar to the military, according to proper etiquette, a *Beamter* should be addressed by his rank, e.g., *Herr Oberinspektor*. It is not permissible for them to go on strike, but neither can they be fired, except under extreme circumstances. In the absence of anything equivalent in the English language or in American society, I will reluctantly use the inadequate term *civil servant*.—Trans.

military service. Personally, I did not wrestle with this question. As to why not, I can only answer by pointing to the fact that I had given my life to my Lord Jesus. Since I had turned my *entire* life over to Jesus as my Lord, I trusted him that he would lead me on the right path in all areas of my life. Sadly, so many people only give their *spiritual* lives to Jesus, but not their *entire* lives. In the following pages I will point out what ramifications this had for me in reference to taking up arms, which, I believe, a Christian should actually avoid. My Lord, in his divine wisdom, guided me much better than anything I could have accomplished with my human understanding. Sometimes people feel pressured to discover, or maybe even contrive, various principles, which they believe to be integral to a genuine Christian life. They desire to live by rules, and if they do not know of any applicable ones, they have a hard time trusting in the person of God himself.

Let me get a little ahead of myself and state now that eventually I was called up for military service, but it was one year later than my peers. By that time several of them had been wounded or had come home because their term was over for the time being, I was still waiting for my draft notification. As I already stated, I did not refuse military service but rather left that matter to my Lord, and he guided me marvelously through the war years.

As mentioned above, our family lived in the Fellowship House of the Christian Faith Community. Because my father had connections to persons in the opposition to Hitler, our family was kept informed of the actions of the Nazi Party and its oppressiveness. When I was sixteen years old, I was ordered to show up for my physical examination for military service. When I was there, I did not mention that I was in the top ten of our regional Reich's Youth Competitions. Instead, I just stood there letting my shoulders droop. As a result I was deferred for one year. But only six months later, I was ordered to report for a re-evaluation, which I knew could only result in my being declared qualified for wartime service. So, I had to change tactics. To the question of the presiding officer to which branch I wanted to be assigned I replied: "medical personnel." I received a severe tongue lashing and was ordered to report back after getting dressed. A sergeant in the medical service, who was assisting the evaluation committees, encouraged me to hold my ground. He did say, however, to call it the "medical corps" rather than "medical service." Ultimately, the lieutenant colonel informed me after some further discussion that I was being drafted into the infantry.

You will recall that I had already received the notice that I had been selected for the Langemark scholarship so that I could study medicine. Naturally, I had made the logical connection that, therefore, I should be employed in the military in a medically related field. For the moment, I continued to pursue my career as an entry-level civil servant in the county government.

Then came the year of 1943 and my seventeenth birthday. Via special messenger from the Hitler Youth, I was ordered to report to the hotel Deutscher Hof immediately. By the time I got there, a number of Hitler boys had gathered there already. A Hitler Youth leader gave the order to form two columns, with the leaders of the Hitler Youth on the left, and everyone else on the right. After we had done so, in walked the *Bann-Führer* (the group leader), to whom Hitler Youth units in the Schlawe region reported. He was accompanied by high-ranking, full-time Hitler Youth leaders from Berlin and several SS officers. The man who carried the highest rank made it clear to us that it was now incumbent upon Germany to muster all her strength in order to win the war. This attempt to rally all available resources included the formation of a "Hitler Youth Division," which would greatly enhance Germany's fighting ability. The *Reichsjugendführer*, Arthur Axmann, a politician of cabinet rank, planned to present the "Hitler Youth Division" to the Führer on his birthday on April 20, 1943. This unit, composed entirely of "volunteers" from the Hitler Youth, was to be an elite unit under the guidance of the Waffen SS (the armed branch of the SS).

Then he challenged the gathered Hitler boys, with the following words: "All those who want to volunteer take a step forward. The leaders do not have to do so because they have already volunteered." I was one of those leaders, yet I had no recollection of ever having volunteered. Nor would this be the only time for this to happen. He continued with the order: "Leader group, turn right, form column right. March!" And so we marched through the back door into the hotel. The hallway that led into a small room made a right turn. Straight ahead, however, was a bathroom. I took the straight path, (this time literally), into the bathroom and locked myself inside. There I waited anxiously for what would happen. Sometime later, when all the commotion had ended, I quietly let myself out and walked home.

A short time later I learned from friends that when I had disappeared, all the SS officers and the Hitler Youth leaders had called my name and searched for me. Later, I also heard from an acquaintance that the SS officers had seized my military file from the recruitment offices. They hung on to these files tenaciously, as I learned later, all the while maintaining that I was one of those who had volunteered. All they needed now was my signature, which they would submit at a later date.

After spending some time in prayer, I made contact with the regional recruitment offices in Köslin. I asked advice on how I should conduct myself since my goal was to become a medical doctor. I was quite convinced that in this situation, just as much as in any other, Jesus, my Lord and Savior, would guide me correctly. The recruitment officer replied that at this time they would not take a stand on the volunteer notice. They requested that I come to Köslin for consultation.

On the train trip, which lasted about an hour, I sat across from a Navy boatswain. In the course of the conversation I told him a little bit about my life, including my shenanigans at the recruitment examination, and a number of other things. Shortly before we reached our destination, he said to me, "You could not know who was sitting across from you. I am a psychologist, who conducts examinations for officer candidates for the navy. You might as well forget your desire to become a physician for the time being. Because of the current state of the war, that will certainly come to nothing. But you stand an excellent chance of being accepted as an officer candidate in the navy. Everything else you can worry about later. Go to the recruiting office, to the navy division, and request the documents for volunteering." And that is what I did. I encountered a number of close acquaintances there, who handed me the forms, but said that there was virtually no chance that I would be accepted.

When I arrived back at home, my grandmother (who also was a devout disciple of Jesus), my father, and I knelt down together and laid my problem before the Lord. Then I sent my volunteer request for officer candidacy off to the navy.

Soon thereafter I received orders from the navy to report to Stralsund for a seven-day evaluation. Trusting fully in my Lord Jesus, I started on my way. What could I expect? Were my acquaintances at the recruitment command post right when they said to me, "With only an eighth-grade education, you might as well not bother"? At the navy base

I was given oral and written tests for six days, and then we spent one day in the gym for physical evaluation. During those tests, my personal studies, which had been motivated as an intended candidate for medical school, helped me tremendously. At the end of the examinations, when the results were announced, approximately half of the aspirants were rejected. On my document it said, "Accepted as navy sea officer candidate. You will receive your induction notice for training at Stralsund. Report to the appropriate recruitment command post." When I arrived at the post, I received hearty congratulations from those who had assured me of the futility of my plans not all that long ago. Then I was issued an ID card and a lapel pin designating me as an officer candidate in the navy.

REICH LABOR SERVICE

By this time some of my classmates, some of them even sporting the Iron Cross, had become battle-hardened veterans and had come home on leave. Meanwhile, being a compliant youngster, I continued to make my daily track to City Hall. I received notice concerning other friends and classmates that they had received a wooden cross and were buried far away from home. I contemplated the irony of this contrast. Had my Lord created a scenario of confusion? And I could not help myself but to think that, yes he had, not only in appearance, but in reality.

I must confess that the relief I was feeling during the subsequent events was tempered with a certain amount of trepidation. My brother Benno had a friend whose mother had worked as a custodian for the city administration. Both boys were a year older than me. My brother was in the Reich Labor Service. One day his friend received a summons to report to the Waffen SS for induction. He refused to comply but eventually was forced to obey. None of us ever found out what exactly happened to Benno's friend, other than that he was shot for refusing to obey orders. Since the Waffen SS considered me a volunteer to serve in their ranks, some of the townspeople, not to mention myself, now felt a certain amount of justified apprehension.

Contrary to the wishes of the recruiting post, the Waffen SS held onto my files because they supposedly needed them to prepare for my induction into the Waffen SS, more specifically into the Hitler Youth division of their group. They were, however, unsuccessful in asserting themselves because my files were also being requested by the navy for my induction as a sea officer candidate. The upshot was that, according to an acquaintance who worked at the recruiting post, who confided in me, my files allegedly could not be located. In order for the official boards to be able to stop having to save face, on December 15, 1943, I was called up to report to the Labor Service at Neddemin in Mecklenburg.

Life is seldom without complications. However, in all situations I sensed the hand of my Lord. One evening, it was my unit's turn to be on watch. The watch supervisor on duty was a volunteer, just like me. It turned out that, of all possible nights, the colonel in charge of all units decided to check up on our performance and make his own rounds. He discovered that the aforementioned watch supervisor had already recorded all of his entries in the log book for the entire night. The information he recorded included his regularly timed rounds to the various guard posts outside. Filling out his log ahead of time certainly saved him quite a bit of time and effort, but it also entailed a great risk, and he had come out on the losing side of this gamble. The colonel was determined to charge our supervisor with dereliction of duty. In order to make his case, he needed my confirmation that our supervisor had not left the watch room all night, and so he turned to me for corroboration because my duties had been inside the building the entire time. If I were to confirm that the watch supervisor on duty had not actually checked on the outside guards, my word would serve as clear evidence of his having falsified the book, which would certainly be considered gross misconduct.

But my own recollections were nebulous. While it certainly seemed to me that he had not ventured outside at any time, I really had not paid close enough attention to swear to it. I could not account with certainty for whatever he had been doing during the times that I was physically present in the room. Also, for the sake of solidarity, I really did not care to testify against a member of our unit and verify the accusation that he had not checked on the outside guards. But I did see an open door. It would be possible for me to manipulate the truth just enough that our supervisor would be spared of any punishment, and he pressured me heavily to lie on his behalf, specifically, he wanted me to assert with certainty that he had not been inside the building at the required times. On the other hand, the colonel threatened that, if I would not confirm his suspicions, I must also have been sleeping on the watch, and I would receive three days of hard labor.

He gave me half an hour to contemplate my options. No matter how I would testify, I would find myself in serious straits. As I prayerfully committed the situation to my Lord Jesus, for the first time in my life, He gave me a clear answer that my prayer had been heard. So I adhered to my minimally truthful testimony, sticking to the exact boundaries of what I could say with certainty, even in the face of punishment. I maintained without reservation that I could not confirm one or the other side based on my direct clear memory. As a result, the supervisor was charged only with falsifying his log book, but not with serious misconduct, and he was arrested and sentenced to three days of incarceration. Needless to say, he was upset with me because I had not lied to save his neck. But now the question was, would the colonel also be angry with me for not supporting the much stronger charges, which he had wanted to bring against the supervisor?

As a matter of fact, he had greater discernment than that. He gave me to understand that he considered my conduct in this case as clear evidence of good character. Temporarily, during the supervisor's involuntary absence, he placed me in charge of the unit, and he gave orders assigning me to the administrative office. This incident so fortified my trust in Jesus as my Lord that it left a strong imprint on the rest of my life. Anyone's faith would profit from such encouragement. I cannot promise you that God will intervene miraculously in your life, but I can say that I would never have had the chance to see him do so if I had taken matters into my own hands and lied.

IN THE NAVY

On February 2, 1944, I was discharged from the Labor Service as a supervisor. Then at the end of March the mailman delivered my induction orders to report to the parent unit of the Third Naval Division in Stralsund. There we underwent a week of testing, the so-called entrance exam, while we were still in plain clothes. The passing of this examination was a prerequisite to the final acceptance as a sea officer candidate. We had to answer questions, both orally and in writing, about a wide range of subjects, such as mathematics, history, biology, geography, etc. With my limited, elementary education it did not seem possible for me to answer all those questions. Then, on my birthday, April 4, 1944, I received my military passbook as a sea officer candidate. Again I had successfully passed an examination.

Having arrived at the training site at Schwedenschanze, we new inductees were assigned accommodations in the barracks. We slept in a room with fourteen companions,[4] and the company commander designated me as "senior." Then came the first Sunday. Because in the opinion of our company sergeant we still had to learn how to walk and to salute properly, we were not given liberty. After lunch we were resting on our bunks. It was sleeting outside, which made any notion of leaving the barracks uninviting.

After a while two of my companions got up from their bunks and sat down at the table. Their conversation drifted through various topics. Then without any discernible cause, their conversation turned to religion. They got quite worked up over the notion that any of their contemporaries could still believe in God and the Bible. The Bible was full of contradictions and mistakes. Modern science and archeology had clearly proven it, and everyone knew that. When the conversation came to a lull, I rose up and asked them, "Tell me, is that really true what you just said about the Bible?" They looked at me with astonishment that I, one of them, who had passed all of the examinations and had to be an intelligent person, even their senior, could ask such a question. Then they asked me, "Do you really still believe in the Bible?" I admitted to them that until now I had always believed in God and the Bible. Maybe they could enlighten me, since the matter seemed so obvious to them. So they stated that everyone knew that the Bible contained many contradictions. I asked them if this judgment also applied to the New Testament. They asserted that in the New Testament alone there were more than one hundred errors. In response, I asked them if they would perhaps point out some of them to me. They replied they could show me at least fifty. Then I pulled my New Testament out of my pocket and said, "Please show me just three." After a time of unsuccessful searching I asked them if perhaps they were looking for "blessed are the weak-minded." Then I showed them that the Bible says, "Blessed are those who are spiritually poor," not mentally poor.[5]

---

4. In German, the natural word would be *Kamerad* (comrade), which does not have the political connotations that it has in English and other languages. In German, the political word would be *Genosse* or *Parteigenosse*. Thus, even though *comrade* would be the most obvious translation, its association with political, particularly communist, movements makes *companion* a better choice. Americans most of the time speak of "army buddies," but that expression is a little too informal for this situation.—Trans.

5. In German there is only one word, *Geist*, which does double duty combining the meanings for both "mind" and "spirit" in English. Usually the context makes it quite clear what aspect of the word is meant.—Trans.

At any rate our conversation ended with these two companions withdrawing their assertion in a high state of perplexity. Everybody sensed the tension in the room. Wasn't it a bit risky, and perhaps unwise, for me to take such a stand this early in our training? This was only the very beginning of this designated time period. We would spend four months together in our basic training. Would my companions, whose squad leader I was, accept their defeat in good grace? Would my superiors, whom I really did not know as yet and whose actions I was not in a position to predict, label me as "religious" and make life difficult for me? I believe that nobody will be surprised to learn that I placed the entire situation, prayerfully and with childlike faith, into the hands of my Lord. I felt a deep peace come over me and enjoyed an excellent night's sleep.

It was now Monday morning. Even today I am still puzzled how the boatswain's mate of our unit had already been informed of events that happened only a few hours ago. But first I had to make my report to the boatswain's mate: "Room four ready! All awake and healthy! Ready for inspection!" The boatswain's mate hardly acknowledged my report and walked straight to my locker. With a swift move he grabbed my books—my New Testament and my devotional book, *Kleinode Göttlicher Verheißungen* (*Treasury of God's Promises*) by Spurgeon. "Well, here goes," I thought to myself. Was I nervous! Then the boatswain asked me a question: "Did you read your devotions today?" I answered in the affirmative. Then he asked me to tell him what it had said. In my nervousness my mind went totally blank. As punishment for my forgetfulness I had to do twenty push-ups.

From here on for the duration of my time in the navy I was known as a Christian and, as I will describe later, Jesus, my Lord and Master, was by my side faithfully and sometimes noticeably. It was certainly clear to me that I could not, like a brazen mushroom, poke my head out of the flower bed. But I was also sure that any mistake in my manners and deportment, as well as my performance, would be very critically evaluated. Such scrutiny, of course, would apply not only to basic training but also to the rest of my career.

We could hardly believe what we heard when the battalion commander in April 1944 informed us that we would be given the normal four months of training with a regular examination at the end, just as in peacetime. The decision would then be made whether we would be appointed for a sea officer candidacy. Right now we were only applicants.

Thus began the so-called drill. We learned to walk, to march, to salute, and to handle a weapon properly. We were drilled in marching with a rifle, which was a carbine 98k. You really learn to appreciate the weight of the weapon after exercising with it for three hours. The exercise area was paved with ground-up bricks, and for reason of its color was called the "blood acre." The amount of the dripping sweat would have to be measured in terms of liters, though nobody ever seriously attempted to assess the amount. A part of our training was learning to master the kind of boats called "cutters," which could be operated by rowing them or by sailing. These vessels were equipped with fourteen oars, and there were seven benches on which the oarsmen would sit.

I will never forget one particular sailing excursion. There were already dark clouds on the horizon when we set out. We were approximately in the middle of the sound when the first gust of wind hit us. A shroud (a side support of the mainsail) was torn out of the gunwale. We continued our crossing in this storm and finally reached the other side of the sound, though our sails had been blown down.

There is one other event that I would like to mention in passing. It was only a very minor event, but it had required a lot of self-control on my part. It was a test of my ability to maintain control of the fourteen recruits with whom I shared sleeping quarters as their senior. There were few times outside of duty when somebody did not come up with a stupid or off-color joke. You could almost get the impression that it was an inevitable necessity for these young men to air out their brains by continuously displaying some manner of filthy thinking, and over time it had a negative impact on the morale and unity of our group. Basically, I had the respect of the group as a whole, but how could I rein them in this time? The matter was turning into an issue of my (albeit limited) authority. This repulsive behavior was in full swing on one particular Sunday morning at breakfast time. Finally I said, "The next time one of you cracks a dirty joke or makes an off-color remark at the table, I will do something that you will remember for a long time." The reply was a gale of laughter. Now I had to be smart; otherwise I would never be able maintain respect. So I got up and stepped right outside of the front door. There I turned over a small rock. Underneath it I found a little earthworm. I picked it up and, concealing the worm in my fist, walked back to the table. Now I asked if they were finally done with all of their dirty jokes. In the interim, of course, one of them had dredged up a special joke for me and proceeded to tell it. I got up from my seat and said, "Everyone, look at me." Then I took the earthworm, dangled it in front of my mouth, dropped it in, and swallowed it. The immediate reaction went in two directions: some men were downright sickened with disgust, while others gave me a round of applause. Either way, I had made my point. Henceforth there was no more dirty talk at our table. And, interestingly, no one ever mentioned the event.

Not far from base Schwedenschanze was the airdrome Parow. It was a training facility for pilots who received instruction in the handling of light aircraft. Every now and then we could see them flying overhead. Once we were at rest from parade duty and were watching the maneuvering aircraft. Suddenly two of them made wing contact. One of the pilots bailed out and drifted to earth dangling from his parachute. The other one tried to land his damaged aircraft in a field not too far from us. We raced to the plane to render aid. However, the crash landing had killed the pilot, who was still strapped into the seat. I picked up a piece of the wing. The wood was extremely light. By applying just a little bit of pressure I was able to snap it in two. I should not have done that.

I discovered that a little splinter had penetrated the middle finger of my left hand. I quickly pulled it out and thought no more about it. A few days later, however, my finger started swelling, so I went to the aid station where a medical officer gave me a local anesthetic, lanced the infected site and drained out the puss. This was the week before Easter. By Good Friday the finger had swollen to twice its normal size. However, it was not until the holiday was over that I was taken to the base hospital. By then it was Tuesday morning. (In Germany Easter is observed for two days. Both Sunday and Monday are holidays.) This time I was given a general anesthetic, and a surgeon sliced open my finger. Later I found out that only the fact that I was an officer candidate made the military doctor hesitate and finally decide against amputating my finger. If there had been an amputation, I would have been able to return to duty a lot faster. As it was, it took five full weeks for the wound to heal. During the time of my recovery I was excused from participation in rifle drills and physical exercises. This time of recovery, however, caused me to fall behind my companions in my physical abilities.

Naturally, during rifle drill on my first day back I stood out, though not in the way one usually wants to. Consequently, every day after hours and on weekends I practiced with the rifle and spent time in the gymnasium working out in an effort to catch up with the rest of my group. I made noticeable progress, but I also pushed myself too hard. While marching with the rifle in the July heat the platoon leader repeatedly called out, "Corduan, hold the rifle tight." During a break he called me over and told me that he had been watching me for several days. He had noted my efforts and eagerness to perform on the same level as the rest of the company. In my zeal to make up for the training I had missed, I was going beyond my physical strength. He ordered me to go see a doctor at the infirmary. The doctor prescribed a daily dose of Sympatol and prohibited me from training after hours. He also reassured me that everyone, all the way up to the commander of the unit, recognized my eagerness. I complied with the order, and, once I allowed my body to function on a normal level, it didn't take much longer for me to regain the same level as the rest of my companions; I had turned into a strapping young soldier, and all rifle drills were snappy.

Finally the four months of basic training came to an end. Our military pass books were collected and our new rank was entered. This notation documented the fact that we had successfully completed basic training. For those who did not pass, the rank was ordinary seaman. The rank in my passbook read: "Sailor and Officer Cadet."

We now transferred to Danzig (Gdansk) to the naval base Danzig-Neufahrwasser, where we reconvened next on the training sail ship *Albert Leo Schlageter*. "Oh my, how tall the masts look!" I thought. Now we started our actual seamanship training. Everyone was assigned a sailing station. My station was the main topmast staysail. Do not think for a moment that when I was standing sail watch and a storm came up, I was exempt from having to secure the sail. Many, many times I had to climb up and lower the topsail, no matter what the conditions were. Because of the ship's motion from side to side, there were moments when I was able to look straight down onto the water, alternating from port to starboard and back again to port and then again to starboard, and so forth. A basic principle on a sailing vessels is this: "one hand for you and one hand for the ship." That sounds good, but try to imagine hauling in a sail with only one hand. As is the case so often in life, there is a wide gap between theory and practice.

This part of our training was conducted by a different set of officers and chief petty officers, no longer the ones that had given us our basic training. I was wondering whether these officers and chiefs had been informed about my religious attitude, which was generally considered idiosyncratic. No one gave me any hint at all. My companions, of course, already knew me. My section leader had been a sailor in the merchant marines prior to being conscripted by the navy. He had already crossed the oceans on sail ships for quite a while. I had no idea how he regarded me. Then came a Sunday morning in port. All hands reported for swabbing the decks and tidying up the ship. I put on my dress uniform, and reported to the petty officer on duty: "Seaman Corduan reports departing for Sunday services." He acknowledged my intention with the remark, pray for me also, and handed me a liberty pass. My companions, of course, took note of the incident. The next time we were in port on a Sunday morning, after I had received my liberty pass, a second seaman stepped up to the petty officer. As I was walking away I could hear the chief bellowing, "You lazy dog, you, get back to where you belong and start swabbing the decks!"

It is, of course, understood that I made every effort to bring honor to my Lord Jesus by taking my training very seriously. Quite often it is the little things that are so important, as I will illustrate in a moment. First, however, I need to describe the duties of a sailor on watch.

Onboard a sailing vessel one distinguishes between two types of watches. One is the regular sea watch. At the bow, there is a slightly raised platform, on which the lookout sentry stands. He has to call out to the officer of the watch all markers or lights as well as other ships that may have come into his sight. Then there is the bridge sentry who maintains his position right next to the officer of the watch. The stern sentry stares at the water in back of the ship, and the cabin sentry does his best to stay awake at the door of the captain's cabin.

It appeared that, as far as the officer of the watch was concerned, the lookout was the most important sentry. If the officer was able to spot the buoys or lights before the lookout, the cadet would have to write an essay of at least one page in length about the duties of the lookout. During the entire time that I spent on the training sail ship, I was the only cadet who always called out the cans, buoys, and, at night, the lights of the lighthouses, before the watch officer had identified them. The officer had a great advantage in that he was equipped with binoculars and, furthermore, knew where to look. As a cadet I did not get to look at the charts that would give notice of any upcoming signals, such as the old-fashioned lighthouses in which large fires were burning.

The other watch was the sailing detail, which was mobilized in addition to the regular watch, when the vessel was powered by sails alone. The crew of a training sail ship included approximately two hundred cadets, and these were divided into four watches. To which watch a cadet belonged was determined by where he hung his hammock at night. There were two starboard watches (one forward and one astern) and two port watches, again one forward and one astern. I was in the second port section. The duty of the sailing detail was primarily to set the sails so that the ship maintained the intended course. Much of the time there was nothing to do.

As most everyone knows, sails are moved by means of ropes. Therefore, during a maneuver it was very important to know the function of each rope in order to follow the orders of the sailing officer. Furthermore, it was necessary to know the various cleats to which each of the ropes is fastened. All that really fascinated me. During the sailing watch, when there was nothing else to do, I repeatedly questioned my section leader, Chief Petty Officer Wilde, about the ropes, their names, their functions, and their respective cleats. I made every effort to remember all of that information, until one day I knew exactly what each one was called and how it functioned. I was interested because I knew that someday I might have to carry out an order which was critical for the welfare of the entire ship. No one, including me, ever suspected that this little bit of private education would also bring any personal advantage to me. And so, I was greatly surprised when exactly such a thing happened just a short while later.

Our daily routine on the training sail ship was physically quite demanding. Since I was healthy, and since I was of the conviction that this was the path to which God had directed me, I applied myself with a great deal of enthusiasm. Adjusting the sails during the maneuvering provided a good workout. Once you had learned how to get into a hammock, sleeping in it gave you a good rest and was quite restoring. Even in heavy seas the ship's motion was not noticeable in a hammock. The up and down motion of the ship was slow enough that one could hardly feel it. Gravity kept the hammock stationary while the ship rolled from side to side. In the evenings out at sea, as we were quietly sailing along, the cadets would get together for singing. It was quite romantic. At least that is the way I felt about it. The executive officer had appointed me to lead the singing. When it was time for turning in for the night, the chief of the watch would give me a signal. We would then end our evening with the singing of the "hammock waltz," namely the well-known Brahm's lullaby: "Guten Abend, Gute Nacht." Of course it was modified to fit our particular situation. Our last line was "Tomorrow morning, if God wills, you'll be back at the wheel."

About the life and the duties on the cadet training vessel I could tell many a story. But since my desire is to tell you about the way God has led me, I do not want to get bogged down in details. My supervisors as well as my companions appreciated my work and contributions. There was also a certain amount of respect towards me as a Christian, though it was often combined with a little teasing as well. Throughout my life I have adhered to the principle that it is not my job to force my beliefs on somebody else. I always conducted my regular times of devotions and prayer in such a manner so as not to provoke anyone. But now and again I had the opportunity, usually in response to a question, to be a witness as to how wonderful it is to be under God's guidance. But my companions could not leave well enough alone and kept looking for opportunities to entrap me somehow. When we were in port in Gotenhafen (now Gdiynia) on the Helau Peninsula we were given liberty to go ashore. My companions said to me, "Bruno, why don't you join us tonight. We really want to show you something." Soon we came to an establishment, the nature of which I could easily guess from the attractive young ladies that were loitering there. After having a good laugh and warning them not to catch anything, I wished them a good evening and went on my way.

After we had been on the training vessel for approximately two months, there came a very special day. All of us, that is, all two hundred cadets, were called out for formation in our dress uniforms. Formations were nothing unusual, but formation in dress uniform was something special. At that time all of us had the same rank: seaman, sea officer candidate. The officer of the watch reported to the executive officer that everyone was present. Then our captain, Kapitän Asmus, whom we hardly ever saw, appeared. When the executive officer reported to him that all cadets were present, he said, "Seamen, I have asked for this formation to announce the first ten seamen who are being promoted to the rank of sea cadet." When my name was called I marched up to the captain, who shook my hand in congratulation and handed me the insignia of sea cadet. Why was I the only one in our section who had been promoted? That, of course, was the question my companions asked our chief. They readily acknowledged that I had faithfully done my duties. But now they were told, that in addition to whatever other qualifications I had, I was the first, and so far only, cadet who knew the names and functions of every rope on the ship.

LIFE IS LIFE

A person who has decided to live his life as a disciple of Jesus and who goes through life with the assurance of being fully in Jesus' care, is still subject to all the normal vicissitudes of life. I, too, have experienced both the ups and downs of life. Up to this point in my narration, recounting the way Jesus had guided me, I may have created the impression that my life was only a succession of successes. I do not wish to leave such an impression uncorrected. The point of the following anecdotes is to show that my life also had its low points. In 2 Cor 7:8 and the following verses, the Apostle Paul, using the phrase "sorrowful according to the will of God," tells us that we, too, have to experience pain and suffering. In this regard there are times when God does not answer all of our prayers. These are times in which God is teaching us.

At this point let me insert a story of my overenthusiasm while in port in Danzig-Neufahrwasser. Our ship had tied up alongside the pier inside the harbor. Our dinghies were tied to the ship on the other side. As I already mentioned, rowing was an integral part of our training. Even when we were at sea, every day two groups were chosen for a rowing race. While in port all of the dinghies were manned. The race started while the competitors were still on the ship. When the starting order was given the cadets chosen to be part of this race would issue a warning cry as they ran for the dinghies. Each team was eager to have all their men on board and to be the first dinghy under way in order to get an advantage in the race. On this occasion I was one of the first to reach the location where the dinghies were tied. Unfortunately, to be one of the first is not to be the first, and that acclaim went to someone else. Just as I jumped down the six feet into my dinghy, one of the others pushed my boat aside in order to get into his. I tried to make a last-minute correction, but nonetheless fell onto the edge of the boat. Nobody thought that I had actually been injured, though for many years I had inexplicable, excruciating abdominal pain. It was not until 1969, in Washington, DC, that the source of the mysterious pain was traced back to this incident and surgically corrected.[6]

TESTIMONY ON BOARD A WRECKED SHIP

It happened on a Friday late in the afternoon. We were tied up at the pier in the port of Danzig-Neufahrwasser, and we were awaiting the order of the chief of the watch, who, after the well-familiar whistle would announce that it was time for the evening meal. Suddenly our group chief burst onto the deck and cried out with utter frustration in his voice, "The rats are leaving the ship! We are going to set sail today! Doesn't anybody know that today is Friday the thirteenth?" He was a well-experienced sailor from the merchant marines. He had sailed the oceans of the world and had participated in the famous "grain races."[7] And, like most sailors, he was highly superstitious.

We were ordered to assemble on the upper deck, where our executive officer informed us that we would be departing in one hour. Furthermore, the officer continued, there were several people on board from a motion picture company, who wanted to get some footage of sailing vessels in stormy seas. We would make the entire trip in the company of our sister ship *Horst Wessel*. The two ships would make identical

---

6. As long as we have made this leap forward in time, let me mention some other situations in which I was not spared from normal human suffering. I had a brother, named Erhard, who was four years younger than me. He had emigrated to the United States and was living in Oregon. While we were living in the United States ourselves, he passed away at the age of 35. The cause of his death was a form of meningitis, caused by a fungus, which could not be controlled because of his diabetes.

I could also mention that at the age of 79 I was suffering from pain in my chest. For the next six months I was treated for rheumatism of my sternum. Finally a cardiologist inserted a Y-stent into my heart to treat a severely clogged RIVA and the rheumatic pain was henceforth gone.

Now, let us return to the time of World War II.

7. The "grain races" were competitions between commercial cargo-bearing sail ships that arose naturally as they were all pursuing a similar route from Australia to Europe. There were no official starts, though, in order to catch the right winds, a ship had to set out sometime in the month of June, and rounding Cape Horne was mandatory. Each year from 1921 to 1939, plus 1946 and 1949, at least one winner was determined according to who took the fewest days to make the voyage. The winning times varied from 83 days (by the *Pamir* in 1932) to 110 days (by the multiple-winner *Passat* in 1949). Both of these ships ended their useful lives by becoming German-owned training sail ships, just like the *Albert Leo Schlageter* and the *Horst Wessel*, the last of their kind.—Trans.

maneuvers. The cameramen would be able to film the detailed rope work on our ship, as well as the corresponding changes in the sail configuration on the *Horst Wessel*. Our ship left port, the sails were set and soon we were a "ship on the high seas." The wind freshened, and by next morning the weather had become stormy. A steady rain was whipping into our faces. The *Horst Wessel* came in sight and the cameramen began their work. In the afternoon my section was on sail watch. Shortly before dusk we received the order: "Strike topsail, set storm sail!" The wind had already reached force 10, and we were anticipating force 12, which is the top of the scale. The sails on the highest yards (the upper and lower topgallant sails) and the large sails (the mainsail and foresail) were secured. The other sails were reefed. When we were back on deck, the chief of the watch said, "Do you call this teamwork?! There are still five men working in the topsail yards." We had not even noticed. It was already getting dark, and, as we were staring up the mast, suddenly there was a fiery flash on the fore ship, and it felt as though the ship had jumped. We had been hit by a torpedo! In the forward part of the ship, as we discovered later, there was a huge hole about the size of a barn door. Additionally, there was a massive rift in the middle of the ship that reached all the way down to the lower deck and yawned with every wave. The ship was in maximum jeopardy! As to the five men who had still been up in the sails, one had been able to hang on tight. Another one had fallen overboard. A third had crashed on the deck and broken his neck. The fourth one had landed on a pile of ropes and had suffered no harm. The last one had dropped onto some cleats and sustained serious injuries. In all we had suffered the loss of about twenty men in various ways.

Our captain informed us about the ship's status and told us that the *Horst Wessel* would come alongside and pick up half of our crew. The names of those who would be rescued were determined by randomly picking serial numbers; the corresponding names were then called out. As I was just standing there, I suddenly had the feeling that I was being gripped by strong hands and pulled away from the group of cadets with whom I had been standing in formation. Against my will I was dragged to the back of the ship into a dark nook where the emergency rudder equipment was stored. No one noticed me. There I was held tight. Again and again the chief of the watch called out: "Sea Cadet Corduan." I could distinctly hear it, but I was unable to move or answer. I could clearly see my companions and the rescue ship lying alongside of us. No one saw me. After perhaps half an hour (I really do not know the exact length of time), the rescue ship turned away. The force that had kept me let up, and I walked back to my remaining companions. They received me with the words: "There you are. You could have been rescued on the *Horst Wessel*." I did not reply. I only felt the strong presence of my Lord Jesus without being able to fathom what was actually happening to me. Such feelings are difficult to describe.

Our vessel was a wreck bobbing and drifting about without any way of controlling it. The wind was now approaching force 12, and the waves were as high as they can ever get in the Baltic Sea. A small destroyer and a tank cruiser repeatedly tried to tow us. However, we were drifting into one of our own minefields. We, that is the cadets, did not know about the minefield and only found out about it after we had reached port. None of the other vessels came close enough to us so that we could catch the small pilot line with which to pull a towing cable aboard. Several times small tugs came bravely alongside and secured a towing cable. They started moving, the cable became taut, trembled, and snapped. This happened with a total of fourteen steel cables, which were so thick that you could not span them with one hand. These attempts continued over the duration of three nights and two days.

When officers asked for a volunteer to keep an eye on the rift in the lower deck, I immediately stepped forward. But I was seldom alone. Now I realized that Jesus had placed me into this situation with a special assignment. I believe that probably every one of the cadets who had stayed on the ship sat with me for an hour or two. (Just consider the number of those who came to me. I am estimating that there were approximately seventy to eighty sailors still on board.) Most of them started with words such as, "Bruno, do you really believe . . . " I was able to talk to many of them about my Jesus and the gospel message. And I prayed with a number of them. Never again did the Lord give me an opportunity to talk with so many persons individually about spiritual matters in such a short period of time. The best part of it was that I was completely at peace and did not have even a moment of fear, even though the executive officer told us that, should the ship break apart, only about 10 percent of the crew had a chance of survival. When I was not standing watch I was on the upper deck assisting whenever I could. I was there to observe each of the attempts to get us under tow, and I was even able to assist in some of them.

During the third night a small tug with only a two-person crew approached us. They had a manila-hemp hawser three times the size of the steel cables. This hawser had a stretch capacity of about thirty percent. Additionally, they added a steel cable for safety. And so, we tried again. The men of the tug threw a small line to the sailing ship. Attached to it was a heavier line by means of which we pulled the manila hawser on board, the dimensions of which made this an "all-hands" situation. The officers of the two ships held a brief conference in order to agree on signals. The small tug set out. Then came the moment of tension. The hawser became taut; it vibrated and trembled furiously and . . . held! Very slowly our wreck started to move. And so began our slow but steady journey to port. Totally exhausted, but now with hope for survival, we fell asleep in the hammocks scattered on the deck. At dawn we could see land. Those two sailors on the tug had risked their lives to tow us out of the mine field into the port of Swinemünde. Finally, after three long nights and two days our vessel was secured at the pier. Those who now said, "Thank God!" really meant it. I also expressed my thankfulness to God for our rescue, and I thanked him for the opportunity that I had had to talk to my companions about his great love and mercy for us during the long hours aboard the wreck of our once so proud ship. I later found out that both our captain and the executive officer studied theology after the war and became pastors.

SPECIAL LEAVE

Swinemünde had been the original destination of our vessel. The majority of our crew (the rescued portion) had sailed on board the *Horst Wessel* into Kiel, where they had been anxiously awaiting to learn how the drama *Albert Leo Schlageter* would turn out. Since Swinemünde had been our intended destination, it was there that a telegram for me was waiting. The courier of the executive officer sought me out and informed me that it had been sent via special military mail. The telegram informed me that my brother Benno had been severely wounded. He had been assigned to Kurland on the eastern front as a radio man. He was now in the military hospital in Danzig-Langfuhr. I was given special leave in order to visit my brother.

Without having had a chance to recover from the strain of the last several days I now found myself on a train heading for Danzig. I interrupted my trip in Schlawe-Pommern to spend the night at my parents' home, and I was planning to continue my journey the next day. My father informed me, however, that my brother had succumbed to his injuries and had found his final place of rest in the military cemetery Danzig-Silberhammer. Even for a nineteen-year-old this was too much—the three nights and two days on the wreck with hardly any sleep, the immediate departure by train, and now the news of my brother's death. I was overcome by the greatest physical and mental breakdown that I have ever experienced. I "crawled" into bed and slept until the next evening. Then I resumed my journey to Danzig, and there, at my brother's grave, I committed my life to the Lord anew. The next several days on leave allowed me to regain my emotional and physical stability.

ON THE AUXILIARY CRUISER *ORION*

In the meantime, our training sail ship had been towed into a dry dock and raised out of the water. When I returned from my leave I took a good look for myself at the entire ship in the dock. The hole that the torpedo had torn was large enough for a truck to drive through. The theory of having struck a mine, which had been the official explanation, had been discounted. The anti-submarine destroyer number 34 had been sunk in the same location by a so-called fan, a spread of three torpedoes. They had not even had time to send out a radio signal.

Several weeks went by. During this time the modifications were made to accommodate two hundred cadets on the auxiliary cruiser *Orion*. Eventually we moved aboard our new training vessel, which now bore the name *Hector*. An auxiliary cruiser is a merchant ship that has been retrofitted into a warship, including armaments. At first site these merchant vessels did not appear to be military ships. However, their armament was usually equal to that of a cruiser. The *Orion* had a so-called hero-cellar in which the sailors were trained to load cannons with grenades in record time. Additionally the vessel had four twenty-seven-centimeter cannons, and we were trained in their operation. At the end of January, the practical, physical part of my naval training was complete. My next station was at the navy training center in Heiligendamm.

FROM STUDENT TO VOLUNTEER

The official name of the training center was the *Marine Schule* (Navy School). The German navy did not have a school that was officially called a war school as the army did. The officer in charge of our group was a second lieutenant, who during his civilian days was a teacher in a *Gymnasium* (high school). Under his guidance I was doing nothing but studying, because in these exams no one cared about your prior schooling. It was strictly performance that counted. Since I was used to self-motivated studying and always tried to get the most out of any training, I had no difficulty in keeping up with the course's demands. Then came the fateful day in April 1945. The entire school was called for formation, and a first lieutenant briefed us. He stated that the supreme commander of the German navy, Admiral Dönitz, had promised the Führer, Adolf Hitler, assistance in achieving the final victory. Dönitz was putting together a special Navy Anti-Tank Brigade and once again wanted to present it to Hitler as yet another birthday present. The brigade would be formed from volunteer officers and officer candidates of the German navy. We were told that this brigade would be equipped with the newest weapons and with a special secret weapon. Then came the order: "Anyone who chooses not to volunteer for the tank brigade, step forward!" And just like that all of us had volunteered, as I had experienced previously for the Hitler Youth Division. One of the cadets who subsequently complained was forthwith transferred to the infantry.

We were all issued khaki uniforms and were trained in the use of the *Panzerfaust*, the German version of the bazooka. I was assigned to the brigade commander as chief accountant and "runner." Then we were ordered to move into the direction of Berlin. It was getting quite serious. We were supposed to be deployed outside of Berlin to stop Russian tank units, and we received detailed instruction on how to approach a tank with a *Panzerfaust*. Apparently the secret weapon was a detail of navy officer candidates sneaking up on Russian tanks. There was little doubt as to what that would mean to us individually. I committed myself into my Lord's hands and was quite sure that he would once again find a way to see me safely through. However, how he did it this time fills me with astonishment still today. I learned later that the entire unit was wiped out completely on their very first mission.

The day before moving out for deployment I was ordered to report to the company commander. He informed me that a member of the replacement company had received word that his mother and sister had been severely mistreated by Russians. He, therefore, requested immediate transfer to the departing unit so that he could avenge himself.

His request had been honored. I was, effective immediately, transferred to the replacement company, which was made up of a handful of cadets. Several days later I received an ID card with the following notation: "Sea Cadet Bruno Corduan is a member of Army Command Weichsel and is on special assignment for the army command. No military command or unit is permitted to detain him or use him for any other assignments. Signed by Lieutenant General Künzel." Furthermore I was ordered to report to a rear area unit of the brigade in Schwerin. This ID protected me from the "soldier snatchers." This was a term applied to the military police who would seize any soldiers that they happened to come across, combine them into an *ad hoc* unit, and send them to the front to wherever additional troops were sorely needed. After presenting this ID, I was able to join a military convoy heading westward to Kriwitz. We were still en route, on May 2, 1945, when we received word that Adolf Hitler had committed suicide. It was now clear to all that the war was lost.

In some nearby woods an infantry battalion was waiting for their commander who was negotiating with the US military regarding surrender. When he returned, all his soldiers threw down their weapons. I joined them and we marched into US captivity. Doing so, however, was not without its problems. Along the way to the US military post, we, who were totally unarmed, were plundered at gunpoint by a Polish gang. To this day I can still feel the pressure of the pistol against my neck, persuading me to surrender my watch.

The next morning, on May 3, 1945, we passed a roadblock and became US prisoners of war. A US captain introduced himself. He stated he was a Jew and the commandant of the camp. The camp was on a small rise, but no one really knew how far it extended. Additional blockades had been established, so that we could travel no further. The grounds were littered with the corpses of prisoners of war who had apparently been shot at various times over the previous three weeks. For cover we had tarpolins, which some of the soldiers had brought along. I was able to find shelter with five other soldiers. Between us we had three shelter halves designed to accommodate three persons. But there were six of us. Our feet stuck out from underneath the tent, which was quite uncomfortable, especially when it rained. During those three weeks we were not provided with anything to eat. We foraged for nettles and ate uncooked sugar beets. Then finally we were moved westward and turned over to British forces. All they could provide us in the way of food was ten "biscuits" (actually ten thin German-made cookies) per day. Eventually, still a prisoner of war, I ended up on the island Fehmarn.

Finally, on August 4, I was released from captivity. I was able to locate my grandmother in Hamburg and found shelter with her. At the job service for displaced persons I tried repeatedly to obtain work. Each time I was harshly rebuffed. Why I was treated so harshly I did not find out until two years later. An employee of the job service, who had also just been released from captivity, had pity on me. He provided me with papers for a position with the British occupation authorities. I was assigned to work in the harbor of Hamburg. Now at last I received a residency permit, ration cards, and authorization to purchase work clothing. In the harbor I was detailed to unload freight barges, but I only lasted three days due to the internal injuries which I had sustained on the training sail ship when I fell on the edge of the boat. All my other attempts to find work continued to be unsuccessful. Finally I was offered a position as conductor on a streetcar.

GRABBING LIFE BY THE NECK

I was nineteen years old and left to my own devices, in charge of my own life. My place of work now was the streetcar, where I was assigned to the Lockstedt terminal. The streetcar company, Hamburger Hochbahn AG, who owned the entire streetcar net, had arranged a shelter at Falkenried Street for those who were homeless. There was room for forty-eight beds; in other words, it was a crash pad. We were on our own for obtaining food. At the shelter there were cooking facilities for the contingency that you might be able to purchase food with your ration card. In that respect, namely having to provide for myself, this was a very trying time.

In the vicinity on Abendrothweg (*Sunset Way*) there was a Methodist church. There I attended services and youth meetings on a regular basis and became active in the church. With time I became a member of the church. Even though I was quite active in the church, my desire to go to seminary was met with a cool reception. There again, just as at the job service, and with my ongoing efforts to obtain a better position working for the city, there seemed to be a problem. But nobody would talk to me about it. Only later did I find out the reason. Then everyone tried their hardest to make up for the rebuffs and found ways for me to obtain job training.

So, for now, I was a streetcar conductor. Regardless of what I was, I always gave myself fully to my job. The station manager tried to make my life and work easier for me. In response to my request to schedule my Sunday duties so that I could attend services, he showed me a compassionate understanding about which I still marvel today.

2

Life with My Own Family

STARTING A FAMILY

For the time being I stayed at the streetcar accommodations and was just letting life happen. I have to confess that it was a difficult time for me. Furthermore, I was really not sure where the Lord was leading me. After all that I had just been through, now I was starting to have doubts. Then I met a girl who went to Sunday school at the same Methodist church that I was attending now. Before long, we started attending services, Bible studies, and youth activities together. Her name? Ursula.

When we attended the birthday celebration of one of my relatives, I introduced my girlfriend Ursula to them. To my great surprise everyone liked her. Three uncles recommended to me that, if we were agreed to spend our life together we should get married as soon as possible so that I could get away from the less than pleasant conditions of the streetcar sleeping hall. On August 25, 1946, we became engaged and requested permission from our respective parents to get married. My parents readily agreed. Ursula's father, however, withheld his consent. He wanted us to wait until October 11 of the next year, when Ursula came of age. Since I was anxious to get out of the sleeping accommodations at the streetcar hall we kept trying to find a way to get married before then. Even today I am still grateful to the pastor of the Ebenezer Church for his understanding and assistance. On April 16, 1947, Pastor Schneck married us.

That was sixty years ago. The three sons whom God has given us, as well as their wives, are disciples of Jesus. And all of them have, by this time, raised their own children. Wolfgang, our oldest, now lives in Alaska. For health reasons he had to retire early and now works part-time in tourism. He continues looking for opportunities to find full-time employment once again. He is an elder in his fellowship and frequently fills the pulpit for his pastor. Our second son, Winfried, is professor of philosophy and religion at Taylor University in Upland, Indiana. His specialty is world religions. On his job as well as through his books he is known as a good teacher, a recognized authority in his field, and a faithful witness for Jesus. Ralph-Rainer now lives in Columbia, South Carolina. He has been active as a singer at evangelistic gatherings in the United States as well as in Germany. In all respects we can see the guiding hand of our Lord Jesus. I cannot say what God might have done under other circumstances, but it is clear that my eventual transfer to the United States and the highly paid position at NATO definitely opened doors for my sons that would have been hard to envision otherwise.

JESUS ACKNOWLEDGES THE DECISION TO SERVE HIM

I continued to look for better employment but continued to be rejected. What shocked me most was the rejection by the Hamburg Police Department. The reason they gave was a supposed spot on my lungs, which, however, a lung specialist could not find. Next, I applied at the Customs Department. The personnel officer gave me great hope and sent me to the head of the department for denazification. Mr. Wiethüchter was half Jewish and had managed to stay alive in spite of the Nazi terror. He believed that his office would be able to provide me with the necessary document quite easily because I was covered under the youth amnesty laws. But he thought he had better check the data bank. I can still hear his exclamation: "Son, what have they done to you!" And all of a sudden the reason why nobody, including the Methodist seminary, wanted anything to do with me became clear. In the official data bank I was listed as an Adolf Hitler Student,[1] a final stroke from the party members in Schlawe to do me ill. Mr. Wiethüchter became my supervisor,

---

1. These were young people who were most deeply imbued with Nazi ideology. They were chosen for their active participation in the Hitler Youth and the life of the Nazi Party. They were then sent to a special Hitler School and trained in Nazi philosophy.—Trans.

and he helped me to get my personnel files straightened out. I was accepted in the civil service of the Customs Department and received my first appointment to the position of customs service assistant. That was the absolutely lowest rank for a *Beamter* (see note 3 on page 13). Let me insert here that this was the first of a total of ten appointments/promotions I received as a civil servant. However, in order to reach a position of senior government official, I had to take leave from civil service and accept a contract with NATO as I will be detailing a little later.

Let me insert just one more comment. After I was able to show that I was not an Adolf Hitler Student, many of the people around me changed in their interactions with me; this included even the church with whom I had felt a bond on account of our common faith and hope through Jesus Christ. Everyone was more open and friendlier towards me. It was not too long before I was elected to the church board. Contact was reestablished with the seminary in Frankfurt to arrange for me to study theology there, even though I was married, which was a consideration at the time.

Now back to my career in the civil service. I was issued the uniform of a customs and border guard. Actually, the entire port area was under the jurisdiction of the British occupation forces, including even the customs office. Thus, initially there was no regular import business for Germans to regulate, and there were no goods on which a tariff had to be collected. Nor was it the responsibility of the border guards at that time to prevent smuggling. The only obligation we had was to stop theft. The British controlled the freighters delivering the materials needed by the occupation forces, as well as relief shipments from England and overseas. There were British soldiers present at all port gates. The only weapon I received for the sake of self-defense was a baton.

But this state of affairs under occupation was only temporary. Once a new government was established in Germany, all of these matters changed, and the import of goods soon flourished again. Pretty soon my days as a patrol officer ended also. I was detailed to a special assignment, which, for the most part, was desk work. I spent the majority of my time in the office of the customs commissioner. But I did get to go out on patrol periodically so that I would not lose the differential pay for outside duty. At those times, my assignments were to patrol the area around the port in plain clothes, for all practical purposes undertaking customs investigations. I am happy to report that I was quite successful in my endeavors, for which I was rewarded in two ways: (1) my superiors gave me recognition through commendations and rewards, and (2) when some of the residents of the area got to know me, on occasion I would receive flowers from them. Since many of these folks made a great part of their living by smuggling, they would toss the flowers at me while they were still in their pots. I learned to avoid such houses.

In order to be eligible for promotion, I was sent to a training course in Bonn from January to April 1953. In February we were all given a few days of leave. I told my wife that I felt certain that I was going to earn an A in this training program and then have a good chance of being transferred to the Federal Ministry of Finance. My premonition became reality. I passed the exams with an A. Soon after my return to Hamburg I received the transfer order to the Ministry of Finance effective June 1, 1953.

A NEW CHAPTER IN OUR LIFE AS A FAMILY

My new position in the Ministry of Finance was the records office in a special section for administration of occupation expenses. For the next nine months I lived by myself, separated from my family. There was an extreme shortage of housing in Bonn. I was able to rent a room in the barracks, which used to be the housing for students at the customs training facility. A colleague named Walter, who had also completed the training with top grades, was my neighbor. He knew that I was a Christian. One day when we were together with several others of the occupants, he decided to crack a joke at my expense. He said in an overly loud voice, "Every Sunday morning I go to a church where the hymn books have handles." But it was my reply that produced the desired gales of laughter, though at his expense. I rejoined, "Then you get to look forward to the heaven where the angels have horns and tails."

My work in the records office did not require great mental exertions, but exactitude. The pastor of the Methodist church was very happy to have me in his flock. Bonn did not have its own assembly but was a part of the Cologne district. Every other week a service took place in a home. There was also a small gathering in Königswinter, a nearby town. I had many opportunities to proclaim the Word of God and to continue my studies in theology. In February 1954 we were assigned an apartment, and I was able to move my family to Bonn. There we were now looking for a spiritual home. Through a tent revival we became acquainted with a Baptist assembly who had acquired a small apartment that had been furnished to hold Sunday services, and it even offered Sunday school for the children. As can be expected, I tried to get a grasp of their understanding of baptism, which was foreign to me. Through my own Bible study, without talking to either the pastor or any member of the church, I came to the conviction that I had not been baptized according to biblical principles. Therefore, I had a conversation with the pastor of the Methodist church in Cologne and provided a written explanation of my newly acquired doctrinal position. The result was that I was accused of having fallen into heresy, and my name was struck from the list of pulpit supply. During further conversations, the Methodist pastor suggested that, if I really wanted to be baptized by immersion, he would baptize me in my bathtub. I never could get a convincing explanation for this compromise: either he thought that believer's baptism by immersion was heretical or not. If it was, he should not have offered to perform it in a private ceremony. If it was not, then why stand in its way? We decided that a separation was unavoidable.

This was a difficult decision for me. Subsequently, on March 27, 1955, my wife and I underwent believer's baptism at the Baptist Church in Cologne and were received into the Baptist Church. The church in Bonn was an offshoot of the one in Cologne, and they had more than enough work for me. I was given the assignment to start a youth ministry. My efforts were richly blessed by Jesus. We started our youth meetings with four young people in August 1955. In February 1956, over the carnival (Mardi Gras) weekend, we went on a retreat to the town of Adenau with thirty participants. Many of the young people requested to be baptized and were received into our church. This group became an important and integral part of our church, a legacy that has lasted up to the present.

Our entire family will remember those days well, because our financial situation was anything but plush. I have already mentioned that I had been appointed to the lowest rank in the civil service. That status, of course, meant that my salary was also at the lowest level. Even after my promotion, this matter did not change appreciably. For a family with three boys there was never anything left over. The Lord did not exempt us from testing. But from the beginning of our marriage we had agreed to give to God what was God's. And he has always cleared the way for us. We had to live frugally. Now I was glad that my dad had insisted that I learn to resole shoes. I spent many a Saturday afternoon doing just that. When that was accomplished I would prepare myself for preaching on Sunday morning.

Then one day it came to my notice that the emerging Federal Ministry of Defense was looking for personnel. Back then, this government entity was still called Department Blank. The official name was the Federal Department for Issues in Conjunction with the Buildup of Allied Troops. The name of the department head actually was Blank. I applied, and on November 26, 1956, I was transferred to their personnel section. On January 1, 1957, Department Blank officially became the Federal Ministry of Defense and Mr. Blank was made the minister. A new German military force was being formed (the *Bundeswehr*), and it was my responsibility to appraise the files of the candidates who wished to become officers. I had to look for certain qualifications and then issue the appropriate certificates. Because of the efforts I made in the fulfilling of this assignment I soon had personal contact with the minister and was given the responsibility to make the preparations for the appointment ceremonies. When Herr Franz-Joseph Strauß became minister of defense, I received a new assignment in the social services section. From July 1, 1958, to March 31, 1960, my duties were spread over several sections so that I would become prepared for an elevated career track. The ministry sent me to a number of courses at the Bundeswehr Administrative Academy in Mannheim. I completed all exams successfully and received the diploma of a certified federal administrator. For a short time I accepted a post with the federal intelligence service (*Bundesnachrichtendienst*), which opened excellent opportunities for advancement. However, after two months I resigned. The anonymity that this assignment required was too difficult for me to handle. It is simply impossible to be active in the propagation of the gospel and live under several different names.

I was transferred back to the administrative section in Bonn and my new obligations were in supply. My responsibility was to furnish the uniforms and equipment for all military personnel in the Bonn region. A total of five storage facilities were under my supervision. Of particular concern was the guard battalion, which was stationed nearby in Siegburg. This unit had the assignment of parade duty during affairs of state, and their uniforms had to be impeccable. I tried hard to meet the expectations and maintained close contact with the officers whenever special events occurred.

On the occasion of the fifth anniversary of the founding of the guard battalion, many guests attended the parade. I also received an invitation to participate in the accompanying festivities. During the event, the general who was responsible for logistics and the equipment for the entire *Bundeswehr* sent a soldier to me requesting me to see him. Since everything had gone smoothly I gladly obliged. After some of the typical small talk he said, "Herr Corduan, I have visited all of our *Bundeswehr* garrisons in all of the various branches. I have inspected many a parade unit. I have always received the same complaint, namely, that the soldiers' uniforms leave much to be desired. The problem is that there are color variations in the fabric of the uniforms. The difference in shading is minute, yet visible. To the best of my knowledge you receive the uniforms for the guard battalion from the same source as all the others, namely the central uniform issue. How did you manage to get all of the uniforms to appear identical in color?" I said, "Herr General, that is an optical illusion." My reply puzzled him, and he did not hide his irritation. "Are you trying to tell me that I cannot see properly, that I am colorblind?" he rebuffed me. "No, Herr General. The uniforms for the *Bundeswehr* are furnished by five different suppliers. Each supplier is adamant that even with their best efforts they cannot produce uniforms of absolutely identical colorations. Now, we have five different suppliers and, as it turns out, we have five platoons in the guard battalion. Before equipping new soldiers I personally drive to the central supply house and load the truck with uniforms from only one supplier. I usually have to lend a hand myself because this is a lot of extra work. Therefore, every platoon has identically colored uniforms from only one supplier. So, if you were to line up the entire battalion according to size without keeping them in the individual platoons you would see the same problem, which you are used to seeing in other units." Swearing quietly, he asked, "Why has no one else ever thought of that?" Then the general thanked me and assured me that I would hear from him again.

The second special event: General de Gaulle made a state visit to Bonn. The guard battalion was supplemented by a company from the navy. During the taps ceremony the torches of almost all navy men dripped onto their light-colored uniforms so that they could not possibly be used at the parade on the next afternoon at 1500 hours. That same evening I arranged for a cleaning firm to pick up the uniforms the next morning and have them delivered, cleaned and pressed, and into the hands of the troops by 1100 hours. The next morning at eight o'clock I drove to the cleaners and made sure that everything was running smoothly.

Simultaneously I ordered the central supply immediately to load a railroad car with the complete equipment (including extra uniforms to accommodate different sizes) for a navy company and send it right away to the railroad station at Siegburg. With a few phone calls early that morning, I determined that everything was being done the way I had requested. And so it was that at approximately ten o'clock I was sitting in my office satisfied that everything was under control. Then I received a phone call from the head of the section in the Ministry of Defense, responsible for the uniforms of all soldiers of the Bundeswehr. Prior to this occasion he had not known me. He was extremely agitated and asked if I was responsible for the uniform outfitting of the guard battalion. Further he said that the state visit of the French president was of highest political significance. Then he asked me why I had not informed him immediately of the unfortunate circumstances of the navy unit's uniforms. I explained to him that this was part of my normal, daily responsibilities, that I had already taken the necessary steps and briefed him on the status of the matter. Around noon all soldiers had their clean uniforms, and the special uniforms from the central supply depot had arrived. As agreed, I informed the section head. He was full of praise.

Through the grapevine I was made aware that both the general for logistics and the section head for uniforms had decided to create a special position in the Ministry of Defense for me and had requested my assignment personally. This would have been a wonderful honor for me. However, Jesus, the Lord of my life, had different plans for me, of which I, of course, was not aware.

3

On Foreign Soil

SPECIAL DUTY IN THE USA

ONE DAY I HAD to tend to some business in the main building of the Ministry of Defense. While there, I also stopped by to see a former colleague. During our conversation about our common experiences during the early days of the ministry, a gentleman came into the room with a friendly greeting. My colleague interrupted our conversation and said: "Herr Backes, I have found just the man for you." Herr Backes then named a series of people and asked if one of those was the person he had in mind. "No," said my colleague, "I mean the gentleman sitting right here." You can imagine the puzzlement on my face in which you could clearly read the question, what are you talking about? I'm sure my facial expression did not improve much when Herr Backes turned to me and asked, "How would you like to go to America?" Now I found out that I was speaking to the head of the *Bundeswehr* administrative office of the German military representative to NATO in Washington, DC. After a short conversation I agreed to it. This occurred on a Saturday morning at about 1130 hours. We arranged to meet that afternoon at 1430 in the restaurant Salvador to discuss some details. As I was driving a car owned by the ministry back to my office, I happened to see my wife and informed her that I would be home a little later than usual.

In the restaurant Herr Backes explained to me what this assignment was all about. For the last four years student pilots of the Luftwaffe had received their pilot training in the military aircraft of the US Air Force. They were stationed at Lackland Air Force Base in Texas and other air force bases in the US. During the first four years of the establishment of the Luftwaffe, the trainees received advances on their per diem and other funds through the German Foreign Ministry. The final accounting of these funds was initially postponed because that particular position had not been filled. After the administrative offices of the *Bundeswehr* in Washington, DC, and branch offices in Lackland AFB and Fort Bliss had been fully staffed, this accounting needed to be done. After several attempts, all three offices declared this task to be impossible. The German office of accounting agreed to send a request to the Ministry of Defense to forgo the accounting. But first they wanted a knowledgeable and reliable civil servant in the elevated track, working independently, to make one more attempt to balance the books. That civil servant would be given six months to complete the task. If he also failed then the request to drop the accounting would be sent to the Ministry of Defense. I was to become that civil servant. After I had agreed, Herr Backes said that in the time since our first encounter that morning and this meeting, he had inquired in a number of offices and talked to several of my superiors. Everyone had responded positively and recommended me for that assignment. He would request the personnel division to order a six-month transfer.

Armed with this news I went home. Naturally I had already lifted all of this before my Lord Jesus in prayer and had received the conviction that I would be spending several years, not months, in the United States. (Was I being presumptuous?) Initially my wife was not excited at all. But then she said that if I was convinced that this was the right thing for me, she would agree. Our whole family started preparing for the move to America, even though my assignment was to be limited to six months.

IN THE NEW WORLD

On October 1, 1962, the Boeing 707 departed from the Bonn-Cologne airport. In Bonn we had just experienced the first night frosts. When I arrived in Washington, DC, I was greeted by temperatures above 80°F. Over the next twelve days I was thoroughly briefed on the previous attempts of balancing the books. I was given the assurance that it would not reflect negatively on me if I was not successful. More than that, they were expecting that I could not unscramble the data and were anticipating a negative report. On January 30, 1963, I was supposed to return to Washington, DC, for an interim report.

On October 13, 1962, I flew to San Antonio, Texas. My office for the next half year would be in the same building as a branch of the *Bundeswehr* administrative office. I will never forget that flight. We were traveling at an altitude of approximately 35,000 feet and could see a tornado underneath. Nor will I forget the temperatures. Over the next three weeks the temperatures hovered around 95°F. My colleagues wanted to do something special for me, and so they invited me to go with them to a special event in Fredericksburg. The next day there was to be a singer fest by various German language glee clubs. This was always a big event. It took place in a large auditorium that was not equipped with air conditioning. It was so hot for me that I was seriously questioning whether or not I would survive the event. The locals folks, however, felt quite comfortable because they were used to these temperatures.

The person in charge of the office at Lackland Air Force Base, just like the others earlier in Washington, DC, tried to convince me that a successful conclusion of my efforts was virtually impossible. He assured me that he would, of course, provide me with any assistance that I might require. He further suggested that I should look upon my time there as a vacation and not work too hard. It would be futile, anyhow. He would help me with the final report. It took me two months to read through all the files and to examine the conditions under which the pilots had been sent here. About the middle of December I started writing.

I made such good progress that I took leave over Christmas and New Year's to visit my brother, Erhard, who was at that time living in Phoenix, Arizona. In the Cactus Botanical Garden I learned about the many different kinds of cacti. I was especially excited about the saguaro, which grows to well over six feet tall. I had already seen them on my drive to Phoenix, and now I could examine them more closely.

Upon my return, I resumed working diligently. The office supervisor, though he was still convinced of the futility of my endeavor, even provided me with an additional assistant. Then I had to fly back to Washington, DC, on January 30, 1963 to report to Herr Backes on my progress. I informed the office supervisor there that I had already verified 90 percent of the advances. I felt sure that I could complete the rest in approximately six weeks. With this assertion I thoroughly angered the assistant office supervisor. He was the author of the previous negative reports to the Ministry of Defense and on account of my success later caused me difficulties. The office supervisor was impressed by my fluency in English. I had used my free time to study English. Furthermore, I had taken a room with an American family, which meant that in my day-to-day affairs I was forced to speak English and receive corrections for my mistakes. I had had no idea that I had any linguistic abilities, but they provided a number of advantages to me for the rest of my life.

My success in learning the English language had a further cause. Sunday mornings would always find me in church. Needless to say, initially I understood very little. But I did not hesitate to attend the Sunday school class for my age group. Additionally, I bought a King James Bible. With it and my German Bible side by side, God used his word to talk to me in church. I am still grateful to my brothers in Sunday school who helped me gain new insights from the Bible texts.

BACK TO WASHINGTON, DC

It was now the middle of March, and I had completed the tracing of expenditures. There were some remaining receipts that I accounted for as best I could. My work was completed, and the time of my assignment was drawing to its close. How would things continue now? I had been sent to the United States for six months for the completion of a special assignment. There was no doubt that a civil servant who had been detailed for a designated amount of time would have to return to his previous assignment at the end of that time. Yet prior to my deputation I had told my family that our entire family would spend several years in the United States. Was I wrong? Did I misunderstand my Lord? No! For in the meantime the supervisor of the office in Washington, DC, had requested my transfer to the USA. On the initiative of Herr Backes, the Ministry of Defense had issued the necessary orders. The anticipated duration of my service in the United States was set at three years.

Now my wife, still living in Bonn, had to accomplish a number of things that for most people would constitute a succession of extraordinary hurdles. Without the usual assistance from me, she had to arrange for our family and belongings to be transferred to the United States. What turned out to be extremely difficult was to meet the requirements for our three sons to fly to the USA. The children needed passports and visas, which are only issued upon application by the father and require his personal signature. But here also the Lord gave us grace. He does not always keep us out of difficulties, but he makes all things glorious. Ursula obtained passports for herself and the boys, visas for "diplomatic dependents," and airline tickets.

Meanwhile, I was traveling the more than two thousand miles from Texas to Washington in my VW. These days, such a trip does not pose any serious difficulties. But back then, work on the interstate system was just beginning. So, upon recommendation of AAA, I traveled on the routes used by the 18-wheelers. Later I told my family that it had been a race between me and the American trucks. Uphill, on account of their big engines they were able to pass my VW. The only chance I had was to overtake them on the downhill. But then they also accelerated. Finally I arrived again in Washington, DC, and after half a year of separation I was able to greet my family at the airport.

Now began a new episode in our lives. The boys—fifteen, thirteen, and ten years old—had to be enrolled in an appropriate school. Wolfgang had taken English classes in school for about five years and Winfried for about three. That was just enough so that both of them could attend high school summer school from June to August. Both of them passed the course, even though Winfried had considerable difficulties. But he was subsequently able to skip a grade ahead. It appeared that there would be no difficulties for Ralph-Rainer. It was recommended to us that he attend the German school in the DC area. We assumed that in the German school they would be speaking German. But no, except for in-class everyone spoke English, and our son had to go through a difficult time during which he was treated as an outsider by his classmates. It helped our youngest to learn to assert himself. Furthermore he learned everyday English in a relatively short period of time. And as it turned out, I also profited from it. In due time we settled into a routine. In order to avoid speaking the mishmash that you usually hear among the Germans in the United States, we instituted the rule that when any one of us spoke, it would be either in English or in German, but a combination of the two was not allowed.

DAILY LIFE

In Our Fellowship

The first Sunday in Washington arrived as Sundays are wont to all over the world. In Bonn it was our habit to go to church on Sunday morning, and so we would in America as well. Now I took a step by which my wife felt herself railroaded. In Baptist churches in America it was customary to close the service with an invitation. When the invitation had been given I said to my wife, "Let's go forward." So the entire family walked to the front. Upon promise of letter we were received into the membership of this congregation. Initially my wife was quite upset with me. However, because we took this step, the members of the congregation felt a responsibility to assist us in getting settled into life in Washington, DC. This was especially important and beneficial for my wife and our children. The boys quickly made acquaintances among the young people, and it wasn't long before my wife, our oldest boy, Wolfgang, and I sang in the church choir (eventually all the family joined the choir, and the bass section had a decidedly German accent). So, immediately we became part of the fabric of the church. At the next election of the board of deacons I was ordained a deacon. It was not long before I was superintendent of the youth. Because of my active involvement I was offered opportunities to take part in courses and seminars. I was greatly interested in such courses and always gladly accepted those invitations.

The congregation officially issued me a license as preacher of the gospel, which allowed me to preach and conduct services. I used this privilege not only to preach in English. Ascension Day is not an official holiday in the United States. But there are many Germans and German-speaking Americans in Washington, DC. So on Ascension Day we used the facilities of our church at Tenly Circle for a German-language worship service, which was well attended. Because of the announcements and invitations sent out prior to the event, my name became known. As a result I was invited to a party that the German ambassador was giving for Germans who were active in the community. I also was asked to attend a senators' prayer breakfast at which I was publicly introduced. This resulted in valuable contacts for me, but also earned me the envy of some of my colleagues.

Professional Life

Initially I was given a general administrative task for the procurement of furnishings and equipment for the German government offices throughout the United States. This included the official residence of the chairman of the NATO Military Committee, General Heusinger, and another head of a different military section who also held the rank of general.

Furthermore, I was responsible for supplying the needs of German soldiers and civilians stationed in sixty-four military offices throughout the United States. I had to ensure that everyone had what they needed to accomplish their tasks, from pencils and paper to the official cars. From mid-1966 on I was liaison officer to the American government department, responsible for the procurement, quality control, and cost analysis of whatever military equipment the *Bundeswehr* had purchased from the United States. My task also included assessing American firms seeking contracts with the Ministry of Defense as to the quality of their product and their capacity to produce enough of it in the time specified by a contract.

I acquired the necessary knowledge and capabilities to fulfill these tasks by taking distance classes. I earned a diploma in credit and financial analysis from the prestigious clearing house Dun and Bradstreet. This diploma is a requirement for every applicant for a credit manager position in any of the large US firms. A prerequisite for these courses is competency in the American bookkeeping system, provided through two extra courses as well as broad knowledge of the US contract law. This subject usually requires college-level training since the US legal system is based on case law, unlike the German jurisprudence, which is codified. The effect of having the diploma proved to be extremely valuable years later when I was given a NATO position in Munich.

There is much more to tell, both good and not so good, about my career. For example, in the kind of positions I held there were many opportunities to receive and accept gifts. At one point, there was an investigation into my practices in this regard. The incident started when I gave a negative evaluation of an American firm, who had applied for a multimillion dollar contract with Germany. The firm's efforts were supported by the prime minister of one of the German states, who filed an official complaint against me with the Ministry of Defense. My report was classified and had been transmitted via diplomatic channels. It had nevertheless been made accessible to a German state prime minister and US security officials. The investigation was complicated and unpleasant for many, but it did not demonstrate any wrong-doing on my part—because there was none. It disclosed that I had always been above board, even in little things.

Family Life

Under this heading I could easily fill many, many pages with experiences that we had. I could talk about the marvelous trips that we took, primarily by car, as we crisscrossed the North American continent. I will just allude to some of them. One time, we drove up to Canada to the Niagara Falls. We took a cruise on a boat that came so close to the cascading wall of water that we were thoroughly covered by the spray, but the ticket price included special vinyl coveralls to protect us and our clothing from becoming totally soaked. We also had the opportunity to visit many of the national parks. We spent several days in Yellowstone National Park, and, like so many other tourists, not minding the signs, we fed "Yogi the Bear." Naturally, we drove all the way down into Mexico. There we climbed the Aztec pyramids and soaked lazily in the warm waters of Acapulco. Much later on, we were even given an opportunity to take a cruise through the Caribbean. Yes, we saw much of the beauty of this earth, and we met many interesting people in our travels. And yet, we are often reminded of the words of a song we learned shortly after we arrived in the United States: "This world is not my home, I'm just a-passing through." And then the thought flashes through the mind, how few people we are able to reach with the gospel, even looking for and using every opportunity that Jesus has laid upon our hearts and given us strength to use.

4

Coming Home

RETURN TO GERMANY

After eight years, which had begun with a six-month assignment, I was recalled to Germany. We moved into an apartment in Koblenz, because I was initially assigned to the Federal Department for Military Technology and Procurement, which was located in Koblenz. The Ministry of Defense designated me as one of the German representatives to a special international taskforce. We were responsible for the evaluation of proposals from various contractors and the selection of firms for the development and production of the multirole combat aircraft (MRCA) Tornado. The supervisory body for the construction of the aircraft, in which several nations within NATO participated, was NAMMA (NATO-MRCA-Management and Production Agency). Such an aircraft consists of approximately 350 pieces of flying equipment. These were built by a roughly equivalent number of specialty manufacturers. The contracts were awarded to the various firms after consultations in meetings of the selection committee. This committee was staffed by an equal number of representatives from each of the various nations involved. A short while later I received an administrative transfer back into the Ministry of Defense without any change in my job description.

Here I would like to mention another peculiar event. I am known to have strong convictions and to go my own way on occasion. That often leaves others wondering about my course of action and intent. But in this particular case, even I did not know the reason for my actions.

We were still living in Koblenz. The beginning of another session of the contractor selection committee, which I was required to attend, was set for nine o'clock Monday morning in Munich. The train ride from Koblenz to Munich takes around five hours. There were three of us who were the German representatives, and we all lived in Koblenz. The two engineers (construction supervisors from the Federal Department for Military Technology and Procurement) and I agreed to meet at the train station Sunday evening. We met on the platform and chatted amicably, since we were well acquainted with each other. The train arrived, and my two colleagues boarded one of the rail cars. I, however, just like on the wreck of the training sail ship, was grabbed and pushed into another car. There I sat wondering what was happening to me. Suddenly the door to the compartment was thrown open and one of my colleagues pushed an American GI into the compartment and said, "Here is somebody with whom you can talk in English." Well, he took a seat across from me and slowly we started a conversation. He told me a bit about his life and that, on account of spiritual confusion, he was at his wits' end. He had been unable to find the inner peace for which he longed fervently, in any of the various religions with which he had had contact. Currently he was investigating the Mormons to see if he could find his yearned-for salvation there. Should he not be able to find his answer there, he was going to take his own life, since it was all useless. We had several hours for our conversation. The two distinguished-looking gentlemen from India, who were sharing our compartment, initially complained that they were forced to overhear our Christian discussion. But then they listened. After a prayer, the GI left the train in Munich with the remark that he was truly happy and no longer had any cause to take his own life.

After many months of intense research and negotiations, the selection of equipment suppliers had at long last been accomplished. Now I was finally able, in April of 1973, to take my previous year's vacation. During my vacation I received a call from a colleague who told me that he was asking, in the name of our common superior, if I would accept a posting to NAMMA in Munich. I told him that I certainly enjoyed the joke and asked him to tell me the actual reason for his call. He assured me that this was not a joke and added that he had been instructed to tell me not to say no right away, but to state under what conditions I would be willing to accept the assignment. These conditions were quickly named but in my opinion were less than reasonable. I would take the position only if I were given a promotion this year (1973) to *Oberamtsrat*. Further, I wanted to be given a position as section head at NAMMA, and finally the written promise in my personnel file stating that upon completion of my assignment with NATO I would return to a post at the Ministry of Defense. I was convinced that after my shamelessly stated, almost outrageous, demands the response would be a definite no. However, much to my surprise, I received a reply over the telephone the very next day. After consultation with the personnel department all of my requirements were accepted.

Consequently I was given leave from my civil service appointment and received a contract with NATO. Under the terms of the Ottawa agreement, I was furthermore given diplomatic status and the immunity that goes with it. I cannot disclose much about my work in this international committee. Suffice it to say that my initial responsibility was to supervise two hundred contracts and ensure that they were fulfilled in accordance with contract law. At first, my colleagues, many of whom had PhDs, envied and avoided me. Some wouldn't talk to me, and some wouldn't even return a greeting. However, by the end of about two years we were almost friends.

SEVEN YEARS IN MUNICH

When we returned from the United States, two of our three boys stayed in America. The oldest, Wolfgang, had married an American girl and stayed in order to complete his university training in classical languages and American Indian language studies. The second one, Winfried, had just obtained his undergraduate degree in zoology and had been accepted to study philosophy of religion at Trinity Evangelical Divinity School in Deerfield, Illinois. So there were only three of us, my wife and I and our youngest son, Ralph-Rainer, when we moved to Munich. That first Sunday after our move, as has been our custom, we went to Sunday services at the Baptist congregation meeting in Holzstrasse. We introduced ourselves as newcomers. The Munich International Baptist Church used the facilities of the German Baptist congregation after the German services had ended. That morning their pastor had just returned from furlough in the United States. We greeted him heartily in his native language, and he invited us to attend the services of the international Baptist congregation. In conversation, Pastor Rudzio, the pastor of the

German church, encouraged me to give whatever assistance I could to the Americans. They really needed a lot of help.

So the three of us attended the services of the international Baptist congregation and felt quite at home. The services were conducted according to the American customs, which we had become used to during our eight years in the United States. As a licensed Southern Baptist pastor I wondered if this might be where I belonged. I remembered Pastor Rudzio's comments when I saw that there were only about twenty people in attendance. I should mention that the Sunday morning activities of the international church started at 11:45 AM with adult Sunday school, and the worship service concluded at 2:30 PM. There could hardly be a more inconvenient schedule. As I will detail below the time for the worship service is not an obstacle for the Holy Spirit to work in any fellowship and to increase it in numbers.

About three weeks later I received a phone call from the pastor of international fellowship in which he advised me that he had to return to the United States because of some family problems. He closed the conversation with the words, "Herewith, I turn the pulpit over to you."

I did not find it difficult to feel myself into the task of pastor of the international congregation. Even though my tasks with NATO demanded considerably more of a time commitment than a civil servant is normally expected to give, I was able to make room for the additional activities. After all, I was no longer a civil servant. And since pastoring the congregation was intended only as a temporary arrangement, I figured that this ministry should not cause me any difficulties.

However, it turned out to last considerably longer than I had anticipated. After several weeks, the pastor returned from the United States. He simply informed me via telephone that he would not be able to resume the work there in Munich, and he had only come to Germany in order to make arrangements for his belongings to get shipped back to the United States. Still, I did not have the impression that someone had just left me holding a task to which I had not been called; all of our callings come from above.

This was a time of many blessings. The membership of the congregation was made up of persons from many countries across the globe. These people had ended up in Munich for business purposes and various other reasons. There were times when we had as many as two hundred persons in attendance for our worship services. It confirmed that what many people would have called a detrimental time schedule, namely right in the middle of the day, and a Sunday at that, did not stop the Holy Spirit from working among us. And also my fear that holding two strenuous jobs would overburden me turned out to be groundless.

My NATO job brought with it difficulties of a nature that are not common in other jobs or professions. Suffice it to say that my name was mentioned during debates in the British lower house (and not in admiration) since my job had placed me in the political arena. It is hard to imagine that, within this turmoil, I managed to provide many a service to many small outlying fellowships of the German Baptist church in addition to preaching in my own church. And yet my Lord, to whose glory and honor I was laboring, gave me more than enough strength. I need to add that every year the foreign mission board in the United States sent me a relief pastor for several weeks or even months. Sometimes it was a retired pastor or, perhaps, a professor who was spending part of his sabbatical in Munich. In this context I especially want to mention the services of a professor from Southwestern Baptist Theological Seminary in Dallas–Fort Worth, Texas, Dr. Curtis Vaughan, whom I much admire. I am especially grateful to him for helping me to expand my knowledge of the Greek language. Also the former president of the seminary in Bangkok, Dr. B. C. Thomas, relieved me for over a year before he went back into missionary service.

After seven years in Munich I requested my reassignment back to the Ministry of Defense for health reasons. At that time the foreign mission board in the United States sent a full-time pastor to shepherd the congregation, which had been solidly established over the last several years.

FOUNDATIONS FOR MY SERVICE IN THE PROCLAMATION OF THE GOSPEL

Due to the circumstances that I have described above, my training was confined to seminars, short courses, and distance education. To give an exact list is virtually impossible and in my estimation not even necessary. If you were to look in the list of pastors of the Federation of Evangelical Free Churches[1] in Germany, under my name you would

---

1. Please note that this organization should not be confused with the denomination named Evangelical Free Church (of America), which is also a separate denomination in Germany, called *Freie Evangelische Kirche* (Free Evangelical Church). The above-

find the following summary of my education: participation in theological courses offered at Dallas–Fort Worth, Texas; the Baptist seminary, Louisville, Kentucky; and the seminary of the Episcopal Methodist Church, Frankfurt (1948 to 1954).

There was no language barrier for me in English. Consequently I could fulfill my services in English-speaking fellowships without problems, which I did joyfully. Several appropriate organizations confirmed my calling and ability and assisted me publicly and through certification. The Wisconsin Avenue Baptist Church in Washington, DC, ordained me on January 26, 1964, as a deacon and confirmed this through a certificate. On October 9, 1968, I received from Wisconsin Avenue Baptist Church in Washington, DC, a license as a minister of the gospel. The Munich International Baptist Church ordained me in Munich on July 15, 1979, as pastor. The chairman of the ordination council was the previously mentioned Rev. Dr. Bill C. Thomas. The secretary of the ordination council was Pastor Gerd Rudzio from the German Baptist Church and at that time president of the counseling committee of the brotherhood of pastors. Since the international church did not belong to the German federation of churches, but was affiliated with the American Southern Baptist convention, the question never arose as to whether I should also be included in the list of pastors of the Evangelical Free Churches in Germany.

BACK TO THE MINISTRY OF DEFENSE

Although having been a civil servant in critical positions, which required a lot of dedication and stamina, I found that carrying out assignments in foreign countries and on international committees requires a lot more. For instance, the British government sends their delegates to such posts for no longer than four years. My work included tasks from which arose tension among the NATO partners. In awarding our contracts to the various competing firms from the participating nations we had to ensure equality in the financial values of the contracts and also to balance the special interests and concerns of the participating nations. The goal was to combine the special technology and know-how that the various nations had developed, so that everybody benefited.

---

mentioned *Evangelische Freikirche* (Evangelical Free Churches) is a federation of local churches, which share common commitments to Christ and the Bible, even though they may belong to different denominations, e.g., Baptist or Brethren. —Trans.

In not a few instances, a nation or government was reluctant to release their special technological developments to others. I negotiated several international contracts for the transfer of technologies. These contracts were then signed by the participating national governments. Germany had already developed the technology for an especially important aspect of aircraft technology. Since the inclusion of this item was part of my area of responsibility I had to conduct the negotiations very cleverly because our government wished to keep that particular technology under German control. Naturally the other participating nations had a great deal of interest in this particular technology and know-how. This type of balancing of many, often conflicting, interests was a normal part of my life during all those years. Thus, after seven years at NAMMA, I felt that my health had reached the point where further participation in the international arena was becoming detrimental. Consequently I let my contract with NATO expire and returned to the Ministry of Defense.

I was assigned to the Contract Negotiation and Agreements in Future Air Technology Department, which was not limited to just the production of military aircraft. Initially I had only limited signatory authority, but that was later expanded to include my entire purview. I would like to mention one little incident. At the time I held the authority to ratify a number of contracts. One of those included negotiations with the industrial firms on behalf of several technical sections in the Ministry of Defense. I often had minor disagreements with one of the technical engineers with regard to the proper technical write-up of his requests. Such explanations formed the basis of the contract and would be appended to it. One day this engineer walked into my office and said, "So, Herr Corduan, now I can prove to you that you made a mistake." My reply: "Really, Herr X? I really do appreciate that you are going to show it to me. You see, I am so good, that I am delighted to actually see a mistake that I have made." He shook his head and left the room without a further word. From then on we always worked well together.

A number of my superiors, both in my area of work and in the personnel arena urged me frequently to attend a two-and-a-half-year training program, which was requisite for a further promotion. I did not see much attraction in this possibility, given that my years were advancing.

5

My Service among the People of God

PULPIT SERVICE IN THE ANDERNACH FELLOWSHIP

With the money we had saved over the years, supplemented by a mortgage, we built a small single-family house. Our property was on the right side of the Rhine River, not far from the town of Linz, but at a higher elevation. We lived in the subdivision Ohlenberg of the small village Kasbach-Ohlenberg. The distance was approximately 7.5 miles from the Baptist congregation in Bonn. Our plan was to return there as our church home. We planned to drive to the services and to enjoy a time of peace and relaxation after the high pressure years in Munich. But again it turned out differently.

One Sunday morning after I had preached in Bonn, the brother whom the congregational leaders in Bonn had put in charge of the offshoot fellowship in Andernach walked up to Ursula and me. He stated that he believed that God was calling us to Andernach because we were really needed there. He extended a special invitation to us to attend the services the next Sunday. By way of welcome, and in an effort to express their desire for our service they played a special recording. The song title was "Hallelujah" and was performed by our son, Ralph-Rainer, who had also written the words and music himself. After the service I told them that I would consider joining the congregation in Andernach, if after conducting a series of evangelistic services, I felt welcomed there. It should be noted that for us to reach Andernach required a 15 mile drive and crossing the Rhine by ferry. The evangelistic services were planned for eight consecutive evenings and were conducted by me. For the first service, which took place on Sunday evening, the meeting room was half empty. The brother who had been chosen by the fellowship in Bonn for the leadership of the Andernach congregation expressed some concerns about my delivery. Monday night we could hardly believe our eyes. The chairs in our meeting room, as well as those scavenged out of other rooms, were insufficient to hold the attendees. And this is the way it continued for the rest of the week. In other words, the Lord Jesus blessed the congregation. Several counseling sessions and a baptism confirmed to us the workings of the Holy Spirit.

I took on several responsibilities in that congregation, but I did not desire to be called as pastor. Under the double obligations in Munich, that is, being a NATO section leader and pastor of the International Baptist Church, my health had been severely impacted. I needed the rest. Then the time for the selection of the congregational leadership in Andernach came around, and I found myself elected without having been previously consulted. The pastor of the congregation in Bonn, to which the branch congregation in Andernach was affiliated, persuaded me to accept the election. So we turned our energies fully toward Andernach. Subsequently, there was some unrest in the congregation, which resulted in my being elected to the position of congregational elder. Even though I was kept quite occupied on account of Bible studies taking place at our own home, I devoted time to this new position. In the meantime a congregation in Linz was beginning to take shape and required my full attention. I had to bow out of my obligations at Andernach.

THE BEGINNINGS OF THE CHURCH IN LINZ ON THE RHINE[1]

While I was serving the church in Andernach, I was also conducting a home Bible study that took place in our house in Ohlenberg and at times in other people's homes. We started this Bible study upon request of two couples who wanted to have opportunity to meet with others of similar faith and hope for discussion and prayer. As time went on more and more people joined the group; after about two years we had twenty or more persons who regularly met together on a weekly basis. On May 9, 1984, our fellowship decided to establish itself as an Evangelical Free

---

1. Linz-am-Rhein is the town's official name so as to distinguish it from a town in Austria, which is also called "Linz."—Trans.

Church congregation. Subsequently, starting November 11, 1984, we held regular Sunday morning services in our home. On May 1, 1985, in the firm conviction that I was following Jesus' leading, I rented meeting rooms in Linz on the Rhine on Asbacher Str. 71. At this time we did not have any other congregation's support. My endeavors to belong legally and organizationally to our federation of churches were realized when the congregation at Imhausen/Sieg adopted us as an independent branch congregation. In 1994 the congregation in Linz on the Rhine became a fully independent member of the federation of congregations.

Our meetings had started as a home Bible study fellowship and grown into a congregation. I initially handled the tasks of both pastor and elder. After an official elder had been elected, the congregation in Linz officially called me as their pastor. The official document of my call was also signed by the chairman of the Organization Southwest Germany and head of the Federation's Department of Missions, Pastor Wilfried Bohlen. When I stepped down at the age of seventy-three, we had thirty-seven members in our congregation. Overall, during the time of my service in the congregation in Linz thirty-six persons, primarily young people, requested believer's baptism.

My service in Linz gave me much joy, even though I had to conduct most of the Bible studies and preach in the Sunday morning services myself. There were a few exceptions when we had guest preachers. That I even had the energy, especially in light of my obligations at the Ministry of Defense, I can only ascribe to the loving care of my Lord Jesus, who has guided me all the way. Bible studies took place on Friday evening. When I arrived at home Friday night from work, in a manner of speaking, I only changed desks. A proper Bible study requires proper preparation. The students from the Bible school Neues Leben in Wölmersen, who participated in our services, ensured that we had many a lively discussion. Of course everyone else, who had unresolved questions, profited thereby. I often repeated my underlying philosophy: "if something is not clear, please ask. I will provide you an answer for every question, even though sometimes it may be, I don't know." Then I promised that I would have a reply the next Friday night. I think it is easy to see that our Bible study evenings often were exciting, and in spite of our efforts to limit them to one hour, that did not always happen.

Government regulations provide that civil servants retire at age sixty-five. So, when I reached sixty-five I was released from all my government obligations. Now I could focus all my energy into being a full-time pastor in Linz. The congregation of Linz on the Rhine officially renewed my call. Upon my request, with the support of the appropriate committees, and upon motion by the Directors of the Federation of Evangelical Free Churches of Germany, I was officially issued the title of pastor on September 14, 1999.

Another source of great joy was the cooperation with the Catholic and Protestant state churches. For a number of years there had been an ecumenical Bible study that took place every three months. Hesitantly at first, but eventually energetically, we became a regular part of these Bible discussions. Additionally, every year there was an ecumenical Week of the Bible. Twice I took the lead for this event. When the churches in town had decided to celebrate the Year of the Bible together, the other churches asked me to conduct the opening services in the packed Protestant church. The cooperation among the pastors of the various churches was refreshingly brotherly. Instead of using the usual formal means of addressing one another, we used the friendly "Du" and first names. It is not necessary to put your faith under a "basket" or even deny it in order to have a friendly relationship with other churches. We need to love other Christians, just as Christ loved all people. That also applies to the adherents of other religions.

Even though we started a new Protestant fellowship, which initially was watched with a wary eye, we achieved brotherly cooperation with other Christian churches and congregations. In our Bible studies and Bible evenings I always proclaimed a clear gospel. Upon leaving at the end of a study evening, one of the Catholic priests told me, "Brother Corduan, I marvel time and again at the freedom and joy with which you represent your faith." The youth groups of the various churches also had regular meetings under the direction of our youth leader. No congregation feared that there would be an attempt to proselytize their young people.

When I announced our impending move to the retirement community, the congregation planned a farewell party. This event was an indicator of the Christian friendship in our city. In addition to our congregation, not just the pastors of other churches, but regular members of the various churches with whom we had worked together, were in attendance. There are indeed brothers and sisters in our Lord Jesus who belong to other confessions.

6

The Evening of Our Years in Pilgerheim Weltersbach

A HOME FOR PILGRIMS

EVEN WHEN GOD FAITHFULLY meets all our needs, it is nonetheless our responsibility to see to it that "the pea soup does not burn." With that reality in mind we had applied for residency in the retirement community Pilgerheim Weltersbach. It was clear to us that we had to live our final years in a retirement home, since all of our boys, as I mentioned above, live in the United States and cannot be by our side to meet the needs of those years. In April of 1999 a residence had become available. After some renovations to the dwelling, we moved into our house in June of 1999. Our new address was Weltersbach 33. We had anticipated quiet and possibly even boredom during the final years of our lives. But such was not going to be the case. The Pilgerheim Weltersbach has a church, the *Christuskirche*, which is located in the center of the village. And that is where our Baptist congregation gathers for the usual services. On one of the first Sunday mornings Pastor Jones approached me just prior to the service and said, "Brother Corduan, would you please officiate at this service. Here is the program." So I was immediately back to serving. And not too long thereafter I was asked if I could fill the pulpit and conduct Bible studies, when the pastor needed relief. Additionally, I was asked if I could periodically conduct the morning devotional program that is broadcast to all the residences in our village.

Some disagreements arose in the leadership of the congregation, and the pastor and the church leadership agreed that the congregational elder and some of the members of the church board would resign and that the pastor would go into early retirement. There was a new election to the church board in which I was elected to the board. The church board in its turn elected me to the position of executive elder. What followed then was a very hectic time. We had to call a new pastor, and until that was accomplished, the life of the congregation had to continue. Certainly there were other pastors in retirement in Weltersbach. But it was important that the regular affairs of the church be managed by one person lest there be confusion (people do not know to whom to go) or, worse, rivalry. Actually we were approaching the Christmas season and the New Year. Instead of quiet and boredom, I once again faced many demands. I should mention in passing that by this time I was seventy-three years old.

Let me hasten to state that I fulfilled my tasks with commitment and much joy. We should never forget that Jesus is the Lord also of our church and gives us strength and comfort. Throughout the course of my life I have never believed in coincidence and have always placed my full trust in him, Jesus my Lord. We were without a pastor for only about half a year. The church board visited a young couple, Sybille and Pastor Christoph Becker, in Marburg. They had been recommended to us, and they expressed the willingness to consider such a calling. We went through the usual procedures of inviting the couple to visit Weltersbach and introduced them to the congregation. Pastor Becker preached that Sunday morning, and when the church board officially called them, they agreed to serve our congregation. They were both forty-three years of age at the time and in the prime of their lives. At the time of this writing, six years later, I can say that the calling of Pastor Becker was a gift of God. And it is an added blessing that Sybille Becker is fully trained and certified in the field of church music.

7

Working Together on the Church Board

Now I had to fulfill the many tasks that are usual for the executive elder of a church in circumstances such as these. I had to arrange for a special speaker to be present for the dedication service. The entire service had to be planned. The guests whom we wanted to have in attendance on that occasion had to be chosen and invited. I must have written at least twenty letters and made many a phone call to arrange all the small as well as the large details. When the big day finally arrived, the service and celebration came off as planned. And thus, effective April 1, 2001, we had a new pastor: Christoph Becker.

Since then our work together has proceeded without friction and with many blessings. The number two church elder, who is also one of the directors of the community, the pastor, and I have met regularly Friday mornings for a conference. There we considered the various aspects and events of our congregation. The entire church board has been working very harmoniously. The board meetings prepared by me have run peacefully, and we have experienced many blessings during the four years that I was the executive elder. Since I have continued to present morning devotionals, preach, and hold Bible studies as well as conduct worship services I have been, as in olden times, constantly busy and served joyfully.

Today I'm eighty-two years old. I still preach, hold worship services, conduct Bible studies, and take turns in presenting the morning devotional message broadcast throughout village. I can joyfully say that Jesus, my Lord, has led me for the entirety of my life, and I am astonished how much I was allowed to accomplish to the glory of the name of Jesus. If I were to recall all the examples of my Lord's guidance and write them all down, it would be a book of several hundred pages. I can assure anyone and everyone that no religion can create such a merciful God as Jesus is. By giving praise and honor to our merciful God I want to conclude this testimony. All that I have recounted here can be examined in detail and will be found to be factual, just as God's word, the Bible, is factual and true in all respects.

8

Closing Remarks

I WAS BORN AS a weak baby in the bleak hut of a day laborer, and my chances for survival, let alone "success" were bleak as well. But in the preceding pages, I have pointed out that God is not dependent on our human qualifications. He can use us without formal scholarly training and degrees. Jesus, my Lord, saved me, and I trusted in him. It was he who enabled me to accomplish all that I have done both professionally and in his service for the proclamation of the gospel. I have recorded some of these events in order to give hope and courage to those who are struggling in their faith. Certainly I could add a lot more. But it might start to sound like boasting of my own abilities, which I do not have. If I may boast I want to do it as the Apostle Paul did in 2 Cor 10:17–18: "'Let the one who boasts, boast in the Lord.' For it is not the one who commends himself who is approved, but the one whom the Lord commends" (ESV).

Part 2

Presentation of Basic Concepts Derived from the Bible

Introduction to Part 2

IN THE FIRST PART of this book, I have given you an overview of my life. I have pointed out some of the episodes through which God has guided me. Jesus, God's son and the Second Person of the Trinity, has been by my side and lead and encouraged me throughout my long life. In this second part I want to demonstrate the support that the Bible, the revelation of my living God, has been to me. I would like to encourage my readers to walk in the way of the good news, called the gospel, with the same trust that I have.

Based on the experiences that I described in part 1, it is a special concern of mine to preface my exposition with this statement: Reading the Bible brings great rewards! For the Bible, and only the Bible, gives us the clear instructions from the living God for making our pilgrimage through this life.

At the same time I can understand if one or the other of those who have read the preceding lines would like to turn to me and say: shouldn't you be putting a question mark in parentheses behind those statements? Many of those who call themselves Christians remember little of what they were taught from the Bible during their childhood. Most have taken only a few concepts and rules of conduct with them into their adult lives, on the basis of which they think of themselves as Christians. When Western European people are asked about their religious preference, they will most likely answer either Catholic or Protestant. As babies, they were baptized in the name of the Father and of the Son and of the Holy Ghost. At the time of confirmation, which was preceded by a course of religious instruction, often referred to as catechism, the pastor as a representative of the church then pronounced them members of the Christian church. At the end of the ceremony they were given a Bible verse to remember, and with a blessing they were sent out into life. And, in normal practical terms, they were also sent out of the church. For so many people there appears to be no further necessity to think any longer about what they have learned in their religious instructions or what might be written in the Bible. Many Christian denominations teach that following infant baptism, that baby is now a Christian. In the so-called worship services, which some attend for various reasons, it is seldom pointed out or taught that there is more to being a true child of God. Many people are of the opinion that they are *entitled* to enter heaven at the end of their life on earth. Very few persons question whether this is true or not. After all, the pastors have studied Christian thought and theology. The normal churchgoer assumes that what the pastor believes and teaches must be the truth.

Therefore I would like to add something to the statements I have made above. The Bible teaches unequivocally that it is faith in Jesus, the Christ of God, who died in our place on the cross of Calvary, that makes us God's children. He, Jesus alone, is the door to the heavenly kingdom. All the piety with which people try to impress and appease God, and all rituals, including pilgrimages and works of mercy, are futile. In regards to piety, with which one tries to soothe an angry God or gain his goodwill, other religions can appear to be much more intense, but their futility is enhanced by their evident misdirection.

How this faith, which is a clear certainty to me, has been expressed in my life I have described in the first part. In part 2 I will describe the fundamentals of my faith, which I have found in the Bible. Please let me emphasize that this matter does not come down to numbers or percentages. How many people believe something or how many people accept something as correct is irrelevant. What is important is to know what God says in the Bible and then to follow his instructions. Otherwise, despite one's piety, or, perhaps even because of one's misdirected piety one will be found guilty before the judgment seat of God.

What a shame it is that Christian churches and associations, in the past, and still today, have believed that they had both the right and even the duty to add to the Bible. They add obligations, doctrines, and rules on top of what the Bible teaches. To pick one hypothetical example, whether it is stated outright or merely implied, they convey the message that pious Christians will be more acceptable to God when they faithfully deprive themselves of various items and, say, attend a lot of retreats. Then they look down upon those who do not implement their blueprint of piety and make their own way of life a standard by which to judge others. As a proof text they may cite 1 Cor 11:28 ("But let a man examine himself...") utterly out of context. And they do not even come to terms with what the verse really says, namely that a man must examine *himself*. It does not assign this task to a committee or a congregation.

Furthermore, a duty-based Christianity is likely to use fear to bring people to repentance. I have always seen it as my obligation to proclaim the love of God, as the Scripture says. The Apostle Paul, for instance, clearly states in his Letter to the Romans 2:4 that God's kindness leads to repentance, and that we cannot earn our justification, but are justified because of his grace through salvation, which is through Jesus Christ alone.

Many rules of conduct and practices, even though their intentions may be pious, are false teachings if they deviate from what the Scripture says, regardless of how many centuries Christians may have been teaching these precepts. Consequently it is my prayer that my exposition will cause the reader of this book to read the Holy Scriptures more attentively.

Let me give you an example. Jesus calls Satan the ruler of this world; however, not a single book of the Bible designates him as the ruler of hell. On the contrary, hell, the lake of fire, is the place into which Satan will be condemned. When I recall how many preachers and pastors I have heard preach against the machinations of the ruler of hell and his minions, I ask, "Are you sure, dear reader, that what you believe is correct?" Believe me, the Bible is not one book amongst many books. The Bible is more than just a book.

ARE YOU SURE THAT WHAT YOU BELIEVE IS TRUE?

Do you think, dear reader, that I could have lived my life in the way I described it in the first part without the assurance of my faith in Jesus? It is my firm conviction that Jesus has guided me throughout my life. But that could only happen because I trusted him completely. This phrase, "I trusted him completely," I think, is clear and understandable. I have always had, and still have, the certainty that Jesus is God's son, is a member of the Trinity, and, in his great love, has showered his love on me and protected me. This should make it quite obvious that I did not follow a religion but rather a person who has given his life for me and many, many other people. The reason why I cannot live life without religious precepts I will comment on in the section "Living by God's Ordinances."

It is well documented, and it is also my personal conviction, that every thinking person has an inclination toward religion. Some people call it a worldview that is part of their personality, which gives them their strength and direction. Some people are satisfied with a little mascot or fetish, such as the replica of an animal. I know many persons who are football fans to such an extent that it fills a major part of their life and replaces religion. For others it is an idea or an unattainable ideal that gives them drive and self-confidence. This phenomenon tends to be especially pronounced among those who call themselves atheists. Just consider the politicians who have succumbed to the idea, and some still are under the illusion, that they can improve the world through socialism, despite the inescapable verdict of the last one hundred years that socialism will not work, cannot work, and—at its "best"—logically leads to totalitarianism. And let us not overlook the religions of the world, which hold people under their sway. These religions intentionally or unintentionally play upon people's inner insecurity and the consequential necessity for a belief in something that transcends the common and ordinary. In areas where people are uneducated, they may, in their ignorance, turn to shamans and their magical abilities. In this context we need to point out that all religions originated in human thinking, even if the founder of the religion claimed divine inspiration or even deity. Whatever these religions promise, the real question is not what piety they demand, but what assurance they can give. And when we attempt to answer *that* question, it becomes clear that that is one thing that none of these religions can achieve, namely release from sin and guilt. Despite the multitude of commands about what to do and what not to do, they cannot provide a measure of when a person has done enough to have attained whatever goal the religion may promise.

Every religion, including the Christian religion, leaves an uncertainty. Rites, pilgrimages, ceremonies, or asceticism (the so-called disciplines) are part of all these religions. They are demanded of the adherents or suggested as guidelines. But no religion offers a clear statement or guarantee that the final goal will definitely be achieved. No priests and no religion can issue admission tickets to heaven, attainment of nirvana, or ultimate identity with an Absolute that is beyond verbal or rational description. That is why I asked quite directly: are you sure that what you believe is correct?

The following anecdote may serve as an example of our underlying need for spiritual as well as physical nourishment. Through one of my needs for medical assistance I met a cardiologist who is the president for the association *Freundeskreis Indianerhilfe e.V.* (Friendship Circle for Indian Assistance), which supports Native Americans. Their mission is to provide medical and material assistance to those who live in remote and forgotten parts of the world. Every year he selflessly offers his skills and abilities for several months among the South American Indians to provide medical care and more. He expresses his disappointment over the fact that the people there, when in dire need, will turn back to the shaman instead of accepting the advanced and scientifically based help that is offered to them. He wrote an article under the column "Quo Vadis FKI" entitled: "Why the Return to the Ancient Rites?" His experience clearly demonstrates that, even in our age of scientific progress, human beings are not satisfied with strictly material assistance.

From my remarks it can be readily seen that it was not the Christian religion that gave me inner strength, but that I was guided and provided for by Jesus, who is God, the Second Person of the one Trinity. In the following pages I would like to lay out the insights from the Bible that make it possible to arrive at a firm faith and to live by it.

I must repeat that no priest and no religion has the ability to guide us through this life to heaven or any other godly goal. No church, no religion, no representative of either church or religion has the ability or authority to hand you an admission ticket into heaven or any other sought-after blessedness. No cleric or adherent of any religion or Christian denomination can obtain the favor of any god by means of actions or rites. The formal admission into a church is no entitlement for entry into a glorious afterlife.

As an example, let me bring up the life and death of a Jain monk because no religion makes stricter demands on its followers than Jainism. Jains believe that their final goal far surpasses that of any other religion, for example that of Buddhism. All of his life, the monk needs to undergo physical deprivation, and his ascetic labors will have achieved their fulfillment only when he has starved himself to death.[1] Then, so teaches his religion, his soul may have possibly cleansed itself sufficiently of karma to attain a state of blessedness. But there is no one who can promise

---

1. This is a ritual called *itvara*, and it is carried out only by monks who supposedly have achieved the highest level of spiritual achievement.

him success. Jainism intentionally rules out the existence of a Supreme Being. There is no certainty that he has achieved his goal or that he will ever achieve it. All that is left to him, as well as to us if we rely on our own accomplishments, is futile hoping and striving.

In the following pages I will be taking a position on several topics that arise out of the Bible. I will show that it is possible to understand God's revelations. I especially want to point out God's love for us, which he has demonstrated in Christ Jesus. He has not just left a mark in my life but has demonstrably guided me.

As an eight-year-old boy I gave my life to Jesus. From that time on, Jesus, the Christ of God, has led me through the ups and downs of my life. And here again I want to state in unequivocal terms that Jesus is not a religion, but a person. To be even more exact, Jesus is a person of the Trinity. It would give me great joy if I could have a part in giving others this certainty of faith in Jesus.

9

Living by God's Ordinances

Our Christian life is based on the idea of living a life pleasing to God; that is to say we seek God's will and strive to live according to it. In this regard, we also tend to assess the lives of fellow Christians. But we always have to ask ourselves, on what basis do we evaluate our conduct and that of our fellow Christians? In the following paragraphs I will lay down some basic conclusions. Some of what I'm about to say may strike you as paradoxical or even inconsistent with the last few paragraphs. But that is true only in appearance. Some further distinctions will make the matter clear.

CHRISTIANITY IS A RELIGION, BUT JESUS IS NOT

In his work, *Church Dogmatics*, the famous Swiss theologian Karl Barth promulgates the thesis that Christianity is not a religion among many world religions, but that it is a revelation from God. I am not willing to accept this statement outright. Our Christian faith is based unreservedly on God's revelation in the Bible. Nothing needs to be added to or taken away from it (Rev 22). We have a fundamental concept of what our lives would be like if we adhered to biblical doctrine in its entirety. Our Christian walk under the guidance of the Holy Spirit is supposed to make visible the new person, who is the result of salvation by grace. Please note that even Christian communities require that individual members live by rules of conduct that cannot necessarily be derived directly from the Bible. But in contrast to other religions, for example Judaism or Islam, true Christianity is not centered on any codified guidelines or rules of conduct. The focus of our Christian faith and life is the substitutionary death of Jesus on the cross of Calvary for a sinful world. That historical event constitutes the basis of our faith. Following our surrender to Jesus, our sinful person is drawn to Jesus, where we receive forgiveness for our guilt and sin and become a child of God. Solely through and in Jesus can we receive forgiveness for sins and adoption as sons and daughters of God.

However, churches, federations, and congregations are also temporal organizations that have to provide for themselves guidelines and basic rules of conduct, as well as a structure. We have done so, in order to make orderly existence in church and congregation possible. These ethical, moral, or socially acceptable rules of conduct are not a revelation from God, but rather were crafted by human beings. They are a part of our understanding of the model Christian believer. They form the solid structure as well as the organization within which we conduct our worship services and lead our daily lives. Still, whatever these moral and ethical rules may do, they are of little spiritual value to us until we have experienced repentance through the working of the Holy Spirit.

At the risk of repeating myself I want to bring out as clearly as possible that Christianity is not an ethics-based religion insofar as there are no rules of conduct, commandments, or directives by the observance of which a believer can obtain God's favor. The Christian faith and the adoption into God's family are based on historical events. God's Son, Jesus of Nazareth, paid the price for our sin by dying in our stead on the cross of Calvary. We receive release from our guilt and sin through accepting these facts and the person of Jesus, not by observing commandments, church attendance, sacrifices, or any other actions. In this respect we are distinctly different from Judaism, Islam, and virtually all other religions. They attempt to pacify an angry God, or, as in the case of Hinduism, try to obtain eternal enlightenment, through pious conduct.

THE BIBLE IS AND REMAINS GOD'S REVEALED AND WRITTEN WORD

The Christian faith is based on the foundation of the written word, the Holy Bible. The life of faith is structured by the ordinances that people have developed on the basis of the Holy Scriptures and that have become normative for the various denominations. Even though the observance of these norms and laws do not provide for us release from guilt and sin, they are not useless or superfluous. God gave Israel his commandments through Moses, and Jesus says in Matt 5:17, "Do not think that I came to abolish the Law or the Prophets; I did not come to abolish, but to fulfill."

As I have already stated above, living decent and orderly lives together in churches and fellowships, as well as leading a life well pleasing to God (once we are reconciled to him), requires that certain rules and guidelines need to be observed, and they are part of our religious understanding. We find ourselves in the situation that we have God's commandments and a significant number of rules and guidelines by means of which we strive to live out our Christian witness and to be pleasing to God. The observance of rules, as I have already pointed out earlier, is not a means of obtaining salvation from guilt and sin. However, at the moment of our conversion to Jesus, something took place in both the inner and outer person, and the world can rightly expect that the character of the regenerated person is manifested by our religious organizations and its members. They want to see a living testimony. Nonetheless, we discover that our human capabilities have limits. The more we attempt to live according to the laws and ordinances, the more the law demonstrates our inability to keep it (Rom 7). We realize that all our striving to be pleasing to God according to the laws and ordinances is bound to fail. The guilt and sin that are made manifest through the law leave us with only one escape, namely to seek refuge in the salvation that Jesus has provided for us. In our conversion we accept the historical fact that Jesus has purchased our liberation from sin. We are born again; we become God's children. Through the agency of the Holy Spirit we are led to the holiness without which no one can see God (Heb 12:14). Only now, as a consequence of our renewal, is the law released to perform its real function. It provides us with an understanding of the boundaries of what is pleasing to God as we pursue a life within God's will. I will clarify this idea more in the next section.

WHAT IS THE SIGNIFICANCE OF THE DECALOGUE FOR CHRISTIAN FELLOWSHIPS?

The biblical text makes it quite clear that the Ten Commandments were given to Israel, God's chosen people. Through the acceptance of Jesus' redemption, Gentiles, also, became children of God, and, according to Rom 11, were grafted into the root of the people of God. Consequently, God's laws and promises now also apply to us. There are various interpretations as to which part of the law applies to the Gentiles who have become God's children. Without a doubt, the Decalogue, that is the Ten Commandments, form a foundation that is binding for us as well. Within the framework of this writing I cannot delve any deeper into this issue.

Let me mention in passing that all world religions have foundational concepts, which in some cases are even similar to the Decalogue. Without a moral foundation there is no order, only chaos. The basic precepts of Buddhism are also ten in number and are similar to the expected biblical conduct, but cannot be compared to the Ten Commandments. For instance, the Ten Commandments prohibit the worship of other gods and command us to keep the Sabbath holy. These issues certainly do not apply to Buddhists. On the other hand the ten precepts of Buddhism contain rules on what may be eaten, as well as how Buddhist monks are allowed to sleep. There certainly is no parallel to those rules in the Ten Commandments.

As Christians we look upon the appearance of Christ as a fulfillment of the prophecies of the Old Testament. In this context I want to emphasize especially chapter 53 of Isaiah, which clearly describes Jesus' redemptive death centuries before its occurrence. And by his death, the commandments of God, as previously mentioned, are not invalidated, but fulfilled (Matt 5:17). What human beings in their sin-tainted nature were unable to achieve, God has accomplished. Look at Rom 8:3 and 4: "For what the Law could not do, weak as it was through the flesh, God *did*: sending His own Son in the likeness of sinful flesh and *as an offering* for sin, He condemned sin in the flesh, in order that the requirement of the Law might be fulfilled in us, who do not walk according to the flesh, but according to the Spirit."

Through God's intervention, which took the form of the sacrifice of his son, and based upon the supernatural working of the Holy Spirit, a person is born again and is led to salvation. And now the Holy Spirit takes control and makes it possible for this person to live a life pleasing to the Lord. God's laws and ordinances become guidelines. Still, this is only possible because the blood of Jesus Christ continues to apply to us day after day.

Let us look at an example of how to understand the ethical injunctions of the Bible. In the Bible as well as in most world religions, marriage is placed under special protection. The Bible does not have any prescription for how a man and a woman enter into marriage. Such regulations frequently are also not found in church, congregation, or denominational rules. But this "absence" should not be viewed as a lack of desire to keep order. The various bodies generally practice the customs as they are established by the legal codes of their particular locality. As each person is accepted into the fellowship, they carry along the legal traditions of their surrounding society. And, thus, even though the Bible does not specify how a marriage must be established, it is clear on the point that, however it is established, once it is in place, it is sacred and may not be violated.

THE NEW SIGNIFICANCE OF THE COMMANDMENTS FOR CHRISTIANS

In the previous section we have already glanced at the significance of the commandments for Christians and have already mentioned, that, thanks to the redemption by Christ and our personal rebirth, the Holy Spirit leads us into holiness. This action by God has produced a new relationship for us in respect to the Commandments. Not through the observance of the law does a person become a child of God but through the righteousness purchased by Jesus.

In Gal 3 and 4 Paul gives us a clear interpretation of the significance of the commandments for us. These instructions come to a high point in this statement in Gal 3:24: "Therefore the Law has become our tutor *to lead us* to Christ, that we may be justified by faith." The Greek word that Paul uses for "tutor" is *paidagōgos*. This term designates the slave who was responsible for the education and upbringing of a son prior to his legal emancipation. In antiquity this slave taught the son not just academics, but acquainted him with the laws, rules, and customs of his society. When the son had acquired the skills and knowledge necessary for adult life and had proven his abilities by passing various examinations, he was pronounced worthy and recognized by the family as a full adult member. This event would be celebrated, and at that time he would be, in a manner of speaking, adopted as an adult by the family to which he already belonged by bloodline. In the same way, the law has brought us into a position in which we recognized the necessity of redemption through Jesus. We accepted the salvation that has been offered, and now, just as in the above example, the Lord adopted us as children, and we were fully accepted into God's family. Here we see once again that God gives us freely, as a present, something that it is impossible for a sinful person to acquire by means of observing the law. To those who have been redeemed through Jesus, God gives the gift membership in his family: "THERE is therefore now no condemnation for those who are in Christ Jesus. For the law of the Spirit of life in Christ Jesus has set you free from the law of sin and of death" (Rom 8:1–2).

APPLICATION, OR THE QUESTION: "HOW THEN SHALL WE LIVE?"

In the previous section we have shown that in the Old Testament, the Bible demands a way of life that a sinful person cannot possibly fulfill. But because of the substitutionary death of Jesus and through his supernatural power, God *gives us* the righteousness that is acceptable to him. Even though we are unable to keep the law, by grace, through faith in the death of Jesus on the cross, God now views us as if we had fulfilled the law. This status continues to be in effect until we reach our goal, and it is manifested as we live on the basis of the work of the Holy Spirit, who leads us to righteousness. The law and the moral regulations under which we have placed ourselves in order to live a life pleasing to God continue to be valid as indicators of what God has done for us, because we can only present a Christian witness within that context. To return to our previous example, such moral rules of the church founded on Jesus Christ also encompass the married couple, husband and wife, who may only live together when they have met the appropriate moral and social rules of marriage. For a Christian, the Christian religion and the Christian ethic are so intertwined that we cannot separate the spiritual laws and the moral and social rules from each other.

This observation leads me to the conclusion that I cannot ignore moral and social rules that are applicable to the assemblies or churches to which I belong without placing myself outside of their fellowship.

10

God's Covenant with Humanity

THE POSITION OF HUMAN BEINGS IN SIN AND GOD'S PLAN

BEFORE JESUS ASCENDED TO heaven he stated in his farewell speech (Mark 16:16 NASB): "He who has believed and has been baptized shall be saved; but he who has disbelieved shall be condemned." The prerequisites for a person's salvation are quite clear in this verse. Jesus had to take the horrible path of sacrificial death on the cross. Those who believe that this was done for them and accept Jesus as their savior will receive eternal salvation. In John 3:16 we read the explanation that God loved us so dearly that he sacrificed his only begotten Son that all who believe in him will not perish but have eternal life. Did God use an unnecessarily complicated way and pay a higher than necessary price? That question also raises the further one of whether God could have prevented human beings from disobeying him and thereby falling under a curse. It should not have been very difficult for God to create a human who did not have free will with which to oppose God. No, God accepted the risk that we, human beings, would use our free will to live independently of God. Initially God created animals, including worms and fish and small life. Do we as people want to make ourselves equal to those creatures? We were supposed to be different, and so we are. In what follows I will look in detail at the development of the relationship between God and humanity, the creature's fall and subsequent separation from God. But that is not the end! God eventually provided for us liberation from the curse, and he did so through Jesus' sacrifice.

God created the human being as a creature upon whom he could shower his love. God's love was so great from the very beginning that he wanted to have a personal relationship with each individual person. God created the human being in his own image. Again: why? God wanted, here on earth, a being with whom he could have fellowship, on whom he could lavish his love, and who could reciprocate that love. And so, in order that we can truly be his partners, and not robots, he gave us a free will. God deliberately risked[1] that we might act contrary to his will—in other words, sin. God wanted to have pleasure in humanity, the beings whom he had created, and we, the human creatures, were supposed to show forth his glory.

However, human beings made full use of this freedom and fell for Satan's tricks. This act of opposition to God's clearly stated command is the original sin that bore destruction with it. The Holy Spirit departed from the human person, and people fell into an abyss. Without God's Spirit we people resembled the animals. Discord and hatred moved in. It led to our dissatisfaction with ourselves and our neighbors. We can read and hear daily in the media with what hatred people destroy one another—a direct result of this disobedience.

Can we imagine how much this situation pains God? Yes! That is the reason why God in his immense love prepared, in the very beginning, a way, a means of rescuing humans out of that abyss. God knew human nature from the beginning. He knew the nature of humanity, whom he has chosen as coworkers, children, and friends by offering to us the possibility not only to return to the original condition, but to enter a state of glorification that is even greater. This is what we call God's plan of salvation. When did he choose us?

In the following discussion we will examine the history of salvation and the steps that God went through to bring us back to himself. He made it possible for us to become holy, pure, and beyond reproach once again, and to escape from Satan's domination under which sin has placed us. When did the history of this salvation start? Even though I will be making this statement repeatedly, I want to stress that God, who is in all respects almighty, in his infinite wisdom had already known that human beings would fall into sin. As I already stated above God was fully cognizant of those he would create and the nature of those whom

---

1. Was this really a "risk" in the sense of a gamble whose outcome was unknown to God? In the next chapter we will look at this matter more closely.

he was going to create, before this world in which we live came into existence. Therefore the Bible states quite clearly that God's plan of salvation was established before the foundation of this world. In Apostle Paul's Letter to the Ephesians we read in chapter 1, verse 4: "just as He chose us in Him before the foundation of the world, that we should be holy and blameless before Him." In other words God was in no way surprised that the human beings allowed themselves to be led astray by Satan. Thus, the "risk" to which we alluded above was not a gamble on God's part. Albert Einstein said that God does not play dice. We can amplify that statement by saying that, if God did, he would know beforehand how the dice would land. Having presented these thoughts I would now like to detail God's plan of salvation and the history of salvation as the Bible reports to us.

GOD'S COVENANT WITH NOAH

In looking at the history of salvation, we can find a number of covenants into which God entered with certain men. I would like to focus on four significant covenants. The first one was with Noah. This was a very one-sided covenant. God let all people whom he had created, and all other living beings, drown in the flood, except for Noah, his family, and the animals in the ark. We read in Gen 6:8: "But Noah found favor in the eyes of the LORD." God blessed Noah and his sons. He set the rainbow in the clouds and said to Noah, "I set My bow in the cloud, and it shall be for a sign of a covenant between Me and the earth" (Gen 9:13). At the same time God provided a short list of commandments to Noah, such as forbidding one human being to take another one's life.

GOD'S COVENANT WITH ABRAHAM

The Bible does not give us much information about Abraham's religious heritage. There were many religions and many gods whom people worshipped. In the midst of this tapestry of religions we find one man who recognized God Almighty as his God, to whom God spoke, who believed what God said, and (this is the critical point) acted in accordance with God's directives.

Abraham was receptive to the living almighty God, and God entered into a covenant—we could say a "contract"—with him. Now for a contract or covenant it is necessary that there are at least two parties who agree to certain rights and responsibilities in regards to each other. What was Abraham supposed to bring into this contract? Was Abraham such a good, blameless, and wise man that God could in some way profit by this contract? No! We don't read about any such qualities. Was Abraham at least sinless according to the then-existing interpretation of this expression, in other words, a totally righteous man? Again no. In this regard Abraham was no better than anyone else. His qualification is given to us in Gen 15:6: "Then he believed in the LORD; and He reckoned it to him as righteousness." All that Abraham could point to was his faith in the Almighty God. There is no other explanation or qualification for the choice of Abraham, other than that God had chosen him.

This continues to be the prerequisite for our calling as mentioned above in Eph 1:4. It is God's will that:

1. We believe that God is the Almighty Creator of heaven and earth and that he is a triune God. For without faith it is impossible to please God (see Heb 11:6). Now, isn't it enough to believe that there is a God in order to be righteous? We know that this is not enough. In his letter, James says quite clearly (Jas 2:19): "You believe that God is one. You do well; the demons also believe, and shudder." Abraham did not just believe.

2. We conduct our lives in faithful obedience. Just as Abraham acted upon his faith, in the same manner we are to conduct our lives in faithful obedience. He did that which God expected of him. In the same manner God expects from us, who are in a new covenant, quite simply and clearly, obedience. Many people ask about God's will and even read the Bible and then . . . do whatever they please or whatever they see others doing. That is not obedience! It is only when we fulfill God's will that God will act in our lives. That is a prerequisite for every prayer.

Abraham therefore is an example to us. In obedience he traveled to the land of Canaan, and then God acted on his behalf.

It does not work the other way around, even though many people would like to have it reversed. First they want to see God act, and then they will believe. That is what I experienced during the war as well as later. People suddenly find themselves in a desperate situation. In my example in chapter 1, we were on a wrecked ship, during a storm, drifting on the sea into one of our own minefields. Now suddenly many sailors began to pray, "God, if you get me out of this mess, I will lead a different life." In the same way many pray when they are seriously ill. Later they very often forget all about whatever pledges they may have made to God. Abraham kept his covenant with God, and God gave him the promised son twenty-five years later at the age of one hundred.

We cannot turn this matter into a formula for getting God to do something that he would otherwise not do, but it makes no sense to ask for blessings from God if we do not care about the directions he has given us.

GOD'S COVENANT WITH THE PEOPLE OF ISRAEL THROUGH MOSES

There is a lot to say about God's covenant with the people of Israel in which Moses was the mediator. But, we might ask initially, why should that be important to us? We need to understand that God renewed his covenant with Israel in that he provided commandments, which Moses, in God's name, declared to the people. These commandments clearly outline what God expects from those who want to belong to his people. Even without the written commandments the people knew what was sinful. But from that day on, the day on which Moses proclaimed God's commandments, it was clearly spelled out what is sin. Sin is called by name. Today, as well as back then, people know what is sinful.

But in the renewing of the covenant, something very important was added: the establishment of the great day of atonement. God proclaims: I am willing to forgive your sins. And ever since that day there is not just guilt and sin, but now also forgiveness. God demands a penalty for transgression and provides the way to forgiveness. This is a foreshadowing of the covenant that Jesus, being both God's Son and a man, established. Shortly before his death on the cross, at the Last Supper with his disciples, Jesus proclaimed this covenant.

God's love is particularly exemplified through the establishment of the commandments. Let us read what Moses has to say when God walked past him, right after he received the second set of tablets of the Law: "Then the LORD passed by in front of him and proclaimed, 'The LORD, the LORD God, compassionate and gracious, slow to anger, and abounding in lovingkindness and truth; who keeps lovingkindness for thousands, who forgives iniquity, transgression and sin; yet He will by no means leave *the guilty* unpunished, visiting the iniquity of fathers on the children and on the grandchildren to the third and fourth generations'" (Exod 34:6–7).

What does that mean? God is exacting. Sin must be punished. Every sin remains until the punishment for it has been exacted, even those sins for which the high priest has sacrificed. The day of atonement was, as I mentioned earlier, a foreshadowing of the final covenant that would be accomplished in Jesus. By keeping the commandments of Moses, no person can please God: "because the mind set on the flesh is hostile toward God; for it does not subject itself to the law of God, for it is not even able *to do so*" (Rom 8:7).

Therefore, God himself had to step in and take the initiative, and that is what he did. We read in Rom 8:3: "For what the Law could not do, weak as it was through the flesh, God *did*: sending His own Son in the likeness of sinful flesh and *as an offering* for sin, He condemned sin in the flesh." And so, God established a new covenant through Jesus.

THE NEW COVENANT IN JESUS

What is this new covenant? Jesus himself has put it in place:

> And while they were eating, Jesus took *some* bread, and after a blessing, He broke it and gave it to the disciples, and said, "Take, eat; this is My body." And when He had taken a cup and given thanks, He gave it to them, saying, "Drink from it, all of you; for this is My blood of the covenant, which is poured out for many for forgiveness of sins." (Matt 26:26–28)

Subsequently Jesus walked to Gethsemane and from there, to the trial before the spiritual leaders of Israel, who condemned him to death as a common criminal. Jesus walked this way in obedience to God, fulfilling God's will, so that we can become children of God. As we said earlier about God, he is compassionate, gracious, slow to anger, and abounding in loving-kindness toward us to our salvation. He did not even spare his own Son.

I repeat: what we could not accomplish through the keeping of the commandments, God did for us. He sent Jesus, who deliberately made himself equal to us in his baptism by John. He, Jesus, took up our sins and carried them for three years as he walked on this earth. Weighed down with our sins, he was nailed to the cross. Apostle Peter, in his letter (1 Pet 2:24) expresses it this way: "and He Himself bore our sins in His body on the cross, that we might die to sin and live to righteousness; for by His wounds you were healed." Jesus was punished for our sins.

I am punished in Jesus, because I am in Jesus:

> Or do you not know that all of us who have been baptized into Christ Jesus have been baptized into His death? Therefore we have been buried with Him through baptism into death, in order that as Christ was raised from the dead through the glory of the Father, so we too might walk in newness of life. (Rom 6:3–4)

But we have to enter into the covenant with Jesus. He says in Matt 26:28: "[F]or this is My blood of the covenant, which is poured out for many for forgiveness of sins." Yes, not for all, but for *many*—those who will accept Jesus' offer.

How can one enter into this covenant?

1. By depositing one's sins by faith where Jesus has picked them up. Jesus has made himself equal to us at the Jordan River and in this act of obedience took our sins upon himself. It is to this Jesus that I must confess my sins. This is what we call conversion, and it is the prerequisite for acceptance into the new covenant.

2. By making a covenant with God, through Jesus. Jesus states in John 6:37: "All that the Father gives Me shall come to Me, and the one who comes to Me I will certainly not cast out." God responds to my request for acceptance into the covenant by letting me be born again. Therewith I am grafted into Jesus. Now I know that I am a part of Jesus.

3. By undergoing baptism as an external sign that we have entered into the covenant. By this act we confirm his covenant before man and God. Just as a man and a woman become husband and wife only through the public wedding ceremony, in the same way God established baptism. In baptism we declare that we are now free from guilt and sin through the blood of Jesus and want to be part of Jesus and his church. This is not a ritual. This is an act of the will, which God demands of us.

Dear reader, God has entered into that covenant with us, sinful people. In this covenant we become acceptable, pure, and holy before God. As his part in the establishment of this contract he gave his only begotten Son. Jesus died on the cross of Calvary in our place. My and your sins he has taken upon himself. Now we can become children of the living God by entering into this contract. Many of us have already become part of this covenant. Some, however, have become lukewarm and lethargic in their following him. Others have rejected the offer God has made them. They draw back timidly from conversion and baptism. We all have to remember that we are living in God's time of grace. The love of God is still available to us. Now, all those who have become lukewarm and lethargic in their walk can renew their commitment to the covenant. Those who want to enter into the contract can acquire that which God in his love provided for us in Jesus. There is a day coming, and no one knows that date except God himself, when the time of grace is over, and at that point the possibility of receiving God's offer ceases.

11

God, the Trinity

THE NAME OF GOD

In Exod 3:13 Moses asks God for his name, and in verse 14 God gives Moses the answer and calls himself יְהוָה or "Yahweh." In the Greek translation of the Old Testament the name is given as Ἐγώ εἰμι ὁ ὤν, or "Egō eimi ho ōn." In English we translate the name as "I am" or "I am who I am" or "I will be." As we can see, the single Hebrew word requires several words in order to capture the meaning of the original language in Greek or in today's English. And even that is only an approximation. Such is frequently the case in translating from one language into another.

The Israelites, based on the second commandment (Exod 20:7), had a reverential awe for the name of God and never used this name in their conversations. They used the more generic names El, Eloa, and Elohim and replaced occurrences of "Yahweh" with those alternatives. In general, in the Greek manuscripts the name was represented as *Theos*. It is similar in the written language. Since in Hebrew only the consonants are written we will find in the sacred writings Y-H-W-H.[1]

During the Middle Ages, Bible translators struggled to come up with a Latin equivalent for J-H-W-H. It was unknown at the time that the letter A always follows the Hebrew consonant that we now represent

---

1. In the Hebrew above, vowels have been added by means of the dots and lines underneath the four consonants, often referred to as the *tetragram*, which means "four letters." The vowel marks, which you can see in the Hebrew script at the beginning of this section, do not exist in the original Hebrew text.

with a *j*. Actually, in Latin it would have been an *i*. Eventually the word *Jehovah* was coined. In the Authorized Version and in many other English translations, the convention was adopted to represent the tetragram by the word *Lord* with all capital letters.

GOD THE FATHER

The Concept of Father, Son, and Holy Spirit

To begin with, we need to consider that the Bible was written by human beings for human beings at the behest of God. That means that words and expressions were chosen that belong to the human language and could be understood by people of all ages. When the Bible talks about God the Father it is not referring to a person who, together with a woman, had children. Neither is he an old man with a long white beard. Rather this expression is used to clarify that God is preeminent and preexistent to all that we see, hear, and feel. In our language the closest expression to this concept is "Creator of all things." Jesus tells us in John 4:24: "God is spirit, and those who worship Him must worship in spirit and truth."

The same logic applies to the designation of Jesus as "God's Son." Jesus has always, in eternity past, been a member of the triune God. We will talk more about that later. In the same way, the expression "Holy Spirit" does not initially convey much. He also is a member of the Godhead. Again, we'll come back to that.

The Being and Actions of God

The Bible does not teach us a religion with rules and directives on how we can placate an unknowable and capricious God. We know that, according to 2 Pet 1:21, a human person under the influence of the Holy Spirit spoke in God's name and wrote the holy Scriptures. That means that God gave this person the responsibility or assignment to write about him, namely God—his being and his doing. In the beginning was the triune God (Gen 1:1); everything was created through the Word of him, who was in the beginning (John 1:1), and without the Word nothing was made that was made (John 1:3). Here we can sense the mystery of the Godhead. We have to admit that our human understanding has great difficulty to follow divine thinking. This singular God is the Source (Father) and Creator of all things and exists from eternity to eternity.

Since God cannot doubt his own existence, there is, consequently, no necessity that he explain himself or prove his own existence. As Paul states in Rom 1:20, it is, however, possible to sense God's invisible being and his eternal power and Godhead since the creation of this world occurred through his own works. With so-called scientific methods we, as humans, cannot prove the existence of God, nor provide proof that he does not exist. God can only be experienced. God reveals himself (provides us information about himself and what he does) in the Bible. The entire Bible is gospel— the good news that God announces to human beings (Rom 1:1-4). The Bible contains three important pieces of information:

1. God's plan of salvation for humanity
2. The history of God's dealings with humanity
3. The redemptive acts of Jesus for humanity

JESUS, THE SON OF GOD

Jesus as a Member of the Trinity

Since the Bible writes about Jesus as a human being, it is difficult for us to keep in mind that Jesus, God, exists forever (in our way of human thinking, without time or beginning). We cannot but think in human terms. Jesus himself declares to us in John 8:58, ". . . before Abraham was, I am" (ESV). John, in the beginning of his Gospel, 1:14, points to the fact that the creative Word of God, Jesus, existed at the time of creation and subsequently became flesh. In 1 Cor 10:4 we read that the spiritual rock that traveled with the people of Israel and out of which they drank was the Christ (see also John 18:6 and Mark 14:62 for Jesus' "I am" statements). Jesus is "the image of the invisible God" and "by Him all things were created" (Col 1:15-16).

To his disciples Jesus initially appeared to be no more than a human being. That he simultaneously had the same nature as God the Father was something his disciples could not comprehend at first. It is easier for us to come to terms with this because, in contrast to his original disciples, we now have the entire Bible, which contains Jesus' explanations. We read in John 14:8-9:

> Philip said to Him, "Lord, show us the Father, and it is enough for us." Jesus said to him, "Have I been so long with you, and *yet* you

have not come to know Me, Philip? He who has seen Me has seen the Father; how do you say, 'Show us the Father'?"

At the same time we have to maintain the unity of the Trinity. The unity can be expressed through the concept of *nature* and the triadity by the word *person*. Theologically it is expressed this way: the one God is one nature in three persons. In Christ we find a person with two natures. This has been established doctrinally in two councils. In the Council of Nicaea, the term *Trinity* (one substance in three persons) was described. The Council of Chalcedon described the "hypostatic union," namely "the person of Jesus and his connection as God and man." In order to understand what I have just said, it is important to remember, as I stated earlier, that the concept of Father and Son are not identical to what we mean when we talk of human fathers and sons. Those are simply attempts to somehow capture the divine concepts with human language. We have in front of us (as in a number of places in the Bible) a mystery, which our human understanding can only partially comprehend.

Jesus as a Man on Earth

Because of the fall of humanity—Adam's sin—human beings lost their spiritual connection with God. Specifically this meant the departure of the Holy Spirit and thereby a human's capability to maintain a connection with God. Only he, God, is capable of bridging this gap. He reached out and still reaches out to humanity across the chasm that sin had created. He wants to reestablish communion with each human being. He has given us instructions to accomplish this reunion, and he has provided us with everything that is needed. According to God's word we were condemned to eternal death. God's justice could only be satisfied when the sentence of death had finally been carried out. However, a human person's death was not God's desire. So, since God's holiness demanded justice, God established a rescue plan. As part of this plan God made himself equal to human beings, in that one of the three persons, namely his only begotten Son, actually became a man by joining himself to a fully human nature. Jesus relinquished some of the prerogatives of his deity for the time of his sojourn here on earth in order to accomplish this work of salvation. When Jesus said to John the Baptist by the Jordan River, ". . . Permit it at this time; for in this way it is fitting for us to fulfill all righteousness . . ." (Matt 3:15), Jesus took upon himself our sin and bore it for three years on this earth (1 Pet 2:24). For the rest of his life on earth Jesus was now equal to human beings in every way (Heb 2:17; Phil 2:5–11). He carried our sin but was without any sin of his own (2 Cor 5:21; 1 Pet 2:22; Heb 4:15). In his execution on the cross he fulfilled the justice that God demanded.

What we have just said constitutes the good news, that is, the gospel: when sinful people believe that Jesus is the Christ and Son of God, when sinful people by faith deposit their sins where Jesus has already picked them up, they become children of God. This is repentance. God responds with the gift of the Holy Spirit. The sinful person is reborn and God actually creates a new person. This process will reach its culmination when we shall see Jesus as he is and become like him. In 1 John 3:2–3 we read:

> Beloved, now we are children of God, and it has not appeared as yet what we shall be. We know that, when He appears, we shall be like Him, because we shall see Him just as He is. And everyone who has this hope fixed on Him purifies himself, just as He is pure.

People testify to their entrance into the new covenant with God through baptism. All this is only possible through God's plan of salvation, which he himself established. He gave Jesus the task and authority to complete this plan of salvation against the will of Satan. Satan, the regent of this world, sower of discord, and accuser, has been expelled from heaven (John 12:31). He still rages on this earth (Rev 12:10–12); however, he does not have any authority over those who have committed themselves to Jesus (John 10:27–30). With the gift of the Holy Spirit the human being is connected to Jesus and reconnected with God (John 14: 23).

After the completion of his mission, his resurrection from the dead, and triumph over Satan, Jesus ascended into heaven and left behind his disciples, some of whom still doubted.

Jesus Seated on the Right of His Father's Throne

Jesus came to earth in order to take upon himself the curse of God, which was actually ours. He took our curse upon himself and died in our stead. He did so voluntarily (John 10:17–18). He had received from God all power and authority to accomplish God's will—his plan of salvation—in heaven and on earth (Matt 22:44; 1 Cor 15:25). However, before he ascended into heaven, he explained to his disciples how he would continue to maintain contact with them. By means of this representative he would make his power, as well as his Father's, available to his followers (John 14:14–18). This is the Third Person of the Godhead, the Holy Spirit.

THE HOLY SPIRIT

We will remember from what we have said already that God is Spirit. We can only think in terms of human concepts and thought patterns. God's manifestations, however, are not tied to our concepts; they reveal his divine majesty in manifold variations.

The Holy Spirit in the Old Testament

We are aware that through the fall in the garden of Eden the relationship between God and humanity was broken. There is a deep chasm between human beings and God (Luke 16:26). In order to accomplish his plan of salvation, God, now as well as then, reaches out across this chasm. The Bible tells us that God appeared to people in a variety of ways, for example, to Abraham at Mamre (Gen 18:1) as well as to Gideon (Judg 6:25). It is not totally clear whether that was God himself or an angel, but that doesn't really matter. Whether God speaks through an angel with a human appearance or a donkey is not the central concern. The crucial point is that God has spoken his Word, and that *God's Word is his Word*.

In the Old Testament, God filled people with his spirit on particular occasions. We read that this happened with Samson and Samuel and, in the New Testament, also with Zacharias and Hannah. Through Jesus, God's Anointed, these cases were exceptions in the execution of God's plan to restore a person to the relationship he would have had before Adam's sin. Here we have to remind ourselves that from the beginning God was not trying to create faithful servants and children. If that had been the case he could have prevented humanity's fall into sin. God's goal was to make us fellow heirs with Christ, that we may be glorified with him (Rom 8:17). To this end God gave us free will so that we can, equipped with God's glory, live as God's representatives and glorify him. Here we find the final vocation of God's children, not as keepers of commandments but as glorifiers of God.

The Holy Spirit Poured out after Jesus' Victory and Ascension

In the Old Testament God revealed himself to the prophets. He joined himself to various individuals in the person of the Holy Spirit for special circumstances. When God's timing and preparation had been accomplished (Gal 4:4), God revealed himself through his Son Jesus. Jesus accomplished his mission and sat down to the right of his Father. With his work of salvation, he has eliminated the chasm, which sin had created between God and humanity. Now the way has been cleared. God reestablished the connection. But Jesus is no longer personally present on earth.

Jesus explains this matter to his disciples and us when he says, "I will not leave you as orphans; I will come to you" (John 14:18). Furthermore, Jesus says, "And I will ask the Father, and He will give you another Helper, that He may be with you forever; *that is* the Spirit of truth . . ." (John 14:16-17). That means that Jesus was the representative and plenipotentiary of God, the Father, while he was here on earth. Following his redeeming death God raised him through the immeasurable greatness of his power. He placed him on his right hand in heaven above all realms, authorities, might, powers, and whatever else there might be, not just in this world, but also in the one to come and has placed all things under his feet (Eph 1:21-23). Jesus' representative is the Holy Spirit, who will be with us until Jesus returns as the ruler of his kingdom.

IN THE END, GOD ALONE IS GOD

In the preceding pages, we have drawn a picture of what sin has done to humankind. God had fashioned humanity for his honor as his almost-equal, just "a little lower than God" (Ps 8:5). Through sin, humanity came under the curse of death. In his plan of salvation God prepared for himself a people out of one man (Abraham) and out of this people he chose his Son Jesus as Redeemer for the world. Jesus was God, yet he made himself equal to us. God laid everything at Jesus' feet so that he could achieve victory for God and re-conquer all that had been lost through Adam's fall. "And when all things are subjected to Him, then the Son Himself also will be subjected to the One who subjected all things to Him, that God may be all in all" (1 Cor 15:28).

12

The Visible Beginning of the Plan of Salvation

For the scriptural basis of what follows in this section you may want to read Gen 22:1–13, Rom 8:31–34, and Rom 8:38–39.

INTRODUCTION TO THE PLAN OF SALVATION

God's plan of salvation culminated in the arrival of Jesus. In order to understand why this is the high point of God's plan we need to look for the starting point, a necessary feature of any narration or report. Thus, if we begin at the beginning, the first eleven chapters of the Bible are a good launching pad for our further thoughts. In these chapters, we observe human beings living aimless lives, which twice ended in catastrophe.

The first installment of human beings became so utterly polluted that God sent a flood to eradicate them. Then, later, the descendents of Noah and his family, the only survivors of the flood, attempted to build a tower that would reach all the way to heaven. God put an end to this hubris by fracturing the human race. Up to then they had all spoken the same language, but God scrambled their languages so that they could no longer communicate with each other, thereby dispersing the people all over the globe. Having demonstrated the apparent incorrigibility of humanity, we then see in chapter 12 how God set his plan in motion with one man: Abraham. This man, chosen by God, was obedient to God and carried out God's commandments.

Thus, through the depiction of Abraham as a man who obeyed God (most of the time), the beginning of God's plan becomes visible for the first time. Crucially, we find that Abraham was not only a model believer but also the progenitor of the chosen people through whom God was going to implement his plan of salvation.

In contrast to the speculations that are at the bottom of other religions, the biblical story of salvation is also a historical narration. If human beings had scripted it, it probably would look very different and be easier to understand. Nevertheless, the first segment of this history carries special significance because we start to get an outline of God in the role of Savior and Redeemer. God reveals himself as a god who enters into a covenant with a man but then severely tests him twice to see if he will keep this covenant.

To begin with, God promised Abraham that he would have a son by his wife Sarah, but then he made him wait for twenty-five years for this birth to occur. Then, to top it off, once Abraham had his son Isaac, God gave Abraham the assignment to sacrifice him. This story is recorded right there in the Bible and is an actual, historical event. Please allow me to underscore this truth again: the Bible is God's word and is true! God stands by his word. Patriarch Abraham experienced this truth throughout his entire life.

The book of Genesis is factual history, contrary to the assertions of negative critics. Scholars have questioned the truth of many passages, which is a good thing to do per se, as long as they are willing to accept the results. However, when the apparent conclusions do not fit their preconceived negative results, they have resorted to thoroughly implausible theories of authorship, revised the dates of authorship of the various biblical books, and even rerouted the course of history, in order to gloss over their failure to find the historical errors they had been looking for. On the contrary, in their research to prove the narratives untenable, scholarship has proved time and again the accuracy of the biblical accounts. The Bible contains God's plan of salvation, and God brings his plan to fruition, regardless of what a mere human being may pontificate about it. The Israelites' walking through the Jordan River dry-shod and the fall of the walls of Jericho were part of God's plan and are historical facts. *In the same way*, the sacrificial death of Jesus, God's sacrifice of his own Son, really happened. God has no need to impress anyone by signs and wonders; the bland data of history already give overwhelming testimony for the trustworthiness of his word.

WHO WAS THIS ABRAHAM?

Abraham grew up in Mesopotamia near the city of Ur. It is unlikely that he lived inside the city itself because he was a Bedouin and raised sheep, cows, and camels. There are archaeological documents indicating that well-to-do people in that time would send their children to school where they learned not just to read and write but also received instruction in mathematical computation.

Archaeologists have discovered thousands of clay tablets, one of which implies a geometric formula that approximates what we now call the Pythagorean theorem. The Greek philosopher and mathematician Pythagoras of Samos lived in the fifth and sixth centuries before Christ, so Abraham's contemporaries at least may have had a hunch of what would later be confirmed rigorously.[1] These archaeological discoveries allow us to conclude with high probability that Abraham could read, write, and also be conversant in some basic mathematics.

These clay tablets also provide a background for what we read in chapter 23 of Genesis about Sarah's death and burial. Abraham purchased the field, which contained the cave of Machpela, for four hundred pieces of silver from the sons of Heth as a burial plot for his wife Sarah. This event is now accepted as actual history, which is significant because for a long time so-called biblical critics maintained that the sons of Heth never existed. It is easy to counter these critical claims, even for me personally because my son Winfried, professor of philosophy and religion, has personally been inside the cave of Machpela, located in Hebron on the Palestinian West Bank, as is possible for anybody else who would like to do so.

There are many other passages that scientists have claimed that are fictional. However, once their facticity has been established, the scholars who attempt to disprove the truth of the Bible simply move on to another passage, without acknowledging that they were wrong in their previous attempt. In spite of the critics questioning and trying to disprove the historicity of the Bible, archeology continually provides proof of its accuracy. Through the excavation of sites and discovery of

---

1. When your system of mathematics starts with a base of sixty, as opposed to ten, which we use, you're starting out with a decided disadvantage. Common people in ancient Mesopotamia used pre-inscribed tables of arithmetical sums and products in their everyday calculations for trade and other purposes.

documents, we now know that Abraham was an educated man who walked the earth long ago.

ANTICIPATION OF THE FULFILLMENT OF GOD'S PROMISE

God had told Abraham to leave his fatherland and his relatives and had promised him that his descendents would become a large nation. For many years Abraham traveled in the land of Canaan as a Bedouin and waited for the fulfillment of God's promise. What is the basic prerequisite for being the father of a large nation? Obviously, one must begin by having at least one child. Thus, first of all Abraham had to become the father of any child, and Sarah had to give birth to a son. After twenty-five years, the long-awaited heir finally arrived. Isaac was born. I think that all of us can well imagine how the aging parents of this "heir of promise" showered him with love and protection. Ishmael, the son of Abraham and the maid Hagar, had to disappear. For God had said to Abraham in Gen 17:19, ". . . Sarah your wife shall bear you a son, and you shall call his name Isaac; and I will establish My covenant with him for an everlasting covenant for his descendents after him." So the bearer of promise grew into a young man. All appeared to be normal.

THE LOSS OF THE VISION

What happened next must have seemed like a nightmare to Abraham. But, again it was true historical reality. God said, "Take Isaac, your only son, whom you love, and go into the land of Moriah and sacrifice him there as a burnt offering." What is interesting is that in the Hebrew text God's statement is not stated as a command but rather a request. Be that as it may, I suspect that Abraham's head must have been spinning. This could not possibly be true.

After waiting such a long time for the great event of Isaac's birth, would all be brought to naught through this sacrifice? I can well imagine how startled Abraham must have been: "God, do you really mean what you have just said to me?" No answer. Then came the conversation between Isaac and Abraham: "Father! Look, here is the fire and the wood; but where is the sheep for the burnt offering?" Somehow Abraham managed to choke out an answer. Each step that he took must have reverberated painfully through his head. But all through his life Abraham had learned to obey God fully, regardless of how painful it may have been at times. Abraham had to separate himself, in his mind, from his beloved son. With Isaac's death, all his hope for the future and all the promises of God seemed about to come to an end.

FOLLOWING GOD'S PLAN

God's plan of salvation was quite different from what Abraham imagined. We read in Gen 22:11–12: "But the angel of the LORD called to him from heaven, and said, 'Abraham, Abraham!' And he said, 'Here I am.' And he said, 'Do not stretch out your hand against the lad, and do nothing to him; for now I know that you fear God, since you have not withheld your son, your only son, from Me.'"

Almost staggering under the sudden release of tension, Abraham looked up, and there, with its horns tangled in the brush, stood a ram. Abraham took the ram and offered it in place of his son. This marks the actual beginning of the story of salvation, of God redeeming humanity. Here is the root of the fig tree that became God's people, the Hebrew people. And out of the Hebraic tribe of Judah would come the Messiah and with him the salvation of humankind. Again and again we have to focus our attention on the fact that the entire Bible describes God's plan of salvation for us human beings. And it all starts right here with Abraham.

ONE PLAN OF SALVATION IN THE ENTIRE BIBLE

Even though many people may deny it, the history of God's dealings with humanity, culminating in Jesus Christ, starts here in the Old Testament. And this event is meant not only to open our eyes and to make us recognize God's provision for our salvation as an interesting piece of information, but, most importantly, to appropriate it for ourselves. I am convinced that this episode is not just a foreshadowing of the events that God performed for us in Jesus. God's covenant with Abraham was the basis upon which God renewed his covenant with Moses and gave the law to the people of Israel. However, God could not have intended obedience to the law, pure and simple, as a way of salvation in its own right. As we read in Rom 8:3, the law was weakened through the flesh, and by keeping the law, humans were not able to achieve reconciliation with God. What the law could not accomplish God did on his own initiative and in his own power, out of love for us.

OUR PIETY IS WORTHLESS

God's own holy nature prevented him[2] from utilizing any other means of freeing us from the curse under which sin had placed us. He had to do what he had demanded of Abraham, to sacrifice his only beloved Son in our place. No law, no religion, no piety, no pilgrimages, and no spiritual disciplines are capable of freeing us from sin and guilt, and, consequently, eternal damnation. The more we strive to free ourselves from guilt through our own work, the more we recognize the vastness of the chasm that separates us from God. Indeed, we can do nothing, absolutely nothing, through our own efforts to save us from the curse. That is why God gave Jesus, his beloved Son, to hang on the cross in our place, to die in our place.

THE GIFT OF SALVATION

What was it that God lost through Adam's fall into sin? His partner. At the cross Jesus not only achieved peace with God for us. He also opened God's loving heart to us. This is affirmed in Rom 8:32: "He who did not spare His own Son, but delivered Him up for us all, how will He not also with Him freely give us all things?"

It is still necessary that all of our needs need to be met by God. If we had been able to achieve the restoration ourselves, Jesus would not have had to die on the cross in our place. But God did that which he had requested of Abraham. He did not spare his own Son. Jesus willingly did what was necessary to make us children of the living God.

---

2. People who are unaware of how Christian theology works may be startled by such a statement because it seems to contradict God's omnipotence. If we have just pointed out that God "is prevented" from doing something, does that not mean that he cannot do everything, and that, therefore, he is not omnipotent? Well, if you just snatch the word "omnipotence" out of the air, define it as "the property of being able to do anything whatsoever," and think that God has this attribute, then the statement would, indeed, be inconsistent with his omnipotence. But there is much more to theology than unraveling words to their supposed logical conclusion. Christian theology begins with Scripture, and if we say that God is omnipotent, that statement must be (a) based on what Scripture teaches, and (b) understood in the context in which Scripture places it. In that case, it becomes obvious that "omnipotence," as applied to God does not mean that he can do anything, but that he can do anything in keeping with his nature. Thus, for example, he cannot override fundamental rationality because that is a part of his nature. So, God cannot make the number five an even number, he cannot not-exist, he cannot become evil, he cannot become a finite being, and—he cannot simply overlook human sinfulness.

God in his mercy wants to give us all things. What does God mean by that? Does God want to bring us back to the condition in which Adam was before the fall? No, more, much more.

THE GOAL OF THE PLAN OF SALVATION

The living God, Creator of heaven and earth, did not spare his own Son but offered him for us, and God desires to present as a gift what Christ had accomplished: to be part of God's family (Rom 8:32).[3]

This new position entails peace and security here on earth and eternal life with Jesus and all the saints. Yes, we will receive more than simply restoration to the condition of Adam before sin entered. We shall be like Jesus, just as he is. That is more than to be a pardoned sinner released from the prison of sin. He has called us to be kings and priests (Rev 1:5-6, 20:6). Paul writes in 1 Cor 6:2: "[D]o you not know that the saints will judge the world? . . ." In the following verse he writes that we will sit in judgment over angels. That is far more than just fellowshipping with God and living under his guidance and direction. We have a choice to make: to possess Jesus wholly and completely or to reject Jesus wholly and completely. We all know the consequence. Humanity without Jesus has upon it the curse of sin . . . and then judgment. It is in this life that we have to make the decision for or against Jesus. What decision have you made?

---

3. Of late, the idea that God sent his Son to die for our sins has come under severe attack. Don't we feel that, if Abraham truly had sacrificed Isaac, that he would have committed a serious wrong, and that, if the command to do so had come from God, then God would have been both the instigator and accomplice in this crime? How much worse that in the case of his own Son, God did not provide a ram at the last moment, but that he sent Jesus to earth precisely to undergo horrible sufferings and torture, and eventually die! Thus God, in the eyes of these critics, was committing "child abuse" of the worst kind, which we would never accept among human beings.

Once again, we need to point out that this critique can only be relevant if we take some theological terminology from outside of the biblical context, pummel it into submission, and then apply it back to God. This critique carries no weight because it is based on a clearly unbiblical notion, namely that the Father and the Son are two separate beings, of whom the will of one overrides the will of the other. But that is not the biblical scheme. This critique is problematic on at least two grounds: (1) it ignores the unity of God in the Trinity as one being—the Father and the Son would have willed identical things, and (2) it ignores the fact that the Bible consistently testifies that Christ came, suffered, and died of his own will on our behalf. God the Father did not somehow shove Jesus out of heaven so that he could be tortured; the idea that "God sent his son" is premised on the fact that the Son was willing and wanting to go (Phil 2).

IN JESUS WE CAN HAVE IT ALL

From the deepest fullness of my heart do I hope that you, the reader, fully understand and comprehend this. Certainly God showed us his love and mercy in Jesus' death. But that is not all. Do you think that the sole purpose of Jesus' death on the cross was that we may intellectually believe the truth of this event? No! The intention of the reports in the Bible is not just that we can assert the fact that Jesus died on the cross for us sinners as an interesting occurrence in history. Much more! We are supposed to receive and accept Jesus as a present, a gift from God. That is more than simply believing in Jesus and being baptized into his name. The Bible tells us in Rom 6:3: "[D]o you not know that all of us who have been baptized into Christ Jesus have been baptized into His death?" The thought continues, and in Rom 11 we read that we have been grafted into Jesus. We have become part of him. Because of the power of the Father's glory we can now walk in a new life. I repeat: we are grafted into Jesus. I live in Jesus! Do we understand that? Then we can also understand what Jesus said in John 15:4 and following: "Abide in Me, and I in you. As the branch cannot bear fruit of itself, unless it abides in the vine, so neither can you, unless you abide in Me. I am the vine, you are the branches; he who abides in Me, and I in him, he bears much fruit; for apart from Me you can do nothing .... If you abide in Me, and My words abide in you, ask whatever you wish, and it shall be done for you."

The most important thing is that we are in Jesus. It is not enough to believe that Jesus has lived—that he was a historical person. An intellectual faith, in the sense of accepting something as reality, does not lead us to become children of God. Believing, in the biblical sense, means accepting Jesus' offer of salvation, putting our complete trust in his assurance that he suffered for our sins and died in our place on the cross of Calvary. Similarly, it is inadequate for us to undergo some rite or ceremony, such as baptism in whatever fashion. What we need is Jesus himself.

WHERE DO YOU STAND?

Dear reader, here is my question: do you have Jesus? I am not asking whether or not you have been baptized in Jesus' name. Nor am I asking whether you have repented. I am asking you, dear friend: do you have Jesus? There are way too many who have repented, but have never gone any further. If I am standing before an abyss and turn around, am I now any further from the abyss? Not at all! I am now facing in the right direction, but only when I start moving in that direction will I move away from the abyss. If I want to enter my home, it is not enough for me to unlock the door, nor is it enough that I open the door. I have to step inside. Analogously, it is not good enough just to repent. Have you ever heard of someone getting married solely because the wedding ceremony is so wonderful? Of course not. In order to start a new life we have to repent and then accept God's gift, Jesus. God gives us new life with Jesus, in Jesus. If I do not have Jesus, what has changed? Nothing! We need to consider that God (and his Son) did not just play out a charade in order to redeem us through Jesus. Jesus had to die a real death. What does it say in Rom 8:32? He did not even spare his own Son, because he wants to live with us.

JESUS CALLS ME HIS OWN

Dear reader, I have accepted Jesus as my redeemer and my guarantor of eternal life. I now belong to him, and he now belongs to me, in this present age. When my life comes to its end and the trumpet calls me forth from the grave, then he will receive me as a child of God. You see, we already know each other, because he was mine already in this life. Then he will introduce me to his Father as the fruit of his righteousness.

It is my wish that everyone who reads this has this assurance of faith. Anyone who is not certain about having Jesus right now should seek out a spiritual counselor. It is worth it, for Jesus himself gives the invitation.

13

Living for the Honor of Jesus in This World

PRECONDITION

Without full assurance of faith, we are exposed to the temptations of this world without any protection. Paul warns us in Eph 6:12, "For our struggle is not against flesh and blood, but against the rulers, against the powers, against the world forces of this darkness, against the spiritual forces of wickedness in the heavenly places." In order to be properly equipped, we must have assurance and certainty in regards to our faith. Therefore we must ask repeatedly whether or not we have certainty in regards to the content of our faith. The response to this question is critically important. The apostle Paul had the same concern when he made the statements I just quoted from the Letter to the Ephesians.

To be a proper disciple of Jesus it is not enough to be concerned about our own assurance. In his parting comments at the time of his ascension Jesus called upon us to be his witnesses and to pass on the good news to others. He says in John 20:21, ". . . [A]s the Father has sent Me, I also send you."

Paul further elaborates on our commission and our responsibility to Jesus in Rom 10:14–17:

> How then shall they call upon Him in whom they have not believed? And how shall they believe in Him whom they have not heard? And how shall they hear without a preacher? And how shall they preach unless they are sent? Just as it is written, "How beautiful are the feet of those who bring glad tidings of

good things!" [Isa 52:7] However, they did not all heed the glad tidings; for Isaiah says, "Lord, who has believed our report?" [Isa 53:1] So faith comes from hearing, and hearing by the word of Christ.

It becomes totally clear that a disciple of Jesus can only fulfill this obligation if he has full assurance of faith.

THE SOURCE OF MY ASSURANCE

The source of my faith and my assurance is simply the Bible. In the year 1992 the Christian churches in Germany agreed to deemphasize the doctrinal differences that characterize us. The objective was to present unity to the world by proclaiming together, "The Bible is the basis of faith regardless of the denomination." This declaration has no practical value if the individual Christian does not read the Bible. The exhortation of Apostle Paul in the Letter to the Romans, which I cited above, must be followed. While anyone can read the call to action in the Bible, if it is not preached from the pulpit, and if the call to be a witness is not followed by action, very little is accomplished. It is indeed true, and I have come to the conviction through the experiences in my own life: God speaks to human beings through the Bible and reveals himself through it.

The Apostle Peter asserts the fact that God talks to us through the Bible and gives us the explanation how he does so in 2 Pet 1:21: "... but men moved by the Holy Spirit spoke from God." It is obvious throughout the Bible that God (almost) always used a human person to deliver his message to other people. The Bible is the good news from God, the gospel, in which God himself speaks to us humans. But he always uses his human messengers. That is why the Bible never attempts to prove the existence of God. It is up to us by faith to accept and experience the very existence of God. In the first part of this book I have talked about my personal experiences of the reality of God.

The Bible is not a history book. Nonetheless, the events reported within its pages are unquestionably true. And that includes the first eleven chapters of the Bible, which many relegate to myth and legend. Obviously much can be called into question. However, even well-defined and articulated questions cannot falsify those reports. Indeed nobody has yet been able to prove that the reports in the Bible are faulty. Remember that the Bible is not a history book for world history.

Rather, it contains the plan of salvation and the history of the implementation of salvation— how God interacts with humanity. In the first three chapters God tells us that he created the world, that on account of sin our relationship with God has been severed and we are now dead to him. In the 1,186 chapters that follow, God's plan is laid out. He tells us how he wants to save us from the curse of sin. We can read about all that he has done through Jesus and is willing to do for those who choose to accept his offer.

The reports from archaeological findings are available to anyone who is truly interested in questions of the reliability of the Bible text. The former director of the Australian Institute of Archeology in Melbourne, Australia, Professor Dr. Clifford A. Wilson, in his book *Rocks, Relics and Biblical Reliability* on page 35 presents the hypothesis that there is no conflict between biblical and secular history. He asserts that they do not stand in contrast to one another but rather complement each other.

THE CENTRAL MESSAGE OF THE BIBLE IS SALVATION THROUGH JESUS

When I pick up my Bible I know that it talks about many events of the past, taking us all the way back to the creation of the earth. It depicts for us the lives of people from the very beginning and moves forward, all the way to today, because the Bible as God's revelation is in full force until the end of time. There are prophecies in the Scriptures that apply to us and some which still have not been fulfilled. That becomes especially clear to those who diligently search the Scriptures and allow its message to continually shape their lives. It becomes obvious that there is a red thread through the entire Bible, namely God's plan of salvation for humanity and the parallel running history of salvation. God's plan has one all-important goal: to restore humanity to intimate fellowship with its Creator. Maybe it is better to say, as the Bible so clearly expresses it, to restore as many human beings as possible to the relationship Adam once had with God. From the beginning it was God's desire that humans should be kings and priests in his kingdom (see Matt 26:28 and Rev 1:5–6).

When we search the Scriptures thoroughly, verses 4 and 5 of chapter 1 of Apostle Paul's Letter to the Ephesians will stand out. Paul says: "[God has chosen us] before the foundation of the world that we should be holy and blameless before Him. In love He predestined us to adoption as sons through Jesus Christ to Himself, according to the kind intention of His will." Based on these verses we can realize that God's plan of salvation was already in place before the world was made and before human beings were created. Here we must remind ourselves that we have a triune God. Jesus, the son of the living God, had already laid the plans for humanity's redemption at the time that Satan believed he was going to triumph. And God has allowed human beings the freedom of choice. We can choose whether we want to obey or not.

God created us with a free will. We need to recognize that, as I have stated before, it would have been possible for God to create persons without free will, so that we could not make any decisions contrary to God's will, that we could not sin. It was fully within God's power to completely prevent the fall into sin. But what would human beings have been without free will? We would have been like robots fully dependent on God's will. And is there something else that would have been lacking in human beings without a free will? There is, namely that they would bear God's image! Human beings would not have been able to be God's partners, freely and voluntarily fulfilling God's will. We would in all respects be fully dependent on God's will, just like a machine that reacts to the push of a button. But having been equipped with free will from the start, people can today, just as in the beginning, exercise their own will. God allowed that Adam fell into sin, that he was banned from God's presence (in the garden of Eden), and that he is no longer that which God had intended him to be. In order to achieve his original goal God created a plan of salvation for and with humans. The Almighty God in his omniscience already knew ahead of time that humans would sin.

Simultaneously we have to take into consideration that Satan, too, was a created being with free will and that God had given him a specific assignment. What assignment? In John 12:31 Jesus calls him "prince of this world" (NIV). What power Satan had received from God in this capacity we can discover in Matt 4. Satan was given the power to tempt Jesus, the son of God. He was given permission to try to cause Jesus to deviate from the plan of salvation. Jesus could have avoided the path of suffering leading to death on the cross. If Jesus had bowed down to Satan, Satan would have turned the world over to him. We read in verse 9 of the fourth chapter: "All these things will I give You, if You fall down and worship me." Jesus could have avoided the death on the cross as well as all the limitations and restrictions that accompanied his humanity, and he could have still become the Lord of this world.

By the way, Jesus' temptations did not cease at this point. Let us remember the night in which Jesus was arrested. Peter tried to defend him with a sword, and Jesus rebuked Peter with these words: "[D]o you think that I cannot appeal to My Father, and He will at once put at My disposal more than twelve legions of angels?" (Matt 26:53). Such an angel or simply a single word from God's Son would have been sufficient to annihilate the band that had come to arrest him. No! Jesus steadfastly walked on, continued to follow the plan of salvation to the cross. His goal was to pay for the guilt and sin of humankind.

Only when we know the Bible properly and have recognized God's goal can we understand the plan of salvation and the historical events culminating in our salvation. And then we will no longer ask the question, why did God allow this or that? Once God has endowed a creature with the capacity to act contrary to its Creator's desires, he will allow the creature to use this capacity. That fact applies to Satan, to the first human beings, to Jesus, and also to us. And we know that Satan and the first humans chose disobedience to God. But Jesus remained obedient and faithful and voluntarily went to the cross to redeem us.

THE IMPLICATIONS OF ASSURANCE OF FAITH

In Eph 2:19 we read: "So then you are no longer strangers and aliens, but you are fellow citizens with the saints, and are of God's household." In this verse Paul is not talking about hoping, wishing, or longing. He states clearly and plainly that through repentance and baptism we have reached a goal of faith. Through obedience and the acceptance of Jesus' sacrificial death on the cross, we, who have given ourselves to Jesus, have become part of Jesus' body. We are now fellow citizens with the saints and members of God's household. Jesus came to proclaim the gospel of peace, specifically peace to us, who as Gentiles were far removed from being God's people, as well as peace to the people of Israel, who were near. In Paul's Letter to the Ephesians we read: "But now in Christ Jesus you who once were far off have been brought near by the blood of Christ. . . . And he came and preached peace to you who were far off and peace to those who were near" (Eph 2:13, 17 ESV).

However, dear reader, are you sure of your living faith? Or to express it differently, are you sure that you are already a part of Jesus and therewith in God's hand? Allow me to phrase the question more pointedly: do you have full assurance of faith, full assurance of salvation? Faith without assurance is like life without consciousness. My remarks in this book are intended to cause us to examine ourselves and, as it becomes necessary, to make appropriate decisions. For this reason I have preceded my biblical explanations and exhortations regarding our relationship to God with my life and walk of faith. It is intended as a reflection on how I conducted my life by giving full control to him, my Lord and Savior Jesus. I had full assurance that I could trust God's leading and directions. I knew that he understood and would show me the best way to go, especially when I had to make decisions in complex and tangled situations. To make it even plainer, I want to state that throughout my life I trusted Jesus not only in spiritual matters but with my everyday affairs. I knew that if I left my decisions to God, he would show me better ways than I could find on my own. In retrospect I can only gratefully acknowledge that my trust has never been betrayed.

And that is why I want to state clearly in these comments on spiritual topics: in order to have firm faith, I have to have full assurance that the triune God is a reality. Further, my assurance must include that I have turned my life over to Jesus and that God in Jesus, based upon my commitment, has saved me and redeemed me out of Satan's stranglehold. Out of this certainty arises what the Bible calls faith. This faith is the firm assurance of that which one hopes and does not doubt, even though one cannot yet see it. Hebrews 11:1 (NLT) describes this faith as "the confidence that what we hope for will actually happen; it gives us assurance about things we cannot see." This certainty also causes me to be obedient to God and Jesus in the manner the Bible demands.

Unfortunately quite often what I am trying to convey here is exactly the opposite of what is being proclaimed from many pulpits and in writing. I, too, was instructed in school and informed in sermons that we make headway on our way to heaven by means of religious conduct. But the path to God and to holiness is not found through observance of commandments and rules of a particular religion but rather solely through the acceptance of Jesus' death on the cross. And this is the message that Jesus' disciples should be proclaiming from the pulpits as the good news, as the Apostle Paul says in Rom 10:17, "So faith comes from hearing, and hearing by the word of Christ[!]" I know that the world exists and that I myself exist. I know that there is a God. I know that this

God is my God and that he has set me free and purchased me through Jesus. The Apostle Paul has provided some illumination for us in the Bible passage Eph 2:1–10:

> And you were dead in your trespasses and sins, in which you formerly walked according to the course of this world, according to the prince of the power of the air, of the spirit that is now working in the sons of disobedience. Among them we too all formerly lived in the lusts of our flesh, indulging the desires of the flesh and of the mind, and were by nature children of wrath, even as the rest. But God, being rich in mercy, because of His great love with which He loved us, even when we were dead in our transgressions, made us alive together with Christ (by grace you have been saved), and raised us up with Him, and seated us with Him in the heavenly places, in Christ Jesus, in order that in the ages to come He might show the surpassing riches of His grace in kindness toward us in Christ Jesus. For by grace you have been saved through faith; and that not of yourselves, it is the gift of God; not as a result of works, that no one should boast. For we are His workmanship, created in Christ Jesus for good works, which God prepared beforehand, that we should walk in them.

ASSURANCE OF FAITH ELIMINATES DOUBT

Doubts concerning God's word would obviously stand in the way of assurance, and we must read and understand the Scriptures in context. The above quote from the Bible is only a part of the Letter to the Ephesians and consequently only a part of the Bible, a part of God's word. A Bible verse ripped out of its context often leads into error. In this particular case the second chapter of the Letter to the Ephesians is a continuation of the thought that had been developed in chapter 1. There the Apostle Paul acquainted us with the glorious promises God has given us, the riches that God has prepared for us through his unfathomable mercy and love. This is the gospel, the part of the good news of the word of God, which again and again leads me into praise and thanksgiving.

Let me summarize in four points what we have said so far. These will serve us as a foundation for further thoughts.

1. God has chosen us before the foundation of the world by Christ Jesus!
2. God purchased our freedom from Satan's slavery through Jesus' sacrifice. We are redeemed. That is a fact!

3. Because Jesus has served the penalty for our sin on the cross, our sins have been forgiven and thrown into the sea of God's love.

4. God, in his love, determined before the foundation of the world that we are to be his children in Jesus. We must accept this truth, as the Bible says, by repentance and baptism. Through obedience we become partakers of God's riches; we are heirs, part of God's household. Either we believe what the Bible says or we do not. If not, we may search for illumination in any religion, but I can say that no religion can provide us with forgiveness of sins and a placated God.

The Bible is the gospel, the good news for all people. Whoever preaches something else will have to give an account to God along with those who allowed themselves to be led astray. We have the offer to accept God's gospel in full obedience. The unconditional acceptance is the prerequisite that it will apply to us.

Let me give an example. Angela Merkel and the political parties in Germany had come to the agreement that she should become chancellor of the Federal Republic of Germany. The president had signed the document of appointment. Was Frau Merkel now the chancellor of the Federal Republic? No! Frau Merkel became chancellor at the moment that she accepted the document and all its consequences. It is the same with God's offer. We only become children of the living God when we accept his offer. The Bible tells us how.

The Letter to the Ephesians was addressed to simple people who came out of heathenism and were accustomed to try placating angry gods through works and offerings. Paul was aware that not everyone could readily understand his message. In those days, just like today, people may have had only a vague understanding of the good news. Every religion provides its adherents with the guidelines on how to attain its goals. Where applicable it may give instructions on how to placate angry deities and specify what sacrifices and pious works have to be performed. Quite often pilgrimages are required to achieve the goal of piety. Preachers and theologians again and again encourage us to use human endeavors, called piety, as a means to achieve God's mercy as part of the gospel. However, on the cross Jesus has already accomplished everything that needed to be done to remove the curse from humanity, to pay for our guilt, once and for all. This I must accept, this I must believe! Then, in repentance, I turn my life over to God. It is only after repentance that

God expects us to endeavor to live in his love. Not beforehand. That is why Paul explains to the Gentile Christians in Asia Minor the gospel in such clear statements.

WE ALSO ARE ADDRESSED

We, who are not Jews, are Gentiles just as the Ephesians were, to whom this letter was written. And so we also may—better yet, we must—appropriate these instructions to ourselves, just as the early Christians to whom the apostle Paul wrote this letter. We are addressed, through God's word as written in verses 1 and 2: we were dead in our sins following the spirit who is leading the "sons of disobedience." This sad state applies to all people in the past as well as today, just as the good news of redemption always has applied and will apply.

God has given to us, the Gentile Christians, life in Jesus. In God's eyes we were dead in trespasses and sins, like all people who live under the influence of the prince of this world. People who do not know this fact or don't want to acknowledge it do not get an exemption from it. Since the time of the fall into sin, the spirit of the prince of this world has been and continues to be at work in those who have not been freed from his influence by obedience to Jesus. Consequently this principle applies still today: all who have not been released through Jesus Christ are part of this world and are dead in this world.

WITHOUT REDEMPTION THROUGH JESUS WE ARE DEAD IN GOD'S EYES

As already mentioned above, what Paul says in the Letter to the Ephesians in chapter 2 applies to all people without exception: you were dead in your trespasses and sins. Consequently all persons without Jesus are dead, even when most people do not acknowledge this truth. Let us look and see what the Bible says about it. We read in Gen 2:17: "but from the tree of the knowledge of good and evil you shall not eat, for in the day that you eat from it you shall surely die." Paul echoes this concept in Rom 6:23 where he states: "For the wages of sin is death. . . ."

One can raise an important question here: Did Eve indeed die after she had eaten? Or Adam? Did they not keep right on living? Apparently so. But in reality life had ended within them, that is, the life of God's Spirit had departed. Did they continue to live? Yes. But now only as creatures, with their bodies continuing to live in the same fashion as the bodies of animals are alive. Nevertheless God did not give up his original plan and implemented the plan of salvation. Here we see the reason why persons without rebirth are little different from animals. Except that animals do not go about killing one another with the kind of malice and hatred as we see in people who are under the devil's control. We, humankind, are born spiritually dead, and we stay in that condition if we do not appropriate the redemption provided for us through Jesus.

THE HUMAN DESIRE TO LIVE

Here is the reason why a person has such a craving for life, which, however, cannot be truly fulfilled outside of a proper relationship with God. What lengths people go to in order, as they say, to get the most out of life! The Love Parades in Germany and the Christopher Street Day demonstrations throughout Europe are examples of the repulsive consequences that have become an integral part of our society. These extremes are heartily approved of by our social and political leaders.

Isaiah already made the observation that people live in the land of shadow and death, a life without content, a life without purpose. They do not hear God talking. They lack the ability to hear and to see and consequently do not recognize their errors. The Bible describes this in detail. The world of those dead before God is referred to in the Old Testament as Sheol, the land of darkness (Isa 59:9–14) and the land of utter gloom (Job 10:22). The dead walk about like shadows (Isa 14:9; Ps 88:4–8). But this is not God's intent for human beings. As already stated, through the second birth God gives us the opportunity to enter into the fellowship that he had originally created.

THE CHASM BETWEEN GOD AND HUMANS

In view of the fact that a dead body can neither hear nor see, it is not at all remarkable that unredeemed people are unaware of God's Spirit—they are dead. That is why Paul says in 1 Cor 2:14 that the natural human cannot discern God's Spirit. The dead do not even realize that they are dead. What kind of good works can dead people perform? None! They merely exude the odor of decay. A person who is dead in God's eyes can do nothing to be pleasing to God. This is what Paul intends to show us when he describes our condition, as we read above in Eph 2:1–10.

In Rom 3:10–18 Paul addresses the same topic, except from slightly different point of view. He writes:

> As the Scriptures say, "No one is righteous— not even one. No one is truly wise; no one is seeking God. All have turned away; all have become useless. No one does good, not a single one." "Their talk is foul, like the stench from an open grave. Their tongues are filled with lies." "Snake venom drips from their lips." "Their mouths are full of cursing and bitterness." "They rush to commit murder. Destruction and misery always follow them. They don't know where to find peace." "They have no fear of God at all." (NLT)

Don't these verses sound like a tragic ballad, like a symphony in a minor key? Yes, perhaps even darker than dark and utterly hopeless.

THE DAWN OF GOD'S SALVATION IN CHRIST

But then we come to Eph 2:4 and here, like a clap of thunder or the blast of the trumpet, the dark fog of our despair is torn asunder with the outcry:

> *But God!*
> We were dead.
> *But God!*
> We were cadavers.
> *But God!*
> We could only perform the works of death.
> *But God!*
> We did not know, it never even dawned on us, that we were dead.
> *But God,*
> who is rich in mercy, had in His great love with which He loves us, made us who were dead in our sins, alive with Christ. (Eph 2:4–7)

Where there is no hope for a person to escape from the curse of death, there resounds through all eternity the call:

> "*But God!*"
> *In Jesus* there is salvation!

THE ACTS OF GOD IN JESUS

Now I would like to summarize what God in his great mercy and because of his great love for us has done for us if we accept his offer. I will detail this in three steps:

1. He has made us one with Christ. Jesus became a man. Then, taking our deserved place, he went to the cross and died there. He was laid into a grave. Then through the over-abundant greatness of God's power, he rose again. In order to benefit from this act, we must, according to Col 2:12, confess that we are dead, and by faith go with Jesus into the grave. Jesus is calling out—we have heard the Spirit of God, who is calling us and admonishing us.

2. After we have accepted his call, God has made us one with Jesus. We are now alive together with Jesus. We now have a part in his resurrection and we now have a new life. We have been called forth from the kingdom of death.

3. God has seated us with Jesus in heavenly places (Eph 2:6). Simultaneously with our relocation from the kingdom of death into the kingdom of heaven we also have become God's children.

The third point, then, includes the fact that all of us who have accepted God's offer now are a part of God's family. God has done all of this out of his grace, out of love and mercy, and is offering us eternal life as a present—for the taking. All this is available to us without piety or having to prove our worthiness by means of "good works." What more could we ask? I wish that each one of us not only understood this as fact, but also accepted it personally.

Only through Jesus can I reach the goal. There are many religions in which millions of people quite sincerely, and often at the risk of their health, search for a merciful God, for illumination and eternal peace. Are all these people following an error? The sad but unequivocal answer is yes! Solely through the good news contained in the Bible can I find a merciful, placated God. Jesus alone has served the required penalty for our guilt and sin. Only through Jesus' sacrifice can I become and remain a child of God.

What is the difference between the Bible and the religions of this world? To begin with, I would like to clarify that in the sense in which the word is used in connection with world religions, I am not a religious person. I do not follow any prescribed rituals in order to be reconciled with God, nor can I do that. What actually is a religion? Here we encounter an initial difficulty. For each of the world religions has set a different goal. The meaning of the word or the concept of religion is not easy to define. That is why I go back and ask, how did the patristic fathers understand this term? Let us take the explanation of the church father, teacher, and philosopher Thomas of Aquinas who lived in the middle of the thirteenth century. According to his writings the task of religion is to bring humans into proper relationship with God. For him, all who are searching for God are religious.[1] For me this means that religion starts with people. In this case, people ask themselves about God and give themselves the answer. Let me emphasize again, that all religions and their rites were developed by human beings. I acknowledge that all their work may be done in good faith and with great effort in order to meet the requirements of their particular concept of God. I recognize that these rites probably were formulated with the highest integrity. Their intent is to achieve either greater enlightenment or to appease an angry god or to accomplish both. Thomas of Aquinas goes a step further and says that religion arising out of a person's search for the transcendent is, in the final analysis, the worship of a god, albeit possibly a false one. So for Thomas, religion is a set of doctrines or actions of human beings by which some version of God is acknowledged, worshipped, and pacified through prescribed, deliberate conduct.

For centuries many people have attempted to appease a god. Today, as well, millions of persons are laboring toward that target. In Jesus' time, the Pharisees, an association of approximately six thousand members, labored to do so. That was the goal of the Pharisee Nicodemus who, according to John 3, came to Jesus by night. Nicodemus was unquestionably a very pious Jew, who, like the rest of that group, had taken a vow to dedicate his whole life to the observance of God's law and the traditions of the elders in every point. Another such Pharisee was, as we all know, Saul of Tarsus, better known to most people as the Apostle Paul. I'm convinced that Nicodemus was quite serious when he came to Jesus. In piety the Pharisees could not be trumped. By what means did the Pharisees think they could conciliate the Holy God, who has revealed himself through the law? They felt sure they could achieve this by means of their piety, that is, deliberate and determined conduct as prescribed by

1. Aquinas *Summa Theologica* 1.1.6.

God's every commandment and its interpretation by men. But what was it that Nicodemus wanted to achieve when he came to Jesus? Perhaps confirmation that in his pious, honest, and God-fearing conduct he was pleasing to God? Maybe Nicodemus wanted to know how he could become even more perfect in order to receive God's authority to do what Jesus was doing. One thing is for sure, Nicodemus made every effort he could to draw near to God. But was God near to him? In the section on baptism we will come back to Nicodemus.

I would like to give Jesus' response in today's vernacular: "Stop being so pious! You cannot please God this way." This is what I would like to shout at many a Christian. This is the way in which Jesus presented it to Paul on the road to Damascus and later as well: "Paul, stop being so pious! You cannot please God this way." People have been destroyed by sin. They are dead men in the sight of God. Human beings cannot refurbish themselves. A repair is impossible. You, man or woman, must be born again! Nicodemus should actually have understood Jesus' preaching quite well. He was a teacher of the law and knew the law better than others. He should also have been aware of Isa 59:10, where it says, "We grope for the wall like the blind; we grope like those who have no eyes; we stumble at noon as in the twilight, among those in full vigor we are like dead men" (ESV).

Such is the human condition in the sight of God. We neither know where we stand nor what we are actually required to do. Everything that we do is and must be misdirected in God's sight because we have been destroyed by sin. Even our will does not function properly, because we really do not know what we want; chances are that we *want* salvation, but we *will* pleasure and our own autonomy. So many people appear to search for enlightenment and justification, but they do so on their own terms. As a result, the person may have devised a purely human religion without divine input, and the people actually believe that they can appease God with something that may meet their standards, but not God's, who has been given neither voice nor vote in the matter—not that he would participate in this game. Then they refer to obedience to the demands of such a self-made religion as "righteousness." Don't they realize that the final result can never be more than pious self-deception, since they did not listen to the deity whom they intend to worship (or, more likely, manipulate)? This wrong-headed thinking, in which people put their desires ahead of God's demands, culminates in a mere human being (a creature) taking a block of wood (another part of creation), shaping it (in compliance with the aesthetic inclinations of human culture), and then worshipping it. The worst of it is that this person actually believes that a divine spirit can take abode in it.

The Bible, God's revelation, understands us human beings, especially our struggle to find our way back to almighty God, after having fallen into sin. However, our striving is in vain. As Isaiah states in 64:6, "For all of us have become like one who is unclean, And all our righteous deeds are like a filthy garment; And all of us wither like a leaf, And our iniquities, like the wind, take us away." To the question as to what we as humans can contribute to our redemption through all our piety and conduct, Rom 8:3 gives the answer: "For what the Law could not do, weak as it was through the flesh, God did: sending His own Son in the likeness of sinful flesh and as an offering for sin, He condemned sin in the flesh, in order that the requirement of the Law might be fulfilled in us . . ." With this idea in the background I want to restate clearly: Jesus is not a religion, but rather a person, through whom we can be freed from guilt and sin.

In this regard the Bible does not transmit to us a religion, so that by meeting its demands we can achieve piety and reconciliation with a consequently merciful God. As an example, many people who consider themselves Christians focus on only a part of the Bible, which leads them not only to believe, but also to proclaim, that God is merciful to all because Jesus has redeemed us from the curse of sin and death.

However, simply from the point of view of the methodology involved, namely that humans put themselves in charge of defining their religion rather than heeding God's word, these people are logically in the same category as those who carve a god out of a chunk of wood, because they, too, create a god to their liking. Nobody is at liberty to pick out certain portions of the Holy Scriptures because they happen to fit into personal spiritual preferences. To get a clear picture of the word of God and his offer of salvation to us, we must reckon with the Bible in its totality. Jesus has, indeed, taken the curse of sin, which rests upon all people, onto himself and served the penalty. However, redemption from guilt and sin applies only to those people who accept God's offer of salvation on the basis of the sacrificial death of Jesus and appropriate it for themselves.

Now, you will remember that I started out with my first point being "Christianity Is a Religion." I explained that churches, federations, and assemblies as organizations in a secular world have to establish guidelines in order to exist lawfully in state and society and in order to conduct their affairs in an orderly fashion. Such rules and guidelines must, however, be based on biblical truth. They may not be contrary to the principles of the Bible nor contain rules or directives (for instance, demands for pilgrimages or exorcisms), which can be viewed as supplements or replacements for Christ's sacrificial death. And most definitely, they can never, ever grant us salvation.

14

Keeping an Eye on the Goal

MY STARTING POINT TO THE GOAL

Every person, with the possible exception of those who, because of advanced age, no longer see any further sense in life, will set certain goals for themselves, be they ever so small, such as preparing for a vacation. In matters of religion and faith as well, most people have certain objectives in mind. Everybody goes through moments (maybe minutes, hours, days, or even years) when they wonder what will be their state after they die. Many Christians trust that their church, more specifically their priest or pastor, is showing them the correct way to the goal. Furthermore, many people believe that the particular minister to whom they are attracted, or the church into whose tradition they were born, represent the correct faith, thereby receiving their assurance from either a human being or a human association. Maybe they are correct, but how can they know apart from their own study of the Bible? Since no church can hand out free passes to heaven, it is fair to continue to raise the question: is their way to attain the goal correct? or, for that matter, are they even taught the correct goal? To rephrase our guiding question, are you certain that you are heading to the right goal in the right way?

My goal is to develop my relationship with Jesus Christ and to become more like him, who is the same yesterday and today and into all eternity. Furthermore I say with Paul, as recorded in Phil 3:13–14: "Brethren, I do not regard myself as having laid hold of it yet; but one thing I do: forgetting what lies behind and reaching forward to what lies ahead, I press on toward the goal for the prize of the upward call of God in Christ Jesus."

Called by Jesus

In all seriousness, we could celebrate any of the great events that form the basis of our Christian holidays, any time of the year. Any day of the year is appropriate for giving thanks. Whether it be Christ's incarnation at Christmas, the crucifixion on Good Friday, the resurrection on Easter, the ascension of our Lord, or the pouring out of the Holy Spirit, all these events are ample reasons to praise our Heavenly Father daily. Yes, we should often thank him for the good news, in which we—yes, even I personally—have been included. But then, as my thoughts continue to wander, they come to a pause at the last day of the year, New Year's Eve. This is not a church holiday. Nevertheless, many of us observe it as a day on which we reflect on the past year. We ponder our present situation, physically and spiritually. We remind ourselves of what we may have accomplished, as well as which intentions we left by the wayside. Many of us make plans for the new year. And again, I am thinking, why limit these thoughts to just one day a year? Wouldn't it be a good idea to do this every morning? I have decided to look forward to every day and continue walking firmly down the path with Jesus to reach the goal of my calling. My desire is to subordinate my every action every day to my goal to live in the security of the Lord Jesus.

Now it is necessary to keep a central question in mind. You can only have aim for a goal if you have chosen a goal. And there is usually—actually I should say "always"—a particular place and time when that decision was made. Without such a decision you can never arrive at a goal because you do not have one. May I remind you that there are two days in our lives on which we can make no decision because we have no control over them. These are two days on which we can do nothing. Absolutely nothing? We would love to seize upon these days, but our grasp must always come up empty! Those two days are yesterday and tomorrow. Yesterday is gone. Whether we will even be alive tomorrow, we do not know. So, there is only one day in our lives in which we can make a decision. That day is always today.

DO WE HAVE A GOAL, AND WHAT IS THAT GOAL?

Many people think that they have a goal. They have decided to become a better person. But that is no goal; at best it could be the outcome of having attained a goal. More likely it is a wish, and if it's tied to achieving a better relationship with God, it's an empty aspiration. Any plan to become more pious and, therefore, to please God is a wasted effort. Jesus died for me on the cross in order to restore my fellowship with God, and if I could do the same without him, just by keeping a New Year's resolution, the atoning death of Christ would have not been necessary. It is by Jesus' wounds that I have been made whole from all the damage that sin has done to me (1 Pet 2:24). I need not have any fear about standing before God in his judgment seat.

This reality is a fountain of great joy and happiness. However, it is at this point that many Christians, or perhaps I should say many people who attempt to be Christians through their own efforts, wind up failing. They do not accept salvation with all its provisions, and consequently, rather than walking joyfully with Jesus, they shuffle along in dread of God's judgment. They are still trying to pay off the penalty for their sins. But that is precisely what Jesus has already done once and for all. If you are living under such a cloud, let me assure you that you can accept what Jesus has done for you and rejoice because Jesus does not reject anybody.

Our goal is and remains to be that one day we will be welcomed by Jesus. When the day of Jesus' return arrives, nobody will ask what degree of piety (or, as A. W. Tozer used to say, "pietosity") we have attained. At that time the only question will be whether we have become a part of the body of Jesus. The sound of the trumpet of the archangel calls all those who died in Jesus out of their graves and summons together all those who are living in him. Those who have pursued their own way apart from Christ, and even may have impressed the world with their piety, must continue to wait for the judgment. Is there anybody who thinks that Hindus, Buddhists, or Muslims cannot be pious? But they have neither the forgiveness of sins nor the hope of eternal life. Even John Wesley, the founder of Methodism,[1] realized that he was pious, but that he lacked salvation. On his return from America he lamented, "I went to America, to convert the Indians, but oh, who shall convert me?" Only in Jesus can we reach the goal of salvation, for that is the goal.

---

1. *The Journal of John Wesley*, ed. Nehemiah Curnock, Standard ed. (London: Culley, 1909), 1:418 (Tuesday, January 24, 1738).

To see Jesus and to live with him is the beginning of my new life. The Apostle John has described our goal quite clearly in the revelation that he received from the glorified Lord. He writes: "Jesus Christ [is] the faithful witness, the first-born of the dead, and the ruler of the kings of the earth. [He] loves us, and released us from our sins by His blood, and He has made us to be a kingdom, priests to His God and Father..." (Rev 1:5–6) "... We know that, when He appears, we shall be like Him, because we shall see Him just as He is" (1 John 3:2).

In order to achieve this goal I must, as described above, have a clear starting point. I must belong to Jesus and live my life with him, as Paul states in Rom 6:19: "... so now present your members as slaves to righteousness, resulting in sanctification." This word *sanctification* means a state of being set apart for the service of God. Paul, in his letters to the church members in Rome, Corinth, and Colossae, addresses them as saints and beloved because he assumes that the foregoing prerequisites have been met. Are we also part of the "saints"?

When we have become saints and those who are beloved by God, have we reached our goal? Oh no! We are still on our journey heading home to a better country. Yes, I have already lived most of my life, striving to move forward in my service to Jesus along the way. But I must say with the Apostle Paul in Phil 3:12, which I have already quoted earlier, "Not that I have already obtained it, or have already become perfect, but I press on!..." (Exclamation mark added.)

Dear reader, it is not crucial whether you agree that Jesus, the crucified, was born in Bethlehem or that you agree with other historical questions. They may be important, but they are not relevant in light of the question, have you allowed yourself to be conquered by Christ? Then let us continue walking on the way to perfection. Yes, perfection is possible! We will be perfect when we see Jesus just as he is, and we shall be like him.

I CAN REACH THE GOAL ONLY BY FOLLOWING THE CORRECT WAY

On my way to perfection I must clearly keep two things in view.

1. I must know my goal.

2. I must be on the right path.

Jesus is my goal, not "Golden Jerusalem." To him, Jesus, must I belong, and upon him must I have my eyes fixed. I must place myself and my life into the light of God's word every day, so that God's word can illumine and test me.

Let us look at an example: I have traveled by car in a lot of different countries; for example, in the United States and Mexico, as well as in Canada, places with which I was not familiar. As a family we have traveled together to Niagara Falls, Acapulco, Yellowstone National Park, and many other sites. How did we accomplish that? We had a clear goal. We knew where we wanted to go.

We did not place our confidence in what friends and neighbors told us, even though they had been to some of those places. We used a map and directions that we obtained from an automobile club. Our goal was clearly marked, and we studied the map and the descriptions carefully. Usually one of my sons sat next to me with the map and the TripTik in hand and kept track of where we were so that we did not veer off the correct route.

It is similar on our way to our heavenly home. First, I must be sure that I have a goal. The name of this goal is Jesus! And then we also have directions and a roadmap to Jesus. That is the Bible. It tells us exactly how we can get to the marriage supper of the Lamb. But I must read these directions, the Bible, which is God's word, and not just devotional books.

WE HAVE BEEN CALLED FROM ETERNITY

In Eph 1:18, Paul asks in his prayer on our behalf, "I pray that the eyes of your heart may be enlightened, so that you may know what is the hope of His calling, what are the riches of the glory of His inheritance in the saints." This has nothing to do with piety. Isaiah has stated already that our righteousness, which we try to gain through piety, is like a stained garment. Jesus, and he alone, provides the righteousness that is acceptable to God. There on the cross of Calvary, wrestling with death, yes with death itself, Jesus cried out, "It is finished!" He accomplished everything that needed to be done so that you can be a child of God. We must get a firm grasp on that reality by faith and show by our lives that we belong to Christ.

JESUS IS CALLING, BUT NOT FOREVER

How often did Jesus call Peter? Once. And Matthew? When Jesus called Levi, the tax gatherer (customs officer), who later became known as Matthew, he said only two words: "Follow me!" And he arose and followed Jesus (Matt 9:9).

Most likely Matthew had heard Jesus preach on a number of occasions. Maybe he had even been baptized by John or one of his disciples in the Jordan. He may have had a moment of awakening and a feeling of redemption. But he had not yet attained the actual goal. There he sat in his customs office and longed for that one great event that would restore him to his people and make him an acceptable Jew again. If Levi had, indeed, undergone baptism in the Jordan, that occurrence might have been that great event for him. But even if that were the case (and we cannot know), it is clear that he was still far away from having a new life. What changed the customs officer Levi into the Apostle Matthew? All hypothetical speculations aside, we do know with certainty that one and only thing about Levi, and it is the event that made him a new person: Jesus came by, he called Levi, and Levi followed him.

Dear reader, it does not matter how many times we have sensed God's holiness and presence. What really counts is not what we feel, but rather what we do, namely, to have our eyes fixed on the goal and to follow the call of Jesus. Specifically, what this entails for a particular individual, what he has to do, each person should know himself. Please, read the Bible!

JESUS CONFIRMS OUR DEVOTION

When we make ourselves fully available to Jesus, we are grafted into him (Rom 11), and we are part of the body of Jesus! Then his love comes into our being. Not only do we love Jesus, but, furthermore, because of his love in us we are now able to love our brothers and sisters who also belong to his body and, beyond that, all people, for Jesus died for all. The Apostle Peter in 2 Pet 1:8 elaborates further, "if these qualities [godliness, brotherly kindness, love] are yours and are increasing, they render you neither useless nor unfruitful in the true knowledge of our Lord Jesus Christ." Let us add to that what the Apostle Paul says in 2 Cor 5:14 (NIV) that the love of Jesus "compels us" to love. What then is the confirmation and affirmation of Jesus' calling? That we bring forth fruit for him. We experience his recognition and acceptance of our labor and, because of his love, we enjoy the fellowship of those who are of similar faith and hope.

JESUS IS THE SOURCE FOR PROVISIONS AND SHELTER

Just as Satan did not shrink back from trying to divert Jesus from his goal, namely his redemptive work on the cross of Calvary, he will not leave us alone. Satan is the prince of this world and wishes to lose no one.

Paul tells us in Eph 6:12 that "we are not fighting against human beings, but against the wicked spiritual forces in the heavenly world, the rulers, authorities, and cosmic powers of this dark age" (GNT). Satan may even use persons that are particularly close to us. These pressures I have experienced as a young man, even as far back as my childhood. As I described in my memoirs, my name was the only one that was not called when all my classmates of equal age were inducted into the party with great festivities in a large auditorium. I had not been found worthy of becoming a party member. I belonged to a religious sect and participated in the meetings of the YMCA. While in the navy, I experienced Jesus' sheltering presence when our ship was struck by a torpedo. Then Jesus gave me the initially incomprehensible assignment to stay on the wreck, even though I was given the opportunity to leave our severely damaged ship. I was to stay on the wreck in order to be able to talk to my companions about Jesus, my Lord, and to tell them of my life with him. I felt fully secure in Jesus.

Dear reader, Jesus would like to give every one of us that comfort, even here on earth. Anyone who does not belong to Jesus here on earth will not get to spend eternity with him. We have to follow the proper order of events. First comes commitment to Jesus. Then comes the redemption from guilt and sin. After that comes the call to discipleship and to service in Jesus' sheltering presence.

"SHELTERED IN THE ARMS OF GOD"

I cannot talk about this sense of comfort without mentioning a man who experienced this reality deeply and expressed it in a hymn: Dietrich Bonhoeffer. In the very face of death he wrote:

> By gracious powers so wonderfully sheltered,
> and confidently waiting come what may,

> we know that God is with us night and morning,
> and never fails to greet us each new day.

Then, a little farther down:

> And when this cup You give is filled to brimming
> with bitter suffering, hard to understand,
> we take it thankfully and without trembling,
> out of so good and so beloved a hand.[2]

Particularly the last verse stands out as something that he could write only out of a security and comfort that we can barely fathom. And he was, as we all know, executed for his faith.

Dear reader, without this comforting presence, which only Jesus can give, no one can steadfastly look into the eyes of death. But he who has this comfort knows that his Redeemer, the Son of God, is awaiting him with eternal life.

---

2. Dietrich Bonhoeffer, "By Gracious Powers," translated by Fred Pratt Green (Carol Stream, IL: Hope Publishing Company, 1974). Used by permission.

15

The Equipment of Jesus' Disciples for Service

THE RIGHTEOUSNESS PRODUCED BY JESUS GENERATES LOVE

The Apostle Paul writes to the Philippians (1:11) of his prayer for them that they will "[be] filled with the fruit of righteousness which comes through Jesus Christ, to the glory and praise of God."

This prayer that the Apostle Paul wrote to the church at Philippi is so rich and so full of godly love that we can focus upon it as a goal for our spiritual lives. It always speaks anew to me, and there is nothing I desire more sincerely than that God would fulfill this prayer in my own life and in the lives of each one of us and bring it into full reality. Because when we accept God's great love, which he has so richly prepared for each one of us, when we allow God to fill us with that love, then our love will be so great and powerful that we will be bathed in God's love, which will then freely overflow to others.

THE WORK OF LOVE IN THE HUMAN PERSON

What then does this love accomplish in us? To begin with, this love will rearrange our priorities. It is now no longer the fear of hell or of divine judgment that changes us, but God's love, which reached its climax in the death of Jesus on the cross. When we have accepted God's love, it will make us into a new person, a totally different person. But we must continue with the question, what will be the result of God's love in us?

Initially it will result in our desire to do the will of God and, therewith, the will of Jesus. And that applies to every part of our lives. In John 14:23 Jesus says, "If anyone loves Me, he will keep My word; and My Father will love him, and We will come to him, and make Our abode with him." This is an enormous promise, because Jesus did not leave things with this simple hypothetical condition, but rather he tells us very clearly in verse 26 of the same chapter what is going to happen: "But the Helper, the Holy Spirit, whom the Father will send in My name, He will teach you all things, and bring to your remembrance all that I said to you." This happens to each of us at the time when we are born again. Once we have received the Holy Spirit, according to Rom 5:5, we can respond back to God and our Lord Jesus with that same love with which he loved us. Through being born again out of God's grace we become children of the living God, as well as a part in the body of Jesus.

Because of this change we can now love not just God and Jesus, but also the brothers and sisters in our fellowship, as well as our marriage partner and our neighbors with all their imperfections. We cannot accomplish this in our own strength. No religion and no exemplary, pious life can empower us to do this. We see daily on the television screen and read it in the newspapers how pious people can advocate hatred and murder in the name of their religion. That is the reason why Jesus needed to dwell in an earthly body, and that is why he paid the penalty for our guilt in our stead, since we were unable to do so ourselves. Now, the Holy Spirit makes possible what otherwise would be impossible.

Our fellow human beings, with whom we live side by side, are also flawed. They are no better off than we are. They, just like each of us, cannot help themselves. Consequently, what do they need? They need love! Our love, which we received from God, is supposed to overflow and touch the lives of others. The apostle Paul tells us how this is supposed to happen. He writes in the previously mentioned Letter to the Philippians:

> I pray, that your love may abound still more and more in real knowledge and all discernment, so that you may approve the things that are excellent, in order to be sincere and blameless until the day of Christ; having been filled with the fruit of righteousness which comes through Jesus Christ, to the glory and praise of God. (Phil 1:9–11)

THROUGH JESUS' LOVE: REFLECTIONS OF HIS GLORY WITHOUT FLAW

In Phil 1:9–11 we see how love expresses itself: we are to be pure and holy, sincere and blameless, always growing and improving, until the day of the return of our Lord Jesus Christ. This is supposed to be an ongoing process because Jesus wants to present us to our Holy God in perfect condition. Is it possible for us to be so pious that we achieve a blameless life? No! No fruit of my own endeavors, no piety, and no offerings count for anything. Then what does? The fruit of righteousness that Jesus has created in us to the glory and praise of God! That will be the climax of the fulfillment of God's plan of salvation, when Jesus will present the redeemed saints to the Father, dressed in the white robes of righteousness procured for us by Jesus. Then a shout of joy will resound through the heavens and the entire universe. We will stand before God in his holy presence. God's light will illumine us, and we will sparkle like the stars in heaven for ever and ever (Dan 12:3).

We shall be sincere and blameless, says Paul. The word *sincerely* (εἰλικρινής, *eilikrinēs*) in the original Greek text is derived from terms that originally meant "to be examined in the light of the sun." We have to imagine the scene of a marketplace in the Far East. A garment may look quite nice in normal daylight, but when you hold it up toward the sun you can see that it is stained and moth-eaten. In a similar manner, God's light will shine through us, displaying the quality of his work in us.

When God carries out this test of our sincerity, will it not reveal the blemishes of our old life and make them obvious? Oh, no! Either all our sins have been washed away through the blood of the Lamb Jesus or we cannot stand before him. This Daniel had clearly prophesied in 12:2: "[M]any of those who sleep in the dust of the ground will awake, these to everlasting life, but the others to disgrace and everlasting contempt."

How will this happen? When we stand before God's judgment, will we receive the righteousness that we could not obtain through piety during our lifetime? No! God's final judgment, about which the prophets in the Old Testament write, and about which so many people talk, will not happen like that.

After Jesus appeared in our flesh and blood and suffered God's judgment on the cross of Calvary, he sat down at the right hand of the Father. When he returns, he will come as the King of Kings. The substitutionary, sacrificial death of Jesus brought about this exchange in which he gave up his life in our stead. That is the high point of God's plan of salvation. The threatening judgment that had hung over us has been averted. Jesus has become Redeemer and Judge. He says to us in John 5:22, 27: "For not even the Father judges anyone, but He has given all judgment to the Son . . . and He gave Him authority to execute judgment, because He is the Son of Man."

Jesus will judge. But for whom will Jesus be the judge? Not for those who are already in him, because they are already covered by his blood. He will be judge for those who rejected him here on earth. For those persons who accepted Jesus' redemptive work and became a part of him, the judgment and execution of the sentence have already taken place. Look at John 5:24: "Truly, truly, I say to you, he who hears My word, and believes Him who sent Me, has eternal life, and does not come into judgment, but has passed out of death into life." It all depends on being in Jesus.

NO ONE IS LOST BECAUSE OF SIN

Neither our pious works nor our pious life, but solely our reliance on Jesus, here on earth, cleanses us from all our sin. What will occur is what is written in Rev 1:7: "BEHOLD, HE IS COMING WITH THE CLOUDS, and every eye will see Him, even those who pierced Him . . ." I would like to add that all those who rejected him will nonetheless see him, not as Redeemer, but as Judge. For, so this verse continues, all the tribes of the earth will mourn. Why? Because so many rejected his grace and his inexplicable love. Then it will be too late. No one will be rejected because of sin! Jesus knew before he took on our flesh and blood that we are all sinners. He also knew that we cannot make it on our own. That is the reason he came. That is the reason he died in our stead on the cross. If our piety could have made us God's children, then Jesus could have simply stayed in heaven.

The good news that the Bible delivers to us is that Jesus, and he alone, had the power to accomplish our release from sin, and he did so. He did it out of pure love. All of those who have accepted his love, by turning their sins over to Jesus, all of those who let themselves be washed by the blood of the Lamb will stand with glad hearts and bright eyes before Jesus and will greet him as their Lord and Savior.

According to Jesus' instructions, we have been given the mission to preach the gospel to all creation. How Jesus will deal with those who, in their lifetime, have not heard the gospel and consequently could not make a decision, the Bible does not tell us. That is not our burden anyway, if we have done our part of the assignment. The fate of those who never heard the good news we will leave to God.

The great Judgment Day will be a day of joy. How will we appear when Jesus will judge the world? Will we be like poor beggars, crying out for mercy? Will we be prostrate on the ground, hoping to be accepted? No! If that were the case Jesus would have to be embarrassed. Yes, God would have to be embarrassed. This is part of the good news. We read in the Apostle Paul's prayer in Phil 1:10–11 that we will be "sincere and blameless" and that we will be "filled with the fruit of righteousness which comes through Jesus Christ." We will expand on this topic further in the context of chapter 23, on the judgment seat of Christ.

For now, let us take note of the fact that we will have nothing to show in our hands when we stand before the Father. Many Christians strive and even pray that they would not stand before God with empty hands. They would like to have something in their hands, would like to show their fruits, which presumably means their achievements. Dear friends and brethren, that is a misguided perception. We cannot impress God with any good deeds, which we may view as fruit. No, Isaiah already said in 64:6 that ". . . all our righteous deeds are like a filthy garment . . ." The hymn writer sings, "Jesus' blood and righteousness my crown and robe of honor is."

But Jesus will present to the Father, as we said only a moment ago, abundant fruit. What, then, is this fruit? We are! The redeemed! That is why Jesus became flesh and blood like us. That is why he had to walk as a human, for three years, on this earth with all of its depravity. After he became equal to us sinners, he took human nature upon himself and identified with us by shouldering our depravity. The highest spiritual representatives of Israel, in a mockery of a trial, declared him to be a criminal and sentenced him to death. He suffered torture at the hands of the Roman soldiers, followed by the indescribably horrible death on the cross. But three days later he brought forth the fruit, which he will triumphantly present to the Father. We ourselves are the fruit that Jesus will present to the Father. For us he endured all the suffering, and for us he gave his life.

JESUS' LOVE IS ALL THAT COUNTS, NOT OUR PIETY

In the light of the above deflation of the importance of our works, are our labors and all of our sacrifices for God worth absolutely nothing? Almost. They have a purpose, but the purpose is not to improve our standing with God. Now, we need to pay careful attention because the relevant Bible passages once again speak of "fruit," but it is still not fruit that we present as trophies before God. Jesus says in Matt 7:20, "[B]y their fruits ye shall know them." (KJV) Fruit in this sense does not come from our work, but the love of Jesus and the righteousness that he acquired for us will produce fruit. The fruit of the Holy Spirit is the desired fruit. As Apostle Paul writes in his Letter to the Galatians 5:22–23 , "But the fruit of the Spirit is love, joy, peace, patience, kindness, goodness, faithfulness, gentleness, self-control . . ." This is fruit that Jesus produces within us. Filled with the fruit of the Spirit, we will stand before God, and Jesus will present us to the Father. So, these are the three aspects in relationship to "fruit" and judgment.

1. We will have no fruit to present to God that would make us worthy of salvation.
2. We ourselves are the fruit that the Son presents to the Father.
3. The Holy Spirit will have produced his fruit within us.

Thus, somewhat paradoxically, looking at statements 2 and 3, Jesus presents to the Father fruit, which is filled with fruit, but none of it is produced by us.

Still, Jesus also says in Matt 7:21: "Not everyone who says to Me, 'Lord, Lord,' will enter the kingdom of heaven; but he who does the will of My Father who is in heaven." Then he continues on in verses 22 and 23: "Many will say to Me on that day, 'Lord, Lord, did we not prophesy in Your name, and in Your name cast out demons, and in Your name perform many miracles?' And then I will declare to them, 'I never knew you; DEPART FROM ME, YOU WHO PRACTICE LAWLESSNESS.'"

Indeed, it is possible to belong to a Christian assembly without having committed one's life to Jesus. It is possible to do great deeds in the name of Jesus and yet perish. Remember, one of the twelve disciples, whom Jesus selected, whom he sent out, and to whom he gave power over the evil spirits, and who even healed the sick, was Judas Iscariot (Matt 10 and Luke 6 and 9). Our goal is not attainable by being linked to an association of people, but to be in Christ and to be a part of his body. Once again I raise the question, are you in Jesus? Solely the blood of Jesus cleanses us from all sin.

JESUS HAD TO COME BECAUSE WE COULD NOT CLEANSE OURSELVES

Perhaps this next section may be a little too theoretical. So, let me attempt to clarify it at the outset with an illustration.

We don't necessarily talk about these matters, but this little scenario is something that most parents encounter sooner or later. Let us imagine a young mother who has a sweet baby, just at the stage when infants can crawl but not yet walk. Mommy bathed her child in the morning and then laid him back into his crib. Later, when she came back to the crib, she found that the baby had thoroughly soiled himself and the interior of the crib with his own waste. What do you think the mother would do? Will she berate him? Will she tell the baby how horrible he is? No! Back he goes into the tub, and a few minutes later Mommy cuddles her happy child once again in her arms, all cleaned up and freshly dressed.

What could the baby contribute in order to renew his mother's love and joy? Nothing, absolutely nothing. What if it had said, "Mommy, I will behave better?" We all know that it could neither say such a thing nor control its behavior to such an extent. This is simply the way babies are. He had to submit to another washing and getting dressed in clean clothing.

Yes, dear reader, it is the same with us human beings. For the removal of the dirt of our sin there is only one solution: the blood of Jesus Christ. It alone can cleanse us from all sin. We do not receive the fruit of righteousness with a pious life. It is grace and a gift through Jesus.

16

Baptism

DOES BAPTISM HAVE MEANING?

EVERYONE KNOWS THAT JOINING a Christian church almost invariably includes baptism. After a short ceremony involving some sort of application of or immersion in water, the child or the adult will be pronounced a member of the Christian church. Whether the new church member, quite frequently an infant, can actually understand the proceedings may not even be considered in some Christian churches, while in others it is explained with a complex set of doctrines, which would also be incomprehensible to the person being baptized. Because of this almost universal practice of baptism without a consensus of why we practice it, the significance of this rite had eluded me for a long period of time.

For me, the question was a personal one, having received the common sprinkling as an infant: had I been baptized according to the understanding of the term by the New Testament writers? That is to say, does my "baptism" line up with the meaning of the concept that Jesus and the apostles would have had in mind when they spoke or wrote about baptism? The answer was not a simple one. Theologically, it had always been pointed out to me that in the sight of God, how much water was being used (ranging from a few drops to an immersion basin) was not significant. In light of the fact that I was baptized as a baby, I had undergone the ritual without any understanding of the meaning on my part. At the time of the confirmation ceremony I had retroactively made the baptism applicable to me. Confession of sins or committing my life to Jesus was neither asked of me nor did I feel any need to do so. Consequently I was never really sure whether I had committed my life to Jesus in baptism. Further, the question arose as to whether I was, without having knowingly undergone baptism, a child of God. I had experienced much with Jesus; I had been led by him and been used by him. One thing was for certain, even if it sounds strange theologically, the church in which I was baptized as well as the one in which I was confirmed gave me neither an admission ticket nor the assurance that I would be able to enter heaven.

OBEDIENCE IN FAITH

In the Gospel according to John we read in chapter 14 these words of Jesus:

> "He who has My commandments and keeps them, he is the one who loves Me; and he who loves Me shall be loved by My Father, and I will love him and will disclose Myself to him." Judas (not Iscariot) said to Him, "Lord, what then has happened that You are going to disclose Yourself to us, and not to the world?" Jesus answered and said to him, "If anyone loves Me, he will keep My word; and My Father will love him, and We will come to him, and make Our abode with him . . ." (verses 21–24)

Here Jesus is speaking to his disciples. From this text and John 17 it becomes clear that he included also those who, through the proclamation of the gospel by his disciples, would later believe in him. From the context we also understand that Jesus here speaks prophetically. He points out that all who belong to him, then and in the future (meaning us), must be obedient to him by obeying his words and his commandments. The relationship between God and the people of Israel, starting with Abraham, Isaac, and Jacob and continuing through Moses, was always established in a covenant. Probably the most important covenant that God entered into with humans is God's covenant at Mount Sinai. In this covenant he established the Ten Commandments, the so-called Decalogue, as the centerpiece of the human-God relationship. We will address this further in a special chapter. What is significant here is the simple fact that each covenant that was entered into was based on mutual trust that the covenant would be honored. God initiated the covenant and stated the parameters in Exod 19:5–6: "Now then, if you will indeed obey My voice and keep My covenant, then you shall be My own possession among all the peoples, for all the earth is Mine; and you shall be to Me a kingdom of priests and a holy nation . . ." What God is demanding here is obedience to his laws. There is also no doubt that all rites and sequences of worship are secondary to the demand of unconditional obedience. We know how God punished his chosen people time and again because they refused to be obedient.

It is not difficult for us to remember that the same God, who punished his own people severely for their disobedience, who did not spare his own Son, has done everything to make it possible that we, as Gentiles, can also become children of God. This same God expects from us what Jesus states in John 14: he who loves me, or to express it a little differently, he who has entered into the covenant with me, will keep my word. What this means cannot be misunderstood: those who declare themselves to be disciples of Jesus have accepted the obligation to be obedient to the words of Jesus. Otherwise calling themselves disciples of Jesus—or as we usually say, Christians—would be inappropriate. To make my point quite clear and to bring it within the parameters of the Bible we will look at the late night conversation between Jesus and the Pharisee Nicodemus. The Apostle John recorded it for us in chapter 3 of his Gospel. Nicodemus is introduced as a rabbi. That means among other things that he is a teacher or professor of the holy Scriptures. He comes to Jesus at night to inquire—not about baptism—but rather about how a person can enter the kingdom of God. Let us paraphrase the conversation to make it come alive a little more:

"Master, what does it take to get to heaven?"

Jesus replies, "I will tell you. Listen carefully; there is only one way to heaven. You have to be born again of water and Spirit. There is no other way."

Nicodemus was astonished. "What is he talking about?" He, the rabbi, the professor, had expected something totally different. Maybe he expected to be directed to God's law, maybe a profound theological assertion. But not this; the words rang discordantly in his ears: "Unless a man is born again of water and Spirit. There is no other way to heaven."

Nicodemus was as astounded as many people are today when we explain the gospel to them in its simplicity. He began to ponder. He knew all the rites, all the Jewish traditions about washings and baptisms.

That last thought may have brought John the Baptist to his mind. Yes, people were going to him to the river Jordan to be cleansed from guilt and sin. Nicodemus, also, knew only too well the human need for being freed from guilt and sin. All human beings, all people, cling to something beyond themselves, be it a god or an ideology. Many have a fetish as a substitute for faith in the true God. There hardly could have been any doubt in his mind that all humankind had lost their position as children of the living God, the way the Bible portrays it in its opening pages. Since that time, all human beings are sinners, living without the Spirit of God. Obviously, we don't know what really ran through the mind of Nicodemus, but this scenario seems to be plausible.

But let's ponder further. Here is the reason why people often behave like animals, often worse than animals. The reason for this is that a human being, without being born again through Jesus, is dead before God. Ephesians 2:1 tells us: you also were dead in your transgressions and sin. (Additionally, consult Eph 2:5 and Col 2:13.) In the sight of God, we are all dead people, spiritual corpses. What can you do to a dead man to bring him back to life? How often do I have to wash a cadaver, or how deeply do I have to immerse a corpse in water in order to revive him? It is totally useless. A corpse must be buried or cremated. Then, maybe, there is a hope that the dead will rise again in the end times.

Picture John, standing on the banks of the Jordan calling out: "Repent, for the kingdom of heaven is near!" And the people came; they confessed their sins, and they were baptized.—Stop!—Back up!—What did the people confess? Their sins. And then John did what? He baptized them as the external sign that they had undergone an internal cleansing. What did the people think? Presumably they believed that they were washed clean from their confessed sins. They believed that their sins were borne away by the waters of the Jordan. No one knew where they went. Maybe they were floating off into the sea of God's great love.

John performed these sacred acts, which were considered to be cleansing based on the confession of sins. Then Jesus of Nazareth, the one and only sinless person, steps up and asks to be baptized just as the other people were. But that does not seem to make any sense. Jesus was not a sinner. There were no sins that he needed to confess. If he looked for cleansing, there is nothing from which he needed to be cleansed. Maybe we are looking in the wrong direction.

Perhaps he wanted to set an example. We can recall what happened when Jesus washed his disciples' feet. Afterwards he said, "If I then, the Lord and the Teacher, washed your feet, you also ought to wash one another's feet. For I gave you an example that you also should do as I did to you" (John 13:14–15) In short, when Jesus did something as an example, he made it clear that he meant it as an example. Not even once did he say, I let myself be baptized in order to give you an example; now do likewise.

There had to be much more to Jesus' baptism by John. Here we have come across another key event in God's plan of salvation. Jesus had to be made like us—sinners—in all things (Heb 2:17). He had no sins of his own, so, in identifying with us, it could only be our sins with which he burdened himself. And then he needed to demonstrate the contrast between sin and obedience to God. Only in obedience to God could Jesus make our salvation possible. Jesus said to John, "Only in this way can righteousness be fulfilled." What righteousness could he have had in mind? As we have said all along, there is only one kind of righteousness that counts, namely the righteousness that results when God removes his curse from humanity. Humankind was, and still is, under the curse of God: "You shall surely die!" This curse was a death sentence. Righteousness can only be restored by execution, the death of the guilty party.

So, on the one hand we have John's baptism, which was a human cry for grace and mercy. On the other hand, in the light of God's curse, the proper judgment could only be a sentence of death on us. But Jesus resolved this apparent conflict.

Jesus needed neither cleansing from sin nor mercy. He came into this world and in the fullness of time stepped down into the waters of the Jordan River in order to make mercy possible for us human beings. Jesus achieved this justification for all of us in that he made himself equal to all of us. He made himself a sinner, so that he could pay the penalty for our sins. As an outward sign Jesus was baptized in the same waters that sinners were baptized in, there at the Jordan River. He, the pure one, the Son of God, went into the water of sinners. Why would he do such a thing?

We know that Jesus came to the world to take up our sins, for which he eventually made atonement on the cross. But these concepts can be abstract in nature and difficult for us to visualize; theologians write theoretical tomes about the nature of the atonement. But at his baptism, Jesus provided a visible act, with heaven and earth observing, that he was about to burden himself with our sins.

Knowingly and with full intent, Jesus fulfilled God's plan of salvation as an act of obedience. With the weight of our sins on his shoulders, Jesus, the Son of God, walked on this earth for about three years, carrying our sins in his own body to the cross (1 Pet 2:24). Sin was not placed upon Jesus; nobody forced God, the Second Person of the Trinity to undergo the ordeal of the incarnation and the atonement. We have here another indicator of God's amazing grace; he voluntarily took on this role himself (1 John 3:5).

When Jesus came out of the water God showed his approval in a special way. A voice rang out, "This is My beloved Son, in whom I am well-pleased" (Matt 3:17). Yes, God's own Son was now carrying sin, the sins of the entire world. Seemingly impossible, but true! Satan and the powers of darkness must have rejoiced and jumped for joy. Satan now had the right to test, to tempt, to try to divert God's Son. The evil spirits could now harass him like any other person whenever they saw an opportunity, and they did so for three long years.

How Jesus must have suffered under this load of sin—yours and mine. Then came the struggle of Gethsemane. Did Jesus really need to be hung on the cross? Wasn't it enough just to be like us: a human being burdened by our sin? No, the Son of God had to go to the cross after he had been mocked, spit upon, jeered at, and beaten, followed by someone placing a crown of thorns on his head.

Why did the son of God have to suffer all of this? It happened according to God's plan of salvation for us, in our stead. For you and for me! He himself had decided to do it (John 10:18) because there is no other way to achieve our redemption. It was so because Jesus loved us so much that he said to God: Father, let me go, because Bruno and Bonnie, Ken and Kathy, or whatever the names might be, are unable to do it for themselves. They are in no position to purchase their own redemption, regardless of their piety.

This is the good news today and every day: Jesus died in our stead, bearing our sins!

At the very end on the cross, Jesus cried out into the world, "It is finished!" What exactly had he completed? He had provided the only righteousness that God can accept! We are guilty, we have been sentenced, and our sentence was executed upon Jesus! I have been punished in Jesus, provided that I am in Jesus! We, you and I, are free once we accept God's offer and all it contains.

What does all this mean? The answer is clarified in the biblical text, Rom 6:3–5:

> [D]o you not know that all of us who have been baptized into Christ Jesus have been baptized into His death? Therefore we have been buried with Him through baptism into death, in order that as Christ was raised from the dead through the glory of the Father, so we too might walk in newness of life. For if we have become united with Him in the likeness of His death, certainly we shall be also in the likeness of His resurrection.

A few moments ago I asked, what is the only thing you can do with a corpse? Well, bury it, of course. As we just read in the text from Rom 6, we must be buried alive in baptism—in Jesus! According to Rom 6, if we are in Jesus, we are through God's grace and by faith not just buried in him, but at the resurrection we will also be like him. As a part of the body of Jesus, we shall arise at the sound of the trumpet (1 Thess 4:16).

When will this happen? What is there to be done? Dear reader, if you have not already done so, throw off your sins today by faith. Throw them into the same place where Jesus has already carried them away. Yes, that is possible! Repentance is, comparable to engagement, the first official step toward union with Jesus. Then come by demonstrating your faith in the act of baptism, and, just as one demonstrates a change in status at a wedding ceremony, proclaim: I am in Jesus and he is in me, buried and resurrected.

The baptismal water does nothing. Its chemical nature is still H_2O. In baptism neither the water nor you are magically transformed. But in the act of baptism we speak to God and God speaks to us. To state it once more: in repentance we turned ourselves over to God and formed a bond with him. In baptism, God places his seal on the bond, and we confess our new state before God and the world. In baptism you declare that the bond that you have formed with God by your repentance is sealed, and you confess in the presence of God and the world:

1. I am now a part of Jesus according to the Scriptures (Col 2:6–10).

2. I have been crucified with Jesus according to the Scriptures (Rom 6:6; Col 2:11).

3. I have been buried with Jesus according to the Scriptures (Rom 6:4).

4. I have been resurrected with Jesus according to the Scriptures (Rom 6:5).

None of these items is accomplished by the waters of baptism. But the baptism shows that our faith manifests itself in obedience, and we demonstrate this new obedience by baptism.

JESUS WAS OBEDIENT

Now I want to point out something very important. Jesus did not die on the cross symbolically. The nails, which were driven into his hands and feet, were not symbolic nails. Blood flowed, flesh tore! It was a real cross! Jesus died a real death. And God allowed his Son to die this horrible death in order to save us. Philippians 2:8: ". . . He humbled Himself by becoming obedient to the point of death, even death on a cross."

This same God is asking the same thing from us: obedience! All rites and all forms of worship are overshadowed by God's demand for obedience. That was the case back then and still is today. We have seen it particularly applied even to Jesus our Lord. Jesus was always the Son of God, the Second Person of the Trinity, and will remain the same for all eternity. For him, the Son of God, it was not easy to take upon himself our flesh and blood. But he did so. The Letter to the Hebrews gives us Jesus' response to God in 10:7: "Then I said, 'Behold, I have come to do your will, O God, as it is written of me in the scroll of the book'" (ESV). Such was the obedience displayed by Jesus, our Lord. He needed to leave his throne by the Father's side, to "clothe" himself with our flesh and blood and to die in our stead, there on the cross of Calvary.

The obedience of Jesus was the only way to open the road for us to become children of God. Just remember that there were several ways in which Jesus could return from the world and return its people back to God. When Jesus left the waters of the Jordan River after his baptism, he was conducted by the Spirit into the desert. This happened so that he could be tested by Satan. The greatest temptation for Jesus probably was when Satan showed him all the realms of this world and their glory and said to him, "All this I will give to you if you fall on your knees and worship me." Jesus could have accepted that offer. He would have spared himself three more years of being a human, would not have had to go to the cross, and would have been able to place the world at God's feet. Additionally, let us remember again the events in the garden of Gethsemane when Jesus was arrested. When Peter wanted to defend him with the sword Jesus said, "Don't you realize that I could ask my Father for thousands of angels to protect us, and he would send them instantly?" (Matt 26:53, NLT). When we remember that a Roman legion consisted of anywhere from four thousand to six thousand soldiers, averaging about five thousand men, then Jesus just said that he could have had sixty thousand angels at his disposal to defend him. In this context let us also remember that actually only one angel would have been necessary to frighten and destroy those who were trying to take Jesus to court so that he could be condemned and crucified. And we also know that only one word from God's Son would have had the same effect. But listen to what Jesus says in verse 54: "But in that case, how could the Scriptures come true which say that this is what must happen?" (GNT). In other words, only by his chosen path could God's plan of salvation be achieved. In obedience to God he set aside his might as God, and, thus, went to the cross as a man, voluntarily, so that he could stand in our place and fulfill the requirements of God's anger. That is what he did—voluntarily.

Did you catch that? Only through obedience, which originated in divine love, did Jesus come. He took on our nature as man and died as a man in our stead on the cross. And even today he is still calling out to each of us: "Be obedient just like I, Jesus, was. And Jesus said, "He who believes and is baptized will be saved!" Have you given Jesus your response?

It is God's desire that all people be saved and come to an understanding of the truth. And what is that truth? John 3:16: "For God so loved the world, that He gave His only begotten Son, that whoever believes in Him should not perish, but have eternal life."

A SUMMARY OF THE EFFECTS OF THESE ACTIONS

In order to ensure that there will be no misunderstanding, I would like to highlight four important facts:

1. There is no holy water in the world. There was nothing holy about the water in the pool of Bethesda in connection with the incident recorded in John 5. A sick man had been waiting for healing for thirty-eight years and then was restored to health by Jesus. Nor was there holy water in the pool of Siloam where Jesus sent the blind man in order to wash his eyes so that he could regain his sight (John 9:7).

2. There is nothing mystical in connection with baptism; the water as such has no particular power, regardless of whether someone was

sprinkled as a baby or fully immersed in water as an adult.

3. It is not through the act of baptism that anyone becomes a child of God. Neither baptism nor communion are sacraments in the sense that they cause anything to happen. They are symbols of the believer's union with God through the person of Jesus. Baptism is simply and solely an outward sign that God has given us as a concrete action to represent our union with Jesus. As we alluded to above, it is similar to a wedding ceremony insofar as it is a public declaration. The believer wants to proclaim that he and Jesus are one. The Bible very clearly brings this out, and unless we read it, we cannot hear the word of God as it has been recorded. We must read it. We must let the word of God speak to us just as it is written. Traditions receive no status as prophetic promises in the Bible, and they cannot provide saving grace.

4. Regardless of the type of baptism that an assembly or church may practice, no church or fellowship nor any pastor or priest has access to a switch, that, when clicked, opens an automatic door to heaven. Only the acceptance of the substitutionary sacrifice of Jesus on the cross, as demonstrated by our obedience, is acceptable to God. But on these terms God promises us adoption as his children.

17

Scientific Critique of the Bible

THE CHRISTIAN (CATHOLIC) CHURCH, especially prior to the time of the Reformation, had, by means of issuing doctrinal statements, established very clearly what Christians had to believe and how they had to conduct their affairs in order to be admitted to heaven. These rules and guidelines were set out in writing and were accorded the status of *de fide*, which meant that they were considered to be incontrovertibly true. Violations would lead to excommunication so that the offending individual was no longer a member of the church. Not infrequently some rules and dogmas were in conflict with the Bible. Beginning with his posting the ninety-five theses on the church door in Wittenberg, Martin Luther pointed out some of the discrepancies between what the clergy was currently practicing and what the Bible stated. He even called the authority of the pope and the ecumenical council into question because they, too, were mere human beings. His initial actions were intended to be reform the church, but it quickly became the "Reformation," which split the Christian church once again (the previous split having been the one between the West [Roman Catholic] and the East [Orthodox]). Ever since, Protestantism has existed alongside the Catholic Church.

Protestantism is neither a church nor a union of churches. The word is derived from the fact that the German princes who supported Luther lodged a protest against those who remained loyal to the Catholic Church. In 1526, at the Council of Speyer, the various princes of Germany, divided over religion, came to the compromise solution that in the Holy Roman Empire, each province would follow the preference of the one who governed it. However, in 1529, once again at Speyer, the Catholic princes rescinded the previous agreement, and once again insisted that Luther and all those who followed him should be under the imperial ban. This decision obviously aggravated their opponents, and they sent a firm letter of protest to the emperor, Charles V. Thus, they became known as "Protestants," which became the general designation for all the forms of Christianity that arose out of the Reformation period. Basic to the demands of the Reformers was that all people should have free access to the Bible. The roughly contemporary invention of the printing press greatly enhanced the dissemination of the Bible. It made it possible to turn out large numbers of copies of the Scriptures, which had recently been translated into German by Luther and Melanchthon. For the first time after the Middle Ages, the Bible was (quite often literally) unchained from the churches and universities and their noble custodians and placed into the hands of commoners. Now many people had an opportunity to read at least some of the Scriptures.

Due to the fact that the Catholic Church no longer was the sole authority on how people must conduct themselves, many scholars now felt free to question and scrutinize the statements and doctrines of the Christian church. They began using what they considered to be scientific methods to examine the Bible. Now, we must be careful to distinguish between textual criticism (sometimes called "lower criticism") and the methods of analysis used by these scholars (often referred to as "higher criticism"). Textual criticism has existed as long as the Bible itself. The textual critic reconstructs what the original manuscript must have said on the basis of the many later manuscripts that are available to consult. This effort should always be considered positively. Because of it we can view our biblical text as fully reliable. Since there are thousands of manuscripts and there are reliable methods of adjudicating the differences between the manuscripts, we can say that, for all practical purposes, when we read the Bible we are reading the text as it was originally composed under the inspiration of the Holy Spirit by the human authors.

The emerging higher critics had something very different in mind. Now that the Bible was no longer under the sole guardianship of the Catholic Church, the era that we call the "Enlightenment" was setting in, and with it a new spirit of rationalism and skepticism. There was no subject that could not be doubted or questioned. Some writers went so far as to state outright that the biblical reports could not be verified, and that, therefore, they must be considered to be false. Initially, all the Christian churches perceived the publications of such scholars as blasphemous and decried their work as heretical. However, after a time, scientists and theologians started to collaborate. The theologians of the University of Tübingen (initially represented by D. F. Strauss and later under the leadership of F. C. Baur) were foremost in this matter. The final results of their studies were publicized and treated as just as incontrovertible as the dogmas of the church had been earlier. Subsequently a liberal theology, fully supported by scientists, came to the forefront in the universities. What aggravated the situation, particularly in Germany, was the fact that, lacking a counterpart to the Catholic Church's holy office of doctrine, the princes had to rely on the opinions of university professors for doctrinal rectitude. But in the universities, the faculties in biblical studies and theology saw huge leaps of progress being made by other disciplines, such as mathematics and the natural sciences, and could not offer anything comparable within the traditional framework that included belief in the supernatural work of God. They found themselves under great pressure to make progress as well. Progress became synonymous with the search for novelty, and belief in the supernatural and the integrity of the Bible were easily sacrificed for the sake of receiving plaudits for "progress."

It is not within the scope of this book to evaluate the scientific discussions of Bible criticism, and the available evidence, including the Dead Sea Scrolls found at Qumran. Instead I will mention three books that have addressed this issue quite adequately:

1. *Rock, Relics and Biblical Reliability*. This book by the director of the Australian Institute for Archaeology, Clifford Wilson, was published in English by Zondervan in 1977.

2. *The Bible as History*. This book was written by the journalist Werner Keller. It has been translated into twenty-two languages. It was first published in 1955 and has sold over ten million copies.

3. *From God to Us: How We Got the Bible*. This book was written by Norm Geisler and William Nix and published by Moody Press in 1980.

In spite of these and numerous other books, which have been published by scientists or edited by scientists, theologians have not allowed themselves to be diverted from their tendency to follow Bible critics,

Scientific Critique of the Bible 153

partially because they were not taught any better in their seminaries, and partially because they, too, want to be seen as au courant with recent theories. What makes this attitude so difficult to understand is the fact that most theories that challenge the truthfulness of the Bible have been shown to be false, and none of them have been proven to be true. In *Rocks, Relics and Biblical Reliability*, the author talks about the impact of the Dead Sea Scrolls. We read on page 107: "One of the most important implications of the Dead Sea Scrolls to Old Testament studies is that it can no longer be argued that the prophecy of Isaiah should be dated after the time of Jesus, as some severe critics had claimed." In regard to the reliability of the Old Testament canon, he points to the discovery of the Isaiah scrolls. It can no longer be argued that parts of the prophecy of Isaiah were written after the time of Jesus. However, many recalcitrant critics are still asserting such an argument. In the case of Qumran, an Isaiah scroll (Q1Ia) was found that was written at least one hundred years before Christ and has a length of 8 meters. All three of the above mentioned books clearly point out, and actually prove, that the Deutero-Isaiah theory has never been substantiated. The book of Isaiah clearly has been written or dictated by the prophet Isaiah, son of Amos, who is mentioned in other parts of the Bible. The results of the evaluation of the scrolls found in 1947 in the Dead Sea caves are known to all universities, seminaries, and churches.

The first book mentioned above was published over thirty years ago, and many other publications are of about the same vintage and have been available in bookstores for over twenty years. Nevertheless in the year 2007 I heard from the pulpit of an evangelical church the assertion that nobody knows who wrote the book of Isaiah, starting with chapter 40. Liberal theologians (pastors and professors) obviously do not wish to acknowledge (a) that God could have revealed the name of Cyrus to Isaiah (chapter 44) a hundred years before he lived, and (b) that Isaiah's prophecy of the suffering servant of God (in chapter 53) had its clear fulfillment in Jesus. The consequence of recognizing the unity of Isaiah would be that one would have to recognize the supernatural power of God. But then one would have to order one's life in subordination to God, and liberal scholars, priests, pastors, and their disciples are not inclined to do so.

One cannot actually fault the biblical critics for questioning a point in the Bible and then attempting to defend their theories on the basis of logic. If that is how they see their vocation, then that is what they must do. The real fault lies with those people who read those books or articles and take them seriously. No one is forced to read what was written and published in either periodicals or books. The same thing goes for information disseminated through television and radio. Why so many people are willing to accept the unproven speculations and conclusions of Bible critics rather than the Bible is a mystery to me. The Bible is available to anyone who wants to read. Many Bible critics have publicly assaulted the veracity of the Bible. When confronted with evidence that their criticism was false, one would expect that they acknowledge their error. But to do so would involve more than accepting their mistake in this one instance; they would have to repudiate their entire anti-supernatural world view, and that is something that fallen human beings will not do, regardless of the strength of the evidence.

One exception very clearly proves this rule. Eta Linnemann was a student of Rudolf Bultmann and became a highly acknowledged proponent of *historical criticism*, a term that actually signifies the study of the Bible as an *unhistorical* document. Through circumstances that she relates in her testimony, she came to realize that God could perform miracles, and so her entire framework changed.[1] Thus, she became a true Christian, and the Lord gave her the freedom to acknowledge publicly that what she had taught previously was wrong. But it took her experience with the Lord himself to bring her to this point. Such miraculous conversions are rare and exceptional enough to say that the rule is for critical scholars not to acknowledge their errors. The fact that Professor Linnemann lost the respect of her former colleagues also supports this point. Unregenerate scholars would rather go to their graves denying the undeniable than admit a mistake because to do so would imply that they should bow their knees before God, something they will not do. There is no question that Bible critics and liberal theologians use their own presuppositions as a template on which to establish their results.

---

1. Eta Linnemann, "Eta Linnemann Testimony," transcribed lecture, Grace Valley Christian Center, Davis, California, November 7, 2001, http://dcn.davis.ca.us/~gvcc/sermon_trans/Special_Speakers/Eta_Linnemann_Testimony.html (accessed October 6, 2011).

18

The Work of the Holy Spirit

GOD IS SPIRIT AND CREATED HEAVEN, EARTH, AND HUMAN BEINGS

THE BIBLE TELLS US quite clearly that our spiritual life, namely our life with God in Jesus, must be guided by the Holy Spirit if we, as born-again children of God, want to achieve our desired goal. As I demonstrated in the narration of my life, Jesus through the Holy Spirit provided guidance in my spiritual life and my natural life as well. He did that, however, without overruling my free will completely. This demonstrates quite clearly that we still are normal people even when we are lead by the spirit of Jesus.

It is well known and I am fully aware that churches, assemblies, and fellowships organize special activities and worship services in which special healing through the Holy Spirit is promised, particularly under the heading of "the filling with the Holy Ghost." Thus some assemblies and fellowships also offer certain ceremonies in which this baptism in the Holy Spirit is conferred. They state that without this Spirit baptism a person cannot be a complete disciple of Jesus. I would like to clarify that the Bible provides no basis for such special arrangements for those who, like myself, do not see a necessity for such special events. In my general observations, I would like to express clearly when and how the Holy Spirit enters into us and how he equips us with his gifts.

To begin with, in order to get some basic understanding of this topic, we should remember what Jesus said, apparently off-topic, to the

Samaritan woman at Jacob's well. Even though the remark appears random, it has deep significance. The statement is recorded in John 4:24: "God is Spirit, and those who worship Him must worship Him in spirit and in truth." With this assertion, Jesus makes it clear to us that God is not a being whom we can fully comprehend with our limited human understanding, but he is Spirit. We also know from Exod 33:18–23 that even Moses, a man with whom God spoke directly, was barred from seeing God's glory directly.

In this context I would like to point out that the Hebrew and Greek words for "spirit" introduce a certain amount of ambivalence when translated into English. First of all, both the Hebrew word in the Old Testament (*ruach*) and the Greek word in the New Testament (*pneuma*) can mean "air" as well as spirit. The context usually leaves little doubt as to what is meant. But there is a grammatical difference between the two words: *ruach* is feminine in gender, and *pneuma* is neuter. In these days, where the difference between biological sex and grammatical gender has been intentionally obscured, it could be easy to fall into the trap of thinking, that, therefore, the Spirit is a female person in the Old Testament, and a thing or a substance in the New Testament. This is nonsense, of course. Grammatical gender does not transfer to biological sex, and God has revealed himself in certain grammatical forms, but he is neither male nor female.

What does the Bible tell us about the work of God's Spirit? Let us start with the Old Testament in the first two verses of the Bible: "In the beginning God created the heavens and the earth. And the earth was formless and void, and darkness was over the surface of the deep; and the Spirit of God was moving over the surface of the waters" (Gen 1:1–2). When God created Adam in his image and gave him living breath (*ruach*), humanity was complete and was equipped with God's Spirit. At the time of the fall into sin, Adam lost God's Spirit; however, because of God's great mercy, he may receive him back on account of Jesus' sacrificial death at the time of repentance and rebirth. Now the union with God is reestablished, and God can lead and guide a person. We read in the Bible that God can actually extend his rule into the kingdom of the prince of this world in order to complete his redemptive plan (Rev 20–21), but he has not yet stripped the evil one of his power. Consequently, we are in need of the protection of Jesus; we must rely on his guidance and direction in order not to miss our goal of spending eternity with Jesus.

GOD ACTS THROUGH HIS SPIRIT

Now let me repeat: God is Spirit and acts through his Spirit. No one has an unobstructed understanding of what God is, and how he acts through his Spirit. The Bible tells us, however, about the work of God's Spirit in the Old Testament. Let us look at some examples. Throughout the seventy-year captivity, as well as afterward, God promised his people in a vision the reestablishment of the kingdom of Israel and the rebuilding of the temple. He confirmed this promise through the prophet Zechariah. We read in chapter 4:6: ". . . 'Not by might nor by power, but by My Spirit,' says the LORD of hosts."

THE SPIRIT OF GOD IS WORKING IN HIS PEOPLE

The fact that the Spirit of God is working in his people is a constant theme in the Old Testament. That King David knew how important the presence of the Spirit was is seen in Ps 51:11 when he prayed, "Do not cast me away from Thy presence, And do not take Thy Holy Spirit from me." Gideon, Elijah, Elisha, King Saul, and other important figures in the Old Testament are specifically credited with being empowered by the Holy Spirit.

We could cite other straightforward examples but will refrain from doing so. After all, in a book that is meant to serve as an incentive for Christians to study the Bible, I should not simply recite all of the facts of the Bible, should I? But I'm going to leave it with the examples referred to above so that we can look at some of their implications.[1]

In the Old Testament, whenever we see people empowered by God's Spirit, we are invariably looking at individuals whom God had chosen to participate in the fulfillment of his plan. The Holy Spirit gave them all of the strength they needed to carry out their calling. Two individuals who are technically not in the Old Testament, but still fit into that economy, also received the enablement of the Holy Spirit. They were John the Baptist and Simeon, the latter of whom went to the temple under the prompting of God's Spirit. How, specifically did the Holy Spirit work in those cases? Such things are beyond our understanding. We can only assert what God has revealed to us through the Bible itself. In other words:

---

1. As you read the Bible, please read it for more than just for the evident devotional content. Be sure to make use of the help that most Bibles contain, such as marginal notes or cross references. You will find that, the more time you invest in studying the word of God, the deeper your intimate relationship with the Lord will grow as well.

we will only comprehend as much of God's will as the Lord deems necessary, and that leaves a lot of unknowable territory.

I mentioned above that, under the old covenant, God only provided the help of the Holy Spirit to the extent necessary for a person's calling. This apportionment of the Spirit's power is exemplified in Num 11:11–25. There we find Moses complaining in his prayer that the responsibility of leading the people of Israel is too large of a burden for him. Then God has him summon seventy elders from among the people to come to the tabernacle, and he says to Moses, ". . . Then I will come down and speak with you there, and I will take of the Spirit who is upon you, and I will put Him upon them; and they shall bear the burden of the people with you, so that you shall not bear it all alone . . ."

Here we can clearly see that, in contrast to the way God will work in the new covenant, these elders did not enjoy the fullness of the Spirit. Instead, God distributed the Spirit that rested on Moses, and each person received as much strength as God deemed necessary for them to fulfill their obligations.

Joel 2:28–32 prophesies that the Holy Spirit will come as a person. There we read: "And it will come about after this [t]hat I will pour out My Spirit on all mankind; [a]nd your sons and daughters will prophesy, [y]our old men will dream dreams, [y]our young men will see visions . . ." This passage promises something special for us in the redemptive plan. The history of salvation reaches in an extraordinary way into the future. The people of Joel's time had no inkling of what it would be, and it is only in his farewell address, as recorded in John 14, that Jesus broaches it.

Can you imagine how puzzled the disciples must have been when Jesus said to them that he was leaving them? The very first time that Jesus gently alluded to his departure from the people of Israel comes up in John 8:21. As Jesus mentioned his departure from earth, he did not say anything about sending anyone in his stead, and none of his listeners could have actually understood his words. Consequently, the Jews reacted in normal human fashion. We must remember that in those days people did not own a personal Bible, which they could consult on the spur of a moment. They said, "Is he talking about killing himself when he says that we cannot go where he is going?"

JESUS PROMISED TO SEND THE SPIRIT FROM THE FATHER

It was not until John 14:26 that Jesus became more explicit. Then, in chapter 15:26 he made it even more evident: "When the Helper comes, whom I will send to you from the Father, that is the Spirit of truth, who proceeds from the Father, He will bear witness of Me." Here it becomes clear that Jesus was talking about the Third Person of the Trinity.

Now, we have already clarified that God worked through the power of the Holy Spirit during the time of the Old Testament. So, what could Jesus have been trying to explain here? He is not speaking about the power of the Spirit of God now, but rather he is referring to the Person who will come from the Father when Jesus would no longer be present on earth. We need to pause here for a moment because this is an essential part of the topic.

The word *Helper*, which has also been translated as *Comforter*, is *parakletos* in the original Greek. This was a familiar word to Greek-speaking people, and it meant "advocate," "solicitor," or "empowered deputy." Jesus said that he was going to leave and go to the Father. However, he would send an empowered deputy from the Father, the Spirit of Truth. John 14:18 sheds further light on this promise: "I will not leave you as orphans; I will come to you." In other words, Jesus said that he was going home to the Father. However, he would not leave his followers behind like orphaned children, but he would be with them in the form of an empowered representative, the Holy Spirit, whom the Father was going to send on his request.

GOD SENT THE HOLY SPIRIT AS PROMISED BY JESUS

The coming of the Holy Spirit occurred at Pentecost. We all know the story. Now we can ask ourselves who it was that received the Holy Spirit when Jesus sent him as his representative. The answer is that the recipients were those who were waiting for him, the disciples. Jesus had ordered them not to leave Jerusalem, and they were gathered in the upper room when the Holy Spirit took possession of them.

The meaning of this event will become clearer when we recollect the further work of the Holy Spirit in the early church, as recounted in chapters 3 and 4 of the book of Acts. The Holy Spirit filled the people, and the consequences in their lives become manifest. Peter and John gave testimony concerning the resurrection of Jesus before the Sanhedrin, and the entire church was backing them up with prayer. Undoubtedly, the Holy Spirit had changed the people. That much is clear. But how could he have done so? There is a significant point here that we should not miss. Had he changed the impetuous and choleric Peter into a quiet and thoughtful person? Hardly! Peter was still Peter, and, as we know, he still got into a spat with Paul later on (Gal 2).

What, according to Jesus, is the role of the Holy Spirit? Jesus explains it to us in John 14:26 and 15:26.

1. He will teach us all things.

2. He will bring to our remembrance all that he said to us.

3. He will make us his witnesses.

At this point the Holy Spirit expressed himself through the disciples in spectacular fashion. The people who witnessed it were quite agitated. We read in Acts 2:6: "And when this sound occurred, the multitude came together, and were bewildered . . ." We read further in verse 12: "And they all continued in amazement and great perplexity, saying to one another, 'What does this mean?'" It is not that the disciples had instantaneously changed, but that God was working through them. God himself was acting, and when God acts, people feel very small and insignificant in his presence. Simultaneously, the objects of God's action in this case were the human beings. The disciples spoke in other languages and praised God. These shy and fearful men, who had shut themselves in on account of their dread of the Jews, now stood fearlessly in front of the assembled multitude, witnessing to God's mighty deeds.

ONLY WHEN EQUIPPED BY THE HOLY SPIRIT DO WE HAVE JESUS' AUTHORITY

Was the miracle of Pentecost restricted to the apostles? Not at all. The Prophet Joel proclaimed in the name of God, "It shall come to pass afterward, that I will pour out my Spirit on all flesh . . ." (ESV). Peter explained this to the people when they inquired, "Brethren, what shall we do?" The answer is recorded in Acts 2:38: ". . . Repent, and let each of you be baptized in the name of Jesus Christ for the forgiveness of your sins; and you shall receive the gift of the Holy Spirit."

What, then, is required in order to receive the Holy Spirit? Is it the participation in charismatic assemblies or Pentecostal meetings? No! The requirement is clearly detailed in this passage:

1. Acknowledgment of sin and guilt.

2. Obedience to what the Bible says, including baptism, in which we participate consciously in a visual symbol of devotion and obedience to God in the face of heaven and earth. Let us remember that Jesus would have been God's Son, even if he had not gone to die on the cross. He could have said in the garden of Gethsemane, "It was good enough that I, God's Son, had to suffer the fate of human beings in this miserable body of flesh and blood for the last thirty-three years." Also, as he pointed out to Peter in the garden of Gethsemane, he could have asked his Father for more than twelve legions of angels. That would have put an immediate end to the charade perpetrated by the authorities. Surely Jesus would still have been God's Son. But he was obedient for our sake and paid off our penalty in our stead, there on the cross of Calvary.

Now sin and its effect, the curse, have been removed, and we are invited to accept this work. But acceptance remains a crucial condition.

Dear reader, I cannot help but repeat myself. The gospel is not a religion, but a person, namely Jesus. When we convert to Jesus he assimilates us into his body. Jesus has served the penalty for all the guilt and sin that we have confessed. And the result is our regeneration. We receive the Holy Spirit and become a new person. Romans 5:5 states: ". . . [T]he love of God has been poured out within our hearts through the Holy Spirit who was given to us." When that has happened, when we become part of Jesus, the Holy Spirit uses us to the honor of Jesus' name and to the glory of God.

How does this work out in practical terms? The Bible gives us a good example in Acts 3 and 4. There we read that Peter and John healed—in the name of Jesus and through the power and authority of the Holy Spirit—the lame man at the gate Beautiful. But that is not where the matter stopped; we need to bring to mind what further happens, as recorded in Acts. Because of this miracle in the name of Jesus, the apostles were hauled before the high council or Sanhedrin. Let us not forget that these were the same seventy elders who had sentenced Jesus to death only six weeks before. Peter utterly astounded these assembled sages with his courage and candor.

THE HOLY SPIRIT TURNS SINNERS INTO EMPOWERED SERVANTS OF JESUS

Something definitely had changed, and it was not the fact that John and Peter now had the capacity to heal disabled beggars—that was an attention-getting side issue. Far more important was that this event fulfilled exactly what Jesus had said would happen. The Holy Spirit, whom he would send from the Father, was now at work in the disciples. Consider the fact that here we are discussing the same two disciples who, a mere six weeks earlier, had followed Jesus into the high priest's yard, keeping a safe distance all the way. And Peter had qualified himself as a first-rate coward. When one of the maids recognized Peter and merely mentioned that he was a follower of Jesus, he cursed himself. The other disciples did not shine with bravery either. We read about them in John 20:19: "When therefore it was evening, on that day, the first day of the week, and when the doors were shut where the disciples were, for fear of the Jews, . . ."

Now these very men were standing before the same supreme council and were proclaiming Jesus. This occasion is exactly what Jesus predicted to them. Matthew 10:19: "But when they hand you over, do not worry about how or what you are to say; for it will be given you in that hour what you are to say." (NASB95) The Holy Spirit had given them the courage to testify, and additionally, he had provided them with the right words to say.

Let us not think that the Holy Spirit is restricted to providing us with the courage to testify. We cannot ignore in what fashion and why the Holy Spirit was poured out. Galatians 4:4-6: "But when the fullness of time came, God sent forth His Son . . . that we might receive the adoption as sons. And because you are sons, God has sent forth the Spirit of His Son into our hearts . . .!"

The most important requirement for becoming children of God is redemption from our sins through Jesus. But how do we even know that we are sinful and in need of redemption? Who opens our eyes to our state? This is also a work of the Holy Spirit. For when the Holy Spirit has truly entered someone's life, he sheds his light on the person, who then cannot help but realize: "I am a sinner." The Holy Spirit will give us no rest until we confess our sin and lay it at the foot of the cross.

This truth also applies to believers, God's children. As long as we are on this earth we will continue to become guilty before God and our fellows. The Holy Spirit shows us what we have to set right and leads us to our daily "foot washing," so to speak, namely, to leave all of our sins and shortcomings at the foot of the cross.

STRIVING AFTER SPIRITUAL GIFTS

According to Matt 28:19 and Mark 16:15–18, as well as Acts 1:8, Jesus commands his disciples to go into all the world, to preach the gospel, and to be his witnesses. Jesus will manifest the power of his Holy Spirit in the process. When Jesus gave this command, he also promised certain signs that would follow those who were obedient to his commands. This statement has caused many Christians to seek after signs and gifts that he mentioned at those times. But here emerges an attitude that the Apostle Paul already had to confront as a problem among the early Christian churches. So, in order to keep ourselves from becoming entangled needlessly in unhelpful issues, let me set these promises into context and clarify them.

Jesus has ascended to the throne of his Father and has left us in the realm of Satan, the "prince of this world." But that does not mean that we are now vulnerable to Satan without any protection. Because Jesus is no longer with us in person, he has sent another person of the Godhead from the Father—the Holy Spirit—who will, according to Jesus, be the representative of the Trinity during his physical absence. The essence of what Jesus taught in John 14 is that the presence of the Spirit is all-inclusive, and that everyone who has become a disciple of Jesus by repentance and rebirth will be blessed with the Holy Spirit. Jesus says quite clearly, ". . . If anyone loves Me, he will keep My word; and My Father will love him, and We will come to him, and make Our abode with him." (John 14:23). Thus, a disciple of Jesus is part of God, and God (the Father) and Jesus (the Son) are a part of the disciple through the Holy Spirit.

Let us now return to the healing of the lame man at the beautiful gate of the temple. The Holy Spirit gave the two disciples the conviction that they should do something. We can also rephrase that statement and say that the Holy Spirit, who reigned in the lives of the disciples, acted through them and then continued to work in and through them before the supreme council.

Now, we need to realize that this event was not really special. The Father and the Son dwell in the disciple while the Holy Spirit controls his life and actions. Are people who are equipped with the Holy Spirit strange and peculiar? Certainly not. Look at my life. I am a normal person and that includes making mistakes. Just ask my children, my neighbors, and my colleagues, and my late beloved wife, who would certainly have endorsed that sentiment. But guilt and sin are no longer reckoned to me. Jesus has already paid the penalty for those, and by faith I take any new sin to Jesus on the cross as quickly as possible.

Yes, Christians make many mistakes, and one of them is that they want to determine what the Holy Spirit has to do. And in this context many Christians have the sincere desire to be able to experience spectacular events such as the disciples did at Pentecost. At that point, God—through the Holy Spirit—worked an event for his glory and for the fulfillment of the next step in the plan of salvation. However, if our wishes and pursuits are centered solely on the gifts, and not on the glorification of the Lord, it is possible to invite a false spirit. The prince of this world is also able to send miraculous signs. Let us make sure that we do not belong to those of whom Jesus says in Matt 7:23: ". . . I never knew you; DEPART FROM ME, YOU WHO PRACTICE LAWLESSNESS." That would be most horrible.

19

Grace Is Greater than Reward

GOD IS MERCIFUL, BUT WHAT DOES HE EXPECT OF US?

Let me state right up front that aside from accepting his offer, that is to say, appropriating the substitutionary sacrifice of Jesus for oneself, God expects nothing more of us in order to join his family. Even at the risk of overemphasis or redundancy, let us inscribe the fact firmly in our minds: being a Christian, or being a disciple in the service of Jesus, is not a religion.

There is no religiosity or achievement with which I can impress God. There is nothing, absolutely nothing, through which I can earn God's favor. What God expects of me I have already mentioned in chapter 16, on baptism. There I emphasized that, once we are his children, God expects us to be obedient to his commandments. While I can practice religion in the context of my worship, I have pointed out several times that there is no code of conduct with which we can turn away God's judgment and earn his mercy. The Bible does not provide us with any such teaching but rather points us to Jesus, through whom we have a merciful God and in whom we are made righteous. Regardless of what I do, the Bible tells me, God is mercy. Luther in one of his hymns writes, "All our deeds are in vain, even our most pious living."

ENTITLEMENT TO WAGES

In Matt 19 we read of Peter approaching Jesus with this question: ". . . Behold, we have left everything and followed You; what then will there be for us?" It is quite likely that many people have asked this same type of question. I have often been tempted to wonder, when I was sick and feeling low, was giving up my strength, my time, my money, and now even my health, worth it all? To top it off, the leader of a Christian missionary organization told me, "Bruno, what you are doing is sin, the way you are ruining your health. That is not God's will." Of course I was shocked, and I did some serious soul-searching. Was I doing all of my ministry for myself, so that my reputation would shine forth? Or was I doing it to let God's glory shine forth as I fulfilled his commission. God gave me a clear answer, and I continued fulfilling my duty. And then I remembered the Apostle Paul. He enumerated what he had suffered in his service for Jesus:

> Five times I received from the Jews thirty-nine lashes. Three times I was beaten with rods, once I was stoned, three times I was shipwrecked, a night and a day I have spent in the deep. I have been on frequent journeys, in dangers from rivers, dangers from robbers, dangers from my countrymen, dangers from the Gentiles, dangers in the city, dangers in the wilderness, dangers on the sea, dangers among false brethren; I have been in labor and hardship, through many sleepless nights, in hunger and thirst, often without food, in cold and exposure. Apart from such external things, there is the daily pressure upon me of concern for all the churches. (2 Cor 11:24–28)

What reward did Paul expect in return? To what wages can those who offer up their selves, their strength, and their health in the service of God be entitled?

Dear reader, let me come right out with it and not skirt the issue. What reward has God promised to those of us who follow him, serve him, and suffer for him? None! That's right! Nowhere in the Bible does God promise us wages. Neither does he offer specific compensations for the performance of the various duties of his faithful children. In the Greek of the New Testament, the word for "wages" is *misthos*. This word always means the recompense for a certain service performed. The *misthōtos*, a day laborer, receives his wage. Being a disciple of Jesus is something entirely different.

THE GIFT OF SONSHIP

The gospel is God's promise to those of us who have turned our lives over to Jesus that we will receive something much more worthwhile than a wage for our efforts. Whatever God promises that will he also do. And his promise is truly astounding. We read in John 1:12: "But as many as received Him, to them He gave the right to become children of God, even to those who believe in His name." God has adopted us and not just returned us to our previous standing, that is to say, the condition prior to the fall into sin. We have been freed from all of our sin. And there is more! Our situation is not just similar to a person, who, having been released from prison, can now return to a normal life, a point on which we will expand below. Paul calls out to the Galatians, and to us as well, in chapter 3:26–27: "For you are all sons of God through faith in Christ Jesus. For all of you who were baptized into Christ have clothed yourselves with Christ."

This is the greatest of gifts from the living God to all those who have turned their lives over to Jesus. Children are not day laborers; children do not receive wages for expressing their love to their parents. Could you imagine that someone would pay Crown Prince Charles of England a wage? His allowance, which is called his "appanage," is not a reward or wage but comes with being the child of a queen. In the same manner, we became children of the King when we accepted Jesus' sacrifice.

THE SIGNIFICANCE OF BEING A CHILD OF GOD

Everything involved in being a child of the living God is difficult for us to comprehend. The Bible does not tell us everything. We read in Apostle John's first epistle 3:2: "Beloved, now we are children of God, and it has not appeared as yet what we shall be. We know that, when He appears, we shall be like Him, because we shall see Him just as He is."

Can you imagine being like Jesus? That is why the Apostle Paul says in Rom 8:18, "For I consider that the sufferings of this present time are not worthy to be compared with the glory that is to be revealed to us."

Wages? No, dear reader, we will not be given wages. Wages are paid to workers who have been hired to perform a particular task. In Jesus we are children of the living God and not his employees.

This is the answer that Jesus gave to Peter, and we need to look at it closely because many people miss the point of this text. We do not receive wages for discipleship. Rather we enter a new status with certain consequences. This status is given to us as a gift when we turn our lives over to Jesus. It is the consequence of a mutual relationship based on love between us and God through Jesus Christ.

OUR POSITION AS CHILDREN OF GOD

Let us shed some further light on the concept of being a child of God and its significance. A child always holds a special position in the family, and we can mention some of the things that this fact entails. In Matt 19 Peter asked Jesus what the disciples will receive in return for all they have given up. Jesus gives Peter a clear answer. As we read in Matt 19:28:

> And Jesus said to them, "Truly I say to you, that you who have followed Me, in the regeneration when the Son of Man will sit on His glorious throne, you also shall sit upon twelve thrones, judging the twelve tribes of Israel."

Also in 1 Cor 6:3: "Do you not know that we shall judge angels? . . ."

As children of God we will hold a position much higher than the angels before God's throne. That certainly is an awe-inspiring promise. But we should still not think of it as a "wage." You might say that it is a reward or an inheritance to which we can look forward in the world to come. Yes, it is something that was promised to us, and it is recorded for our sake in the Bible. It is certainly hard to imagine why some people hesitate to accept this offer or even outright reject it.

Consequently, the question of how I can appease God and obtain his mercy is utterly absurd. This is what Luther discovered at the end of his long inner struggle. It is impossible for me to make God, who is offering me his grace, more favorably disposed toward me. It would be the equivalent of asking my father to become my father, because of certain things that I might have done for him. He already is my father.

THE GIFT OF GRACE

Paul tells us clearly in Eph 2:8–9: "For by grace you have been saved through faith; and that not of yourselves, it is the gift of God; not as a result of works, that no one should boast." It is God's gift. God has remitted all our guilt and all of our sin. Jesus took our guilt upon himself and paid the penalty on the cross. If I believe that I have to earn additional wages by my good deeds, then I am stating that what Jesus has done for me is insufficient, and, additionally, that God's grace is not enough for me. How can I devalue Jesus' sacrifice in such a way! I would have to conclude that Jesus has died needlessly on the cross. The bottom line is that there is nothing that I can do to influence God to be merciful to me. All I have to do is accept Jesus' act of salvation for me, personally.

Now, this fact does not constitute grounds for laziness. Out of love to him who made me his child, I will labor to further his domain. God invites his children to carry on his work. Paul says in 1 Cor 15:10, "But by the grace of God I am what I am, and His grace toward me did not prove vain; but I labored even more than all of them, yet not I, but the grace of God with me."

Could Paul possibly be talking about wages, favors earned, or payment for services rendered? That would not fit what he is saying at all. In his statement, Paul begins with the grace of God, by which we become the Lord's children. From the personal perspective of an individual, this is where the plan of salvation commences, because that is how one becomes a member of God's family. God has invited every one of us to receive this gift, which is made available through the redemptive act of Jesus on the cross of Calvary. Let us look at the converse of this truth. If I do not accept this grace, which Jesus has achieved for me, if I choose not to repent, then I am missing out on the consequence, namely the adoption by God! Then I will continue to search, then I will continue to slave away at ways of attempting to please God by means of a religious life, hoping to receive God's grace as a reward for my piety. Then I can allow my deep piety to shine before others. But before God I am still a dead man.

Before his conversion Paul was a zealous Pharisee who believed that his ancestry and his strict observance of the commandments were his key to heaven. But by the time that he wrote Phil 3, he knew better. In Phil 3:7–8, he writes, "But whatever things were gain to me, those things I have counted as loss for the sake of Christ. More than that, I count all things to be loss in view of the surpassing value of knowing Christ Jesus my Lord, for whom I have suffered the loss of all things, and count them but rubbish in order that I may gain Christ." Our piety, our attempts at being religious, will only stand in the way of receiving God's gift. Contrary to what so many people think, "being religious" can do us more harm than good.

Only after I had been accepted in Christ, so says Paul, did I realize that all the pious deeds that I performed previously were entirely useless. In the righteousness of Jesus Christ I have found the key to God's pleasure. With God there is no performance-based caste system where the rich get richer and the poor get poorer.

GRACE ENCOMPASSES ALL

Let us explore this idea a little more fully. Paul claims in 1 Cor 15:10 that he has worked harder than all of the other apostles and evangelists. Now, why would he make such an arrogant-sounding assertion? Is he making a case that he is entitled to a better wage or a greater prize? You know by now that the answer cannot be Paul's hankering for a reward. This is the mystery, as Paul explains, that only after grace had done its work in him did his work start to count for anything. Paul gives us here the proper sequence. First he became a Christian, and as such he received a place in God's family. This is the proper order:

1. Acceptance of the righteousness available only through grace. The acceptance of redemption through Jesus' blood. We cannot earn this by means of pious living.
2. Acceptance into the family of God as a child of God.
3. Life as a member of God's family as his child. From here on out work counts, but it would be impossible to obtain a wage or a prize. To return to our earlier example, Prince Charles would be puzzled indeed if the British Parliament offered him a salary.

THE RICHES OF GOD'S CHILDREN

Once we understand this fact, another question will immediately raise its head. Is it possible to earn membership in a royal family, for example, to become part of the family of Windsor? No, you have to be born into it. Similarly, we can apply this illustration to our being members of God's family. The Apostle Peter brings this out clearly. In 1 Pet 1:3 he states, "Blessed be the God and Father of our Lord Jesus Christ, who according to His great mercy has caused us to be born again to a living hope through the resurrection of Jesus Christ from the dead." We are adopted or born again (spiritually) into the family of God.

The Apostle Paul sheds further light on this fact. In Rom 8:17 he continues an enumeration of the blessings that members of God's family receive: "and if children, heirs also, heirs of God and fellow heirs with Christ, if indeed we suffer with Him in order that we may also be glorified with Him." Thus, we are not working for a wage or a prize, but we already are God's heirs and fellow heirs with Christ.

Not everyone can make sense of this fact. Jesus told us in various places that he is the door, the truth, the life, and that no one comes to the Father except through him. He states in Matt 7:14: "For the gate is small, and the way is narrow that leads to life, and few are those who find it." There are many reasons why the gate is so narrow. For some people their unrestrained reason gets into their way, for others the barrier may be something social or cultural, such as belonging to a particular family. But only in Jesus and by being born again as a child of God do we have the hope and the certainty to participate in the marriage supper of the Lamb.

Can you picture this? We are invited to participate in that great feast not merely as guests, but as family members. There we will sit together with Moses, Isaiah, Elijah, Paul, Peter, and many millions of others, and at the head of the table sits Jesus, our Lord, and God, the Father, looks with pleasure upon all who have accepted his gift. Are these words becoming clear to you?

20

The True Pontifex Maximus; or, Jesus, the Bridge to God

DOES THE BIBLE APPLY TO EVERYONE?

In the section on baptism I tried to make it quite clear that our piety will never get us saved, but that our salvation is rooted in the obedience shown by Christ, which, in turn, engenders our obedience. Now I would like to illustrate our position before God prior to our repentance. The baptism represents the graphic illustration of our repentance. Let me use three examples on the basis of which we will then talk about what Jesus actually did for us. Naturally we will let the word of God speak to us. These examples are simply supposed to help us to understand the Bible properly.

We are all well familiar with the responsibilities of the traffic police officer. He may, for instance, stand within the center of an intersection and direct the traffic. Now picture this: I arrive at an intersection blocked by a massive traffic snarl. If I stepped into that intersection, got the traffic all sorted out, and got the vehicles moving again, many might think that was truly wonderful. Everything is running smoothly. Does that make me a traffic cop? It most certainly does not, and, if I pretended that I was, I could even be charged with impersonating a police officer.

Another example: I put on a white lab coat, hang a stethoscope around my neck, and tend to sick people. I even provide them with medication. Some actually regain their health. Does that make me a medical doctor? Absolutely not! I would be in serious legal trouble, and I would likely receive a severe penalty.

Here is a third example. At times, when I have theological questions or want help with the exegesis of a certain Scripture passage, I will turn to my son Winfried, who is a professor of philosophy and religion in America, and he will send me his reply in a letter written in English. Let us say that my question has now been fully answered. Along comes some stranger, who also has questions regarding the interpretation of certain passages in the Scriptures, but different from mine. For some reason, he comes upon my son's letter and reads it. Will the letter that Winfried wrote to me provide the stranger with the answers to his questions? That would be highly unlikely! First of all, Winfried's letter is addressed to his father; second, the letter is in English;[1] and third, Winfried is replying to my questions, not the stranger's. The stranger would not even know the questions to which my son was replying, and Winfried would be aghast to learn that his response to one set of questions was being used as answers to a totally different set of questions.

I think we can all understand what I am trying to establish in these three scenarios: an external action does not change one's identity or position. But here is the startling truth: when it comes to the Bible, many people act in exactly that way. They think that they can appropriate the commandments and promises of God for themselves, and they even lay claim on God himself. But they never ask themselves whether the Bible even applies to them. To most of them this question appears to be superfluous. But again, one could not be more wrong. The books of the Bible, especially the letters in the New Testament, are initially written to God's children by someone who is maintaining fellowship with them from far away, and we should not lose sight of that fact. Just as I first must be a licensed physician before I am authorized to treat people and I must have first earned my badge in order to regulate traffic, I have to know which promises of the Bible apply to me. In fact, here we may find the answer to the questions many people who are nominally Christians are frequently asking: Why are my prayers not being answered? Why are they not accomplishing anything? The answer is quite simply that their prayers and the answers that Scripture promises do not apply to them. Of course, the Bible is written for all people and it tells anyone who is seriously searching how to establish a relationship with God through

---

1. The scenario is set in Germany.—Trans.

THE OLD TESTAMENT IS THE PRECURSOR FOR JESUS, THE REDEEMER

Let me begin with some questions and answers that might at first confuse you. But keep on reading, and the point I am making will become clear.

1. To whom was the Old Testament written? The answer is obvious: to the people of Israel. We read in Exod 20:2: "I am the LORD your God, who brought you out of the land of Egypt, out of the house of slavery." Now let me ask you: do you belong to the people whom God led out of Egypt? If not, then the Old Testament is not necessary or relevant for you.

2. To whom was the Book of Acts addressed? The answer is given in the first verse: to Theophilus.

3. To whom are the Gospels written, the apostolic letters, yes, any of the books of the New Testament? They were sent to particular assemblies and specific persons, who are often named in the document. Not a single letter, not a single gospel was written to the church in Germany or a church in the USA.

4. I want to emphasize again, the Old Testament was written to the people of Israel, that is, the Jews. Where does that leave God's children under the new covenant or those who would like to become God's children? Do I have to become a Jew? That is impossible. If I kept all of the commandments and observed the Levitical laws, if I paid my tithe and faithfully went to the synagogue every Sabbath day, the most I could achieve through all my labors would be to become a proselyte. I could never become a Jew.

Consequently God's commandments and the prophets with all their prophecies do not actually address me. Still, the Jews could not obtain salvation or become righteous before God through observance of the law any more than we can.

If that is so, a reasonable question is why we should even have the commandments and the biblical laws. How do the statements above square with the claim that the Bible is God's word? It would not be surprising if somebody thought, "If I cannot keep the law, since it does not actually apply to me, or if I cannot earn righteousness through the keeping of the law, then why include these matters in divine revelation? For that matter, why should I even bother trying to follow any of those instructions since keeping them will not get me into heaven? I might as well go right on sinning because the outcome will be the same in either case." However, that would be the worst possible conclusion. What is wrong with this attitude? The person who thinks such thoughts is interacting with a straw man. The fault lies with the way in which such a person understands those passages of Scripture.

The words of our Lord Jesus Christ are clear and precise: "For truly I say to you, until heaven and earth pass away, not the smallest letter or stroke shall pass away from the Law, until all is accomplished" (Matt 5:18). So, clearly, even though those books and letters may not be written to us, they must have a great amount of value for us.

THE BIBLE SHOWS US WHO WE ARE AND WHAT WE NEED TO DO

For one thing, the law in the Bible is God's law. It serves precisely the purpose that God intended for it to have in the lives of people. The Bible is not written to us, but it has been preserved for us. The Bible is God's word and has been written for our salvation and blessing, including myself and all other people.

But now this matter seems to be utterly confusing. If the law was not written to us, how can it mean anything for us? What applicability does God's law have to my life? What demand is it making of me, a Gentile? How can I understand the purpose of the law for the Gentiles, when it is not even clear to me what its role was for the Jews, the original readers?

To begin with the Apostle Paul provides a clear answer to us in Rom 3:19–20, which concludes with the following statement: "[T]hrough the law we become conscious of our sin" (NIV). The law makes it obvious that we need Jesus as our Savior and Redeemer. I will now go into more detail on this issue.

On many occasions I have been asked, what actually came first, the law or sin? The answer is not quite that simple. As far as a human being is concerned, the law came first, namely beginning with God's commandment: "[B]ut from the tree of the knowledge of good and evil you shall not eat . . ." (Gen 2:17). Nevertheless, Adam and Eve did so anyway, and their disobedience separated them from God. Before the first pair of people sinned, they lived in the presence of God and according to the guidelines that God had given them. They lived in God's light. There was no shadow caused by sin and guilt.

Then, if there was no sin, how could it originate? It started with putting into question whether God's law was actually appropriate. Then we need to take into account the enticement, which people still experience today, for example in reference to issues such as abortion: did God really say . . . ? Once God's law was broken the human beings had fallen under the curse, as God had predicted, and became sinners. They were driven out of the garden of Eden into the darkness and sin of this world. Oh, what a swamp and mire of sin the world offers! God removed his spirit from them. As I frequently point out, that is the reason why people, now distant from God, often behave like animals or even worse. Human beings no longer have any solid ground under their feet. Disoriented, they are now stumbling through a swamp off the path. In addition to all of those factors there is now a huge chasm between God and humanity. The parable of the rich man and poor Lazarus paints that scene for us (Luke 16:26). There is now no longer a direct connection between God and the human race. The exception has been that, on occasion, God reached across to his prophets and others whom he specifically chose.

THE HUMAN BEING IN THE SHADE OF SIN

Let us take a closer look at the situation. The unregenerate person wanders in darkness, stumbling through the swamp of sin and death. Without God! No law! But filled with a longing for life. Throughout the ages, among all people around the globe, humans have tried to become reoriented and find their way as they are yearning for a life of peace and happiness. The Babylonian epics, which are still extant today, are witness to this longing. We know about Melchizedek, the "three wise men," and our own philosophers, all of whom (some with and some without success) have been searching for truth, or at least a glimmer thereof. God did not take away the human's conscience. Cain knew that he was a murderer, even without the law. Romans 3:10 and the following verses describe the situation for us, beginning with the words, "None is righteous, no, not one" (ESV).

But how do you get oriented in a swamp without a path and in the darkness? That's impossible, right? But God loves his creatures. He called across the chasm to Cain. He told Noah: go and preach to the people. Noah complied, but no one could understand him or even wanted to understand, just as today people turn away from the call of the evangelist. For so many people, whether we are talking about today or the days of Noah, it is enough to live according to what is right in their own eyes. Even back before the flood, there was a "sexual revolution," as the Bible reports in Gen 6. However, the flood put an end to the people who thought they were wiser than God. As truly as there is God's grace, there is also God's judgment. In fact, God's grace only makes sense in the light of his judgment, and people who reject his grace are left with his judgment by default.

Still, God's love towers above all. He saw in his mercy that humans were caught in the mire. He also knew very well about the great chasm. And, he knew that people could not help themselves. That is why he selected Abraham, and the plan of salvation was underway. Why did he choose Abraham? Was Abraham better than other people? No, there is no reason to believe that he was. And that statement implies that Abraham was absolutely not without sin. Did Abraham observe God's commandments? There were, as yet, no commandments.

Abraham was chosen out of God's grace, fully independent of whatever commendable traits he may have possessed. But, once chosen, Abraham distinguished himself: he believed God and was obedient, and God credited this to him as righteousness (Gen 15:6). God reached across the great chasm and made a covenant with Abraham, which later was renewed with both Isaac and Jacob. This covenant was the first light in the darkness of this world. And here is the beginning of the history of salvation, of God reaching out to humanity.

Obviously, God's call of Abraham did not eliminate the chasm. It remained just as deep and unbridgeable as before. A full thousand years went by during which, apparently, nothing significant occurred, except that God's chosen people, Abraham's descendents, became a large nation. Then God called Moses, and through him God provided his people with the commandments. What purpose did the law serve? We have now come full circle on this topic. The law told the people what was right and what was wrong.

PART 2: PRESENTATION OF BASIC CONCEPTS

HOW DOES THIS PLAN OF SALVATION WORK?

We have already commented on a number of aspects of the plan of salvation. Here we want to concentrate on the way in which the chasm between holy God and us, the human person, was bridged. What is the goal, or more precisely, what did God intend to accomplish by his plan of salvation? To begin with, God wanted to reestablish communication with human beings. Further, God wanted to reconcile them to himself. The first step I would like to characterize as the reestablishment of the conditions before Adam's sin. But, as I just said, that is only the first step. I want to emphasize strongly that following repentance and baptism into Jesus we become more than just descendents of God. Our new status is comparable to that of princes and princesses. We find an even better statement in the writings of Apostle Peter: "But you are a chosen race, a royal priesthood, a holy nation, a people for his own possession, that you may proclaim the excellencies of him who called you out of darkness into his marvelous light" (1 Peter 2:9, ESV). But this status is available only in and through Jesus. The observance of laws and commandments, as well as our piety, achieve nothing. The Apostle Paul comments that through the law human beings are able to discover on their own where they are. The law was like a map, a compass, and light. With this aid we can now find solid ground and prevent ourselves from going deeper into the swamp.

But how did all this affect the great chasm between human beings and God? The chasm is still there. All paths that the law helped us to find lead to the same destination, namely the chasm. With the law people are able to orient themselves. They now have found an answer to the question, where is God? Unfortunately, the answer seems not all that helpful. God is on the other side of the chasm. There is no way for a human being to cross it. But now, aware of this situation, we can call out to God for help. On many occasions in the past God stretched out his hands and revealed his presence through the prophets. God also called people to himself by means of the typology of the tabernacle and the temple containing the mercy seat. But the chasm was still there.

What needs to be done so that sinners can find their way back to God and fellowship with him? The chasm must be filled in or a bridge must be built across it. That is something that the law could not do. Somebody had to continue the work started by the law and finish it. But who could do that? That person had to take up the curse of sin through which the great chasm was created, the curse of death and condemnation. Could a man who was himself subject to this curse construct the bridge? Impossible. That is why only God could do it, and he did it through Jesus, his Son (Rom 8:3). Yes, he came to be the great Bridge Builder, and he told us of his intentions in Matt 5:17: "Do not think that I came to abolish the Law or the Prophets; I did not come to abolish, but to fulfill." To John the Baptist, Jesus said in essence: I can only fulfill all righteousness by making myself equal to sinful men and take the curse upon myself (Matt 3:15). Jesus came to let the consequences demanded by the law be fulfilled in him. Let us recall what we have already said earlier on this topic. Jesus was willing to accept the sentence that righteousness required under the law: the execution of the one sentenced to death, to receive the death penalty. He suffered in our stead. He came to complete what the law had started and made himself the bridge across the chasm.

Let us recall that the chasm came to exist by Satan's temptation and human sin. And so it was predictable that Satan would do everything to prevent the building of this bridge and the elimination of the chasm. This was the great struggle between Satan and Jesus, the Son of God. In the end Jesus himself, our Lord and Redeemer, threw himself into the breach, across the chasm. At this moment of eternal consequence, at the very climax of the struggle, God left Jesus all alone, and God's Son cried out in despair, "... 'My God, my God, why have you forsaken me?'" (Matthew 27:46, ESV).

JESUS IS THE TRUE BRIDGE BUILDER

And then came the cry of victory: "It is finished!" The passageway between heaven and earth, between God and his human creatures had been reestablished. The heavens rejoiced. Oh, what a jubilation that must have been. And we can picture the angels were waiting to see who might be the very first one to cross this bridge. A king, perhaps David? A prophet? Perhaps Elijah? No! A criminal! A criminal, who, with death imminent, had thrown himself into Jesus' outstretched arms and with simple words entrusted himself to the Son of God. And sheltered safely in Jesus' arms, he came across that chasm. It was the so-called thief on the cross to whom Jesus said, "... [T]oday you shall be with Me in Paradise" (Luke 23:43).

Dear reader! The bridge to God has been built. Jesus invites all of us to walk across the bridge, sheltered in his arms. Only when we are in

Jesus are we secure, and nothing in this world can rip us out of his hand. Jesus alone is the bridge to God. But we must be in him, in Jesus. Only sheltered in him can we find the way to our goal. In him we can take the path across the bridge. But we must truly move on. Conversion to Jesus is only the beginning. If I am not in Jesus, then I do not live in him, and then I am not protected by his blood, because I am not part of his body. I am defenselessly exposed to Satan's wily attacks. It is God's desire that we should repent. But Jesus does not want just immature penitents in his church. He desires that those who are safe with him will go on to walk with him. Oh, how I wish that we would all be rejoicing disciples, sheltered in Jesus' arms.

21

Receiving Blessings and Being a Blessing

ORIGIN OF BLESSINGS

THE MAIN INTENT OF this book is to make clear who we as human beings are and what our relationship to God is or should be. Certainly we have to start with what the Bible says, namely that God has created us. This, as we have already stated, God did in order to have partners who have free wills that they will submit to his will. God loves his human creatures and shows his love through the mercy and grace that he showers upon us. This mercy and grace we refer to as blessing. Let us remember that while we not only can and should receive blessings, we in turn should pass on the blessings that we have received. Jesus expressed this in the so-called high priestly prayer. He sent his disciples into the world. Their purpose was quite clearly to pass on the blessings, God's loving-kindness, and to proclaim the good news of redemption through his blood. I quote John 17:15–18:

> I do not ask Thee to take them out of the world, but to keep them from the evil one. They are not of the world, even as I am not of the world. Sanctify them in the truth; Thy word is truth. As Thou didst send Me into the world, I also have sent them into the world.

Many people who go to church expect that sometime during the service or as part of the closing formalities of the service a blessing will be pronounced. I wonder how many people really understand what that actually means. I cannot shake the occasional impression that the blessing is supposed to have some mystical significance by which our life will be positively influenced. I am convinced that there is something quite real about the nature of a blessing, and I would like to comment on it.

IN JESUS WE ARE PART OF THE DISPENSING OF GOD'S BLESSING

This is the good news that Jesus brought us, about which the Bible tells us and which we have pointed out several times already: Jesus died in our stead. He took the curse of sin and our guilt upon himself and paid the penalty in full. Now our sins are submerged in the sea of God's great love. Once we have personally accepted this redemptive act through repentance and conversion, we are the children of the living God. We have been cleansed and sanctified. As a response for the acceptance of God's act of mercy and our new birth, we allowed ourselves to be baptized. Now, the question presents itself whether this is all that God expects of us. The answer is no. At that point we have only been born again. But as new children of God, our life with God has only just begun. To stop with the point of conversion and baptism would be equivalent to getting married because the ceremony is so beautiful. But actually this is only where the life of the husband and wife together starts. A similar idea applies to God's children. At the time of rebirth God heaped his favor upon us. Or, to express it differently, we received God's full blessing. But now we have an assignment from God: pass on the blessing; be a blessing. This is why the words of Jesus in the high priestly prayer are so important. John 17:18: "As Thou didst send Me into the world, I also have sent them into the world." We have been blessed, and we are sent out to pass on the blessing.

CONTENT OF THE BLESSING

What actually does it mean, to bless? We really need to address this issue, because when we look around us, it becomes apparent, that not only every person, but every denomination and religion has a different definition for blessing. I will give you the literal translation now, so that we can refer back to it in our discussion. In the Greek and the Latin there are a number of different words available. For right now I'm only going to look at the Latin. From the Latin we get the English word *benediction*.

It is composed of two Latin words, namely *bene* and *dicere*: to say something good, to wish good things. I, who have received "good" from God, can and should pass on this good, namely God's love. In other words, I extend God's favor to others and wish that others would receive God's favor and love.

God in his love and his mercy has so lavishly given that it is difficult to comprehend. In order to make this understandable for us human beings, Jesus tells us the parable of the lost son. The great artist Rembrandt painted a beautiful picture of the event. Three persons are in focus: the younger son, the father, and the older son. The behavior of the younger son, how he squandered the inheritance from his father through his decadent lifestyle and decided to return to his home, is well known. Luke has recorded the entire parable for us in chapter 15 of his Gospel, beginning in verse 11. The impetus for his return was his resolve to confess: "I will get up and go to my father, and will say to him, 'Father, I have sinned against heaven, and in your sight'" (Luke 15:18).

THE FORM OF THE BLESSING

Now we see an incomprehensible act of love. Even before the younger son could utter a word, while he was still at a distance, as soon as the father saw him, the father ran toward him, embraced him, and kissed him. What was it that the father did? He bent down, he "said good" to him, and he laid his favor upon him. That is blessing in its highest form. This is the way Jesus pictured the father for us. Consider what all is included in this act! The old wasted life of the son was buried underneath the father's love, forgotten. He reinstated his son to his previous position. Why? Out of love! We read he "felt compassion for him." Can we imagine that?

This is how Jesus depicts the father for us and wants to tell us that this is the way in which God deals with repentant sinners (yes, us), if only we desire it. But that is not all. His return becomes the cause for celebrating a large feast. In the narrative there is no reference to consultation with the family, nor to the worthiness of the son to participate in a feast, as we in our piety are inclined to expect. For us, it seems humanly impossible to understand the actions of the father, who is a symbolic representation of God. We tend to identify much more readily with the older son who was not at all pleased with his father's conduct.

THE PRECONDITION

What was the prerequisite for the father embracing and kissing his son? There, in that faraway land, the son had beaten his breast and had repented from ruining his life and what he had done to his father. What was the most important item in this scenario? He arose and went. Many people beat their breasts—on many occasions—but never get around to implementing their good resolutions. The son, however, surrendered his life unconditionally to his father and really expected nothing except, hopefully, being tolerated in his father's mercy as a servant.

WHAT DOES THIS PARABLE MEAN TO ME?

God expects nothing less from any of us human beings. Without Jesus we are sinners and remain sinners. Let me express very clearly something that is usually treated as if it were not in the Bible: the sins of which we have repented and which we have confessed, which were taken up by Jesus, are no longer of any interest to God, none whatsoever.

Jesus has died for those sins. In regards to them Jesus has cried out, "It is finished." And there is more: God, the Father, is not going to sit in judgment of sinners. I emphasize: no, he is not. It says in John 5:22: "For not even the Father judges anyone, but He has given all judgment to the Son." The most important statement for us is one that Jesus made in John 6:37: "All that the Father gives Me shall come to Me, and the one who comes to Me I will certainly not cast out." Isn't God incomprehensibly merciful and compassionate toward us, people who are not at all hesitant to take his name in vain, people who, faced with the consequences of our sin, ask, "Why did God allow that?" or when calamity has struck ask, "And where was God?" And yet we live, quite deliberately, as if there is no God.

SELF-RIGHTEOUSNESS AND AFFECTED PIETY SEPARATE US FROM GOD

In the parable the older son comes home from having worked in the field. When he learns about the incomprehensible mercy and generosity of the father toward his brother, he gets angry. He will not enter the house in which the celebration is held. Now, we are quick to say that Jesus is pointing here at the priests and Pharisees but doing so puts us into the position of the older brother vis-à-vis those people. All of us, myself included, are in danger of behaving like the older son. How much pride and self-righteousness we find in us Christians! The older brother appealed to the fact that he has always been a pious and obedient son to his father. He obviously thought that his brother was more deserving of punishment and rejection than a celebration. How do we as Christians treat one another? Instead of blessing each other, instead of bestowing our favor and God's favor on our brothers and sisters, we judge one another and question if some of them are sufficiently worthy to participate in our worship ceremonies. Oh, that we would let the example of the father in this parable speak to us! When the older son angrily refuses to enter into the banqueting hall, the father comes outside to him (he blesses, he says "good" to him) and asks him lovingly and without reproach to rejoice with everyone else. I wish that we had this love of the Father in us. Many Christians step outside when something does not sit well with them. They become angry over the supposed lack of piety.

Here is an example: do we recall the "hippies" of the 1960s? A number of years ago several people who fit that description requested to become members of our Baptist church in America. The church leadership decided to welcome them. Initially a number of church members left the fellowship. Then, when even more "hippies" started attending the worship services, there was a rift in the assembly.

Furthermore, let us look at the many denominations in Protestantism. There is always a group that accuses the others of not being sufficiently pious. Instead of blessing one another we fight about traditions, customs, and formalities. We scrutinize the faith of others to determine whether it measures up to the level of piety we deem appropriate.

AREN'T WE ALL LIKE THE ELDER SON?

Do we now start to see what Jesus was trying to tell us about the older son's attitude in this parable of the prodigal son? It was not Jesus' intent to expose the all-too-human piety of the Pharisees and scribes. All of us stand in danger of drifting from our love of Jesus, our love of God, into a pattern of piety. Recall the accusation that Jesus made toward the rabbis, who were supposed to show people the way to God. Let us look at Matt 23:13: "But woe to you, scribes and Pharisees, hypocrites, because you shut off the kingdom of heaven from men; for you do not enter in yourselves, nor do you allow those who are entering to go in." Evangelical

Christians are prone to do the same thing and consider themselves to be examples of piety.

TOGETHER WITH THE HEAVENS, GOD REJOICES OVER EVERY SINNER WHO COMES HOME

Dear reader, this parable is how Jesus describes the Father for us. And this is God's plan of salvation, as it has been established since the fall. Let us take another close look at the father's actions in this parable. Initially we see the father being on the lookout for his prodigal son. I wish that Rembrandt had painted a picture not only of the return, but also of the father prior to the return, looking, lovingly longing, for his son. He had already forgiven the prodigal son's attitude and actions, because he had started on his way back to the father's house. Yes, this also applies to us. God has sent his Son in our place to the cross, "the cursed tree" and has already pardoned all our sins. He is now merely waiting for us to make our way back to him through Jesus. What are we waiting for? Jesus expresses the Father's forgiveness in Luke 15:7: "I tell you that in the same way, there will be more joy in heaven over one sinner who repents, than over ninety-nine righteous persons who need no repentance." Yes, this refers to our Father in heaven, who wants to rejoice over us.

WE ARE CALLED TO BLESS

Let us allow the entire scenario to impact us. It is addressed to us as well. When a sinner comes to repentance is not the only time that there will be joy in heaven. God wants to rejoice over us always. Our calling is described in 1 Pet 3:9 as "not returning evil for evil, or insult for insult, but giving a blessing instead; for you were called for the very purpose that you might inherit a blessing."

Let us look one more time at Rembrandt's painting. There we see the son kneeling before the father. The father bends down to the son, kisses him, and speaks "good" and does good. This is the best and most impactful picture of God's blessing. God bends down to us and speaks good to us. But let's turn back to what Peter said. We have been called to bless. Can you imagine how many people would be rejoicing if we bent down to them and spoke good to them? Blessing has nothing in common with doing pious deeds. In the parable of the prodigal son we do not read a single pious word. To begin with the father looks for the beloved son. He is waiting. But, and this question is critical to me: did he speak good only to his prodigal son? No, the father went out to the angry older son as well and spoke good to him as well.

We are children of the living God. In Jesus we have been given the gift of the glory of the Father. Now let us take one of the persons in the parable for our personal example. Whose actions are most important to us? Neither the younger nor the older sons are an example to us. Who then? The principal person is the father. We have been called by Jesus to go into all the world, and we are supposed to proclaim the good news. An integral part of this good news is the passing on of the Father's glorious love. And what is included in this call? We need to bend down and speak and do good, just like the Father. As we just read in the verse from Peter, we are called to bless. "Not returning evil for evil, or insult for insult, but giving a blessing instead; for you were called for the very purpose that you might inherit a blessing." And what does it mean to bless? To speak good. Let us seek out those who are shy, on the fringe of our fellowship, put our arms around them, and say to them how much God loves them and what is waiting for them in heaven. That is being a blessing!

LOVE PRODUCES THE JOYFUL DESIRE TO BLESS

To me it is critically important not just to give a proper understanding of blessing, but to see it in action in our daily lives. Just think what it would be like if all members of our fellowship set it as the highest goal to speak good and do good. What a powerful atmosphere of blessing would be the result! Is that achievable? With God's help it is possible. Jesus says to us in John 13:34–35: "A new commandment I give to you, that you love one another, even as I have loved you, that you also love one another. By this all men will know that you are My disciples, if you have love for one another." Once we have accepted Jesus as our Lord, what we read in John 14:23 applies to us: "Jesus answered and said to him, 'If anyone loves Me, he will keep My word; and My Father will love him, and We will come to him, and make Our abode with him.'" When Jesus dwells within us, we can bless one another in his name; we can say and do good.

22

The Return of Jesus Christ

JESUS WILL APPEAR A second time for the salvation of those who wait for him (Heb 9:28). Without fail, when a Christian holiday comes around, various television networks will broadcast "documentaries" concerning the life of Jesus, and, predictably, they will question the veracity of the Bible. Similar critical pieces will often be repeated in news magazines and even newspapers. Some of those critics are atheists. But there are others as well. There are those who are Christians in name only. They were baptized as babies and, since they live in Western Europe (or the United States), have acquired a certain amount of religiosity. Periodically they may roll this heritage out for public display, particularly at Christmas time. As a third group I would like to point out those Christians who, based on the Bible's statements, but in a spirit of doubt raise the question, when will Jesus return? This question is as old as Christianity. Jesus' reply is very clear. Only the Father in Heaven knows the answer. But that Jesus will return is indeed a truth recorded in the Bible.

The church in Thessalonica had questions regarding the resurrection of the dead. Paul, in the fourth chapter of his first Letter to Thessalonica, tries to clarify the issue. Then in chapter 5 he writes, "Now as to the times and the epochs, brethren, you have no need of anything to be written to you. For you yourselves know full well that the day of the Lord will come just like a thief in the night" (1 Thess 5:1–2). Instead of "times and epochs" we could also say "times and events." Then in verse 4 we read, "But you, brethren, are not in darkness, that the day should overtake you like a thief." We will look at this statement in detail in this section.

This sentence does not say that the Thessalonians could predict the coming of the Lord Jesus. Paul did not say that the recipients of his letter were able to calculate when the Lord Jesus would return. Many people, even well-known theologians, have calculated the date and, to no one's surprise, they were wrong.

The well-known theologian Bengel attempted the calculations approximately 250 years ago and, naturally, was incorrect. Many readers will be familiar with the book *Late Great Planet Earth* by Hal Lindsey. He, too, did not pay attention to Jesus' words and wasted a lot of time to calculate and predict Jesus' return in the year in 1988. Sadly, many of his readers joined him in ignoring what Jesus had said and made him a prominent (and financially well-endowed) figure.

The most spectacular event in this regard took place on October 22, 1844, in America. The leader of a pious sect, William Miller, and his assistant, Samuel Snow, gathered their faithful on a mountain top. They were dressed in white clothing and waited there for Jesus' appearance. Naturally, Jesus failed to appear. Now, they should have repented. But they did not do that. Instead their apostle William Miller proclaimed that Jesus had left the throne of grace and entered the heavenly sanctuary. His followership has grown, and his disciples are now found all over the world. Today they are known as Seventh Day Adventists. Similar events occurred in Germany as well. The "Jannowitz Ascension" comes to mind.

The words of the Lord Jesus in Mark 13:32 apply to the Thessalonians just as much as to us today: "But of that day or hour no one knows, not even the angels in heaven, nor the Son, but the Father alone." What is the significance of the reference to "living in the light" and not in "darkness" (1 Thess 5:5)?

A WORD OF ENCOURAGEMENT

The announcement of the arrival of the Lord as a thief in the night is not a threat to the church of the redeemed but the hope on which our faith rests. Consequently this statement should not lead to fear. In 1 Thess 4:17 we read of the rapture of the saints to Jesus. That is the only place where the Bible talks about rapture. The schemes of interpretation that arose out of this statement, with their threats of "being left behind" have no biblical foundation. The second coming of the Lord Jesus is not a threat, but rather the climax of our faith and hope. Hebrews 9:28: "[S]o Christ also, having been offered once to bear the sins of many, shall appear a second time for salvation without reference to sin, to those who eagerly await Him." In his Letter to the Thessalonians Paul says, "Then we who are alive and remain shall be caught up together with them in the clouds to meet the Lord in the air, and thus we shall always be with the Lord. Therefore comfort one another with these words" (1 Thess 4:17–18). The thought of the return of our Lord is supposed to give us great joy.

LIVING IN THE HOPE OF THE LORD'S RETURN IS A GIFT OF GRACE

Let us rejoice in it! Paul says, "You, however, dear brothers, are not in darkness, that the day he returns will come upon you as a thief." In other words, this encouragement that applied to the Christians in the first century applies just as well to those living in the twenty-first century. There is no reason that we should live in fear and tension that we might be surprised by Christ's return. Let me rephrase it this way: we will not be taken by surprise by Jesus second coming. To those who are waiting for him, his return is our salvation. Christians always live in the spirit of Advent, that is, expectation.

These verses are so easily misunderstood because the concept "thief in the night" expresses an event the timing of which cannot be predicted and, therefore, cannot be prepared for. But that is not what Paul is saying. Can the timing of the second coming be predicted? No. Can we be prepared for the second coming? Yes. There is a big difference in the two conclusions. Indeed in the New Testament there are many references to the return of the Lord. Some say that it will come as a thief in the night; see for example 1 Thess 5:2 or Matt 24:43, as well as 2 Pet 3:10. The question is, to whom will Jesus return as a thief in the night?

To the Christians, to Jesus' church, the return of the Lord will not be as a lightning bolt out of the clear sky that catches them unprepared, like a thief in the night. Paul makes the reason for positive understanding quite clear to us in 1 Thess 5:4–6: "But you, brethren, are not in darkness, that the day should overtake you like a thief; for you are all sons of light and sons of day. We are not of night nor of darkness; so then let us not sleep as others do, but let us be alert and sober."

Let me say it again: we cannot calculate the date of the second coming of the Lord, but we can be prepared. Not only can we, but we should be preparing ourselves for the Lord's return.

THE LORD HIMSELF HELPS US TO BECOME PREPARED

In Matt 24 and Luke 21 Jesus himself points our attention to the proper direction. He alerts us to several events that should help us to believe and to watch. In Luke 21:25, he says, "And there will be signs in sun and moon and stars, and upon the earth dismay among nations, in perplexity at the roaring of the sea and the waves." And then he says further in Matt 24:7, "For nation will rise against nation, and kingdom against kingdom, and in various places there will be famines and earthquakes." Now notice what Jesus adds: "But all these things are merely the beginning of birth pangs" (Matt 24:8). Then he becomes even more explicit. When war and terror, starvation and earthquakes increase, since these are called the beginning of the birth pains, we can expect that there will be a continuation and an increase.

Every woman who is a mother knows that from the beginning of birth pangs the frequency and intensity increases until eventually the birth is accomplished. When the first birth pangs occur, she knows, since she is pregnant, that the time of the birth is drawing near. Whether it will occur in a few minutes, several hours, or even days, she is not sure. But let us ask the relevant question: does the birth of the child come upon the pregnant woman like a thief in the night? No. When the birth pangs begin the expectant mother is anticipating their continuation until the birth takes place.

Jesus himself gives his church signs that, like birth pangs, indicate that the final days before his return are here. But he does not give us any indicators that will pinpoint the exact moment when he returns. But his church is not totally unprepared and ignorant. He will not come for his church like a thief in the night. Otherwise what would be the sense of Jesus' words in Luke 21:28: "But when these things begin to take place, straighten up and lift up your heads, because your redemption is drawing near"?

The "last days" began with Jesus' victory. In his farewell words Jesus said, "Now judgment is upon this world; now the ruler of this world shall be cast out" (John 12:31). In a parallel passage we read in Rev 12:12: "For this reason, rejoice, O heavens and you who dwell in them. Woe to the earth and the sea, because the devil has come down to you, having great wrath, knowing that he has only a short time."

As Christians we must be so familiar with God's word, the Bible, so that we can recognize the signs of the times and act according to the Lord's instructions. Mark 13:28–29: "Now learn the parable from the fig tree: when its branch has already become tender, and puts forth its leaves, you know that summer is near. Even so, you too, when you see these things happening, recognize that He is near, right at the door." For whom will Jesus' second coming be as sudden as the appearance of a thief in the night? For those who are not prepared, who are not alert or waiting for him.

COMMENTS ABOUT THE "DAY OF THE LORD" IN THE OLD TESTAMENT

For those Christians who are well familiar with the Old Testament, when they think of "the day of the Lord," this expression is often associated with the threat of God's judgment day. In the Old Testament there is a lot of talk of God's day of judgment. But what does Jesus say in John 5:22? "For not even the Father judges anyone, but He has given all judgment to the Son." For those who have accepted Jesus' redemption, he has already paid the penalty on the cross of Calvary. Jesus took the judgment upon himself in our stead. John 3:18: "He who believes in Him is not judged; he who does not believe has been judged already, because he has not believed in the name of the only begotten Son of God." As I have said before, the second coming of the Lord is no threat to us as Christians, rather it is the greatest of hope. What hope would we otherwise have? Mine is that "Jesus comes to those who are waiting for Him for their salvation" (Heb 9:28).

The statements "for just as the lightning comes from the east, and flashes even to the west, so shall the coming of the Son of Man be" and "then all the tribes of the earth will mourn" (Matt 24:27, 30) clearly refer to the unbelievers. The threat that is contained in them does not apply to the church of the Lord Jesus Christ. For us, Jesus' return completes our salvation!

WHICH OF THE EVENTS THAT JESUS PREDICTED IN MATTHEW 24 AND LUKE 21 HAVE ALREADY OCCURRED?

To begin with, there is in the destruction of Jerusalem and the temple, which occurred in the year 70 and is a historic fact. But we need to go beyond those events and see how they fit into the gospel writer's reproduction of the words of Jesus. I have shown how all of these matters come together whenever I have given presentations on the origin of the gospel of Matthew. Let me summarize the highlights.

Matthew collected notes and summaries concerning Jesus' teaching. But he did not necessarily present them in a chronological order—in actual historical sequence—but rather conceptually; that is, he presented them in topical form. He could have called it "Five Speeches of Our Lord" because that is actually the arrangement of the Gospel of Matthew. There are five main speeches by Jesus, surrounded by narratives. The most important statement that is relevant to us here is contained in the fifth speech, which is recorded in chapter 24 of Matthew's Gospel. We read in Matt 24:15-17: "Therefore when you see the ABOMINATION OF DESOLATION which was spoken of through Daniel the prophet [Dan 9:27, 11:31], standing in the holy place (let the reader understand), then let those who are in Judea flee to the mountains; let him who is on the housetop not go down to get the things out that are in his house." To whom was this addressed?

The concern of Jesus, as well as Matthew, was the protection of his church. Now, if we want to place this event into a chronological sequence, the question that we should ask immediately is where the "abomination of desolation" is supposed to take place, and we know that it refers to the "holy place."

"In the holy place." To the people living at that time this would be a clear reference to the temple. Does this temple still exist? No, it was destroyed together with the city of Jerusalem in the year AD 70, which means that it is an event that took place two thousand years ago. The second question: are we in the land of Judah? This we can quite easily answer, no. We have historical documents that tell us what has happened. As the Roman army approached the city of Jerusalem before the year AD 69 those living in and around Jerusalem gathered behind the protective walls of the city. Their actions, in disregard of Jesus' warning, led to their ruin and demise. Only the Christian church remembered the words of warning of the Lord Jesus, keeping in mind the promise that the Holy Spirit would remind them of Jesus' teachings. Under the leadership of Bishop Simeon they left the city of Jerusalem and moved into the Greek city Pella south of the Sea of Galilee. There they escaped from death and slavery. This has already occurred; it is history. There are several historical documents in which these events were recorded. In particular, the Roman-Jewish historian Flavius Josephus wrote about these events.

WHAT ELSE HAS ALREADY OCCURRED? FALSE CHRISTS AND FALSE PROPHETS

False Christs have been a constant presence in the history of Judaism. The *Encylopedia Judaica* lists dozens of them under the entry, "Pseudo-messiahs." Most of them had a few followers, but little impact, but two of them caused a great amount of damage.

After the fall of Jerusalem to the Romans there was still a small Jewish state. The Jewish leader Simon Kochbar declared himself to be the Jewish Messiah and gained many followers. He called himself Bar Kochbar (son of the stars). Bar Kochbar stormed Jerusalem, and in the years AD 132 to 135 he waged war against the Romans. In AD 134 he was captured by the Roman commander Severus, and from AD 135 until 1948 there was no independent Jewish state.

There were quite a few subsequent self-proclaimed messiahs, but the next one who gained the attention of the whole world was the Jew Sabbatai Zevi. He was born in Smyrna, Turkey, in the seventeenth century. A number of his followers saw in his conduct messianic signs. A young man by the name of Nathan of Gaza publicly proclaimed him to be the Messiah in the year 1665. Many Jews gained hope, and a wave of repentance broke out among the Jews. When Sabbatai traveled to Constantinople in the year 1666, with the intent of proselytizing the Turkish Sultan to Judaism, the Jewish people reached a state of euphoria. However, the Sultan arrested him and promised to spare his life, provided Sabbatai accepted Islam, and he did. He became a Muslim, which unsurprisingly created a sense of despair among many Jews who had put all of their faith in him. Again, this event is also recorded history.

Having taken note of these false messiahs, we can return to the first letter of the apostle Paul to the Thessalonians. First Thessalonians 5:3–4: "While they are saying, 'Peace and safety!' then destruction will come upon them suddenly like birth pangs upon a woman with child; and they shall not escape. But you, brethren, are not in darkness, that the day should overtake you like a thief." As I already said at the beginning, the return of the Lord for his own, namely those redeemed by his blood, will not come as a thief, but only for those who did not think that any of these matters needed to be taken seriously. So the Apostle Paul calls out to the Thessalonians:

> But since we are of the day, let us be sober, having put on the breastplate of faith and love, and as a helmet, the hope of salvation. For God has not destined us for wrath, but for obtaining salvation through our Lord Jesus Christ, who died for us, that whether we are awake or asleep, we may live together with Him. Therefore encourage one another, and build up one another, just as you also are doing. (1 Thess 5:8–11)

A BRIEF SUMMARY

The return of our Lord is not a threat. It should not lead to tension and fear but rather spark the hope and joy of being privileged to meet our Jesus. For Jesus' disciples and his church, the date of his return cannot be calculated. Only the Father knows the day and hour. The angels do not know it, not even the Son. Jesus' disciples and his church should be prepared, watching, sober, and clothed with the breastplate of faith and love and the helmets of hope of our salvation.

23

Before the Judgment Seat of Christ

BASIC CONSIDERATIONS

I HAVE ALREADY POINTED out several times that it is my personal priority to proclaim the fact that the Bible is God's revelation to my fellow human beings. However, we must keep clearly in view that the entire Bible gives us the plan of salvation and a historical record of God's dealings with us. Anyone who wants to be informed and possibly intends to discuss these issues must be familiar with the entire Bible and keep in mind its message in its entirety. To sit down and read the Bible like a novel does not even begin to give a proper overview because the Bible really is not just one book. It consists of sixty-six separate books. Only when I understand the content of each individual book and how it relates to the others will it be possible for me to comprehend the truth that is contained in it. That does not mean that I have to understand the entire Bible in each specific point, such as prophecies and narratives, in order to become a child of God. For salvation I only need to understand and personally accept that Jesus died on the cross of Calvary for my sins. However, it is different if I am trying to determine dates, chronologies, and prophesied events that have yet to occur. Any statement or doctrine on those topics must account for the entirety of the Scriptures in order to avoid erroneous conclusions and possible heresy. Over the years there have been a lot of unsupported sensationalistic speculations that, unfortunately, have been asserted publicly, published, and even taught from lecterns and pulpits.

The Bible informs us of God's plan of salvation and records for us the history of God's dealings with us human beings. The climax of the plan of salvation and its historical development is the incarnation of God's Son. He arrived on earth, just like all people, as a baby. According to God's will, he was given the name Jesus. As he was a person of the Trinity, he himself had no sin within him and never committed any sin. However, he made himself equal to us in that he took our sins upon himself. As an external sign of this fact Jesus had himself baptized by John the Baptist in the waters of the Jordan River. He took his place in the queue of people who acknowledged and repented of their sins and as a sign of the washing away of their sin allowed themselves to be baptized. Taking up and then bearing our sins Jesus continued to walk on this earth for three years, was condemned as a criminal, and paid the penalty of our sin and guilt on the cross in our stead. Jesus did not come to condemn but to save. That is the good news. In anticipation of the speculations about God's final judgment, at which so many people would like to justify themselves before God, I want to point emphatically to Jesus' words in John 12:47: "And if anyone hears My sayings, and does not keep them, I do not judge him; for I did not come to judge the world, but to save the world."

This good news should be the primary content of all messages from pulpits and Christian writings, as well as in Bible study groups. However, it is an undeniable fact that today many sermons, which should be proclamations of the good news, deal with political and social issues. Even apologetics—the scrutiny of the purity and the defense of the validity and veracity of God's word—is given little time. Scientific research has provided us with many clear proofs of the genuineness of the Bible. As a consequence of the publication of scientific reports, especially in the field of archaeology, many portions of the biblical narratives have been validated. Today we can say that the Bible is true! Nobody has yet provided proof that either the spiritual content or the historical narratives of the Bible contain any errors. On the contrary, through their efforts to prove that the biblical narratives are untenable, many scientists have provided us with proof of the veracity of the Bible. Let me remind you, dear reader, that honest doubts do not constitute scientific proof. I already addressed this issue in chapter 17, "Scientific Critique of the Bible."

Fundamentally, the Bible has not been written as a history book. That does not mean that the historical events that the Bible presents are not based on facts. The entire Bible contains the plan of salvation and the historical record of God's dealings with humans. It records for us the good news with the climax that Jesus paid the penalty for our guilt and sin in our stead. Jesus came not to judge but to save. That is why above I already cited what Jesus said in John 12:47. Let me summarize it this way: "Jesus came out of love and not out of anger; he became a human being and died in our stead on the cross." To me this side of the matter appears especially important. Many times when the gospel is proclaimed, there is an emphasis on the horrible judgment from which we need to be saved. As a result many are coaxed into the church by fear. I repeat that it is God's grace that wants to lead us to repentance. In this way we become children of God.

WHO WILL BE JUDGED?

On many occasions Christian have debated the question as to whether all people, including Jesus' disciples, will have to appear before the judgment seat of Christ. There is no question that according to Phil 2:10–11 "that at the name of Jesus EVERY KNEE SHOULD BOW, of those who are in heaven, and on earth, and under the earth, and that every tongue should confess that Jesus Christ is Lord, to the glory of God the Father." This statement establishes that at the return of Jesus everyone will be present. But there still remain the questions: What will the role of Jesus' disciples be when he returns? Where will we stand? We know from the record of the encounter that Jesus had with the Pharisee Nicodemus that whoever believes in the Son of God will not have to face judgment (John 3:18). We will examine this issue more closely.

FOUNDATION FOR OUR DISCUSSION

To make it quite clear from the outset, I want to state that the Bible, and only the Bible, will be the basis for my deliberations. Many misunderstandings and ignorance of doctrinal issues arise from the fact that people do not read the Bible. Additionally, much doctrinal error and downright heretical teaching stems from people interpreting the Scriptures to suit their own purposes. These are well-established facts.

In 1970 the book *The Late Great Planet Earth* by Hal Lindsey was published in the United States. Many Christians read this book, and his theories gained a large number of followers. But he himself failed his own test, which he stated in chapter 2, "When Is a Prophet a Prophet?" On the basis of Deut 18:22 he quite correctly wrote that you can recognize a false prophet by the fact that his predictions are not fulfilled, even if it is only a single false prediction. Lindsey's prophecies, for the most part, did not come true. Most likely he had read the Bible but did not make it the foundation of his thinking and writings. Even though this fact is quite obvious, his books are still best sellers in the United States.

I have deliberately not referred back to various philosophical and otherwise speculative argumentations, for the Bible tells us everything that we need to know. It informs us as to who we, human beings, are and clearly outlines our relationship to God and to Jesus. To restate it one more time: I, myself, have to read the Bible and to treasure God's written word in my heart. Obviously, now and then, I will read other books. But when it comes to the interpretation of the holy Scriptures, everybody should take to heart and do what is written about the Jews in Berea: "Now these were more noble-minded than those in Thessalonica, for they received the word with great eagerness, examining the Scriptures daily, to see whether these things were so" (Acts 17:11).

COMMON UNDERSTANDING OF THE FINAL JUDGMENT

In the minds of most Christians, the return of our Lord Jesus is connected with the judgment. The idea is based on 2 Cor 5:10: "For we must all appear before the judgment seat of Christ, that each one may be recompensed for his deeds in the body, according to what he has done, whether good or bad."

This verse sparks the concept of the all-encompassing final judgment. It leads further to the thought that everyone, whether they are Christians or not, will be judged according to their works. Add to that the well-known statement out of the book of Revelation: "And I saw the dead, the great and the small, standing before the throne, and books were opened; and another book was opened, which is the book of life; and the dead were judged from the things which were written in the books, according to their deeds" (Rev 20:12).

To the superficial reader it appears clear that the previously cited Bible verses combine to give us the following conclusion: when Jesus returns we will all stand before Judge Jesus with our "works." Woe to us if we do not have enough good works. This warning apparently applies to the disciples of Jesus as well. But this is a misunderstanding. It does not apply to the disciples.

Such improperly tying together of verses and thoughts only occurs in someone who is not familiar with the overall themes of the Bible. It is used by certain preachers and evangelists who want to create fear in their listeners. Bible translators, also, contribute to this uncertainty. Certain preachers love to quote the statement in Phil 2:12:

> So then, my beloved, just as you have always obeyed, not as in my presence only, but now much more in my absence, work out your salvation with fear and trembling. (NASB)

> Dear friends, you always followed my instructions when I was with you. And now that I am away, it is even more important. Work hard to show the results of your salvation, obeying God with deep reverence and fear. (NLT)

Putting these verses into practice certainly seems to require work. Salvation is obtained by hard work and fierce struggle with fear and trembling. Granted, the word choice in any given translation is never easy. This is one of those situations. In the Letter to the Philippians the Greek word *meta* is translated as "with." The same word can be translated as "with," "in company with," "among"; "by," "in"; "on the side of"; "against"; "after," "behind."[1] In order to lead people to the point of repentance, fear and trembling may perhaps be expeditious, but it does not lead to a joyful life of discipleship.

Once I have become a child of God, my hope and trust rest in my Lord's love. From creating fear it is only a small step to indulgences and piety through which we want to, and must, earn God's favors. But that is not the joyous message of the Bible! That is not the good news of Jesus who has redeemed and purchased us. In writing this I want to proclaim the true message of the Bible, which the song writer Johann L. K. Allendorf has captured in the following words:

> Jesus has come, our joy's loving fountain
> Alpha, Omega are eternally here
> Godhead and mankind united together
> Oh, Creator of all, you have drawn near

---

1. B. M. Newman, *Concise Greek-English Dictionary of the New Testament* (Stuttgart, Germany: Deutsche Bibelgesellschaft; United Bible Societies, 1993), 114.

Heaven and earth proclaim to the nations
Jesus has come, our joy's loving fountain[2]

In order to fully understand this idea we want to take a closer look at the miserable, unfortunate position all of humankind is in.

THE HUMAN PERSON, AS CREATED BY GOD, WAS GOOD BUT WAS LED ASTRAY INTO SIN

The Bible tells us that God created us in his image, and we read in Gen 1:31: "And God saw all that He had made, and behold, it was very good . . ." Yes, even human beings were good in God's eyes, very good.

But then came temptation through Satan's question, which even today continues to lead people astray. We read, "Indeed, has God said?" And just that quickly Adam became a sinner and came under the curse that God had foretold. Adam and Eve were driven away, out of the garden of Eden and into the darkness and sin of this world. And, oh, what a mire this world has to offer!

How did human nature change from before to after falling into sin and under God's pronounced curse? Initially there did not appear to be any significant differences. Adam and Eve continued right on living, as people still do today. Right? Sure they were still alive, but now only as creatures. The Spirit of God had been withdrawn from them. The truth is that the curse, "You shall surely die!" was fulfilled through the loss of God's Spirit. God had withdrawn from his human creatures that part of the personality that made them into special godly beings, namely the presence of the Holy Spirit. And in that state they continued to exist, as we do today, as created earthly beings, but as godly beings, they had died. This is the reason why there is such little difference between us and other creatures, the animals. And still today, as long as we are without Jesus and unredeemed, that continues to be the situation.

For several centuries now theologians have promulgated an erroneous concept. It is called original sin and is attributed to the church father Augustine. We did not receive any original sin from our forefathers, as though it were a "thing" passed down from generation to generation. It was not the addition of something, but rather the lack of something (or better, someone), that was the consequence of the fall.

---

2. Translated by Wolf Corduan.

We, as human beings, are missing something without Jesus, namely the Holy Spirit. That is why people outside of God's family, as I have already repeatedly stated, resemble animals and behave even worse than such. Let me illustrate this with an example: My forefathers were aristocrats. They were titled and were called Baron von Lettow. In an inheritance dispute one of my ancestors lost his nobility and therewith the title. From then on my great-grandfather's name was Corduan. The "von" designating aristocracy was no longer part of the name. It would be silly to say that I had inherited the disgrace of the common bourgeoisie. Nonsense! The reality is that there is something that I did not inherit. One of my ancestors lost something that was no longer available to my parents. I can only say that I do not have a type of nobility because I have no right to it. One of my ancestors lost that right. The only way that I could regain such nobility would be through adoption by an aristocrat. So, let me underscore it again: we have no original sin as a substance, which, according to the writings of some theologians can be ceremonially washed away by sprinkling an infant. Such an external act, which the infant does not even knowingly experience, cannot wash away anything. Human beings without Jesus lack the Holy Spirit, which God gives us at the time of conversion as a gift.

The Bible tells us quite clearly who we are if we have not experienced rebirth and received the Holy Spirit. In the eyes of God we are corpses. In Eph 2:1 Paul writes to the Christians in Ephesus that they were "dead" before grace reached them. We find the same assertions in Eph 2:5 and Col 2:13.

Since we are dead before God, we have to reacquire life; that is, according to God's plan of salvation, "we must be born again." At the time of rebirth God gives us the status of children, who can bring glory to God and his name. We ourselves are part of God's glory, trophies of his grace. Jesus says to Nicodemus in John 3:3, "Truly, truly, I say to you, unless one is born again, he cannot see the kingdom of God."

THE NEW MAN AND OUR STATUS AS GOD'S CHILDREN

This truth raises the question as to what our status as God's children will be in the heavenly community. What about the saying of Martin Luther? "We are beggars, that is true!" The Bible has a number of things to say about our position. In order that we will all think along the same lines, I want to call to mind some things I have said before. So, please, bear with me as I backtrack for a moment.

The living God, the Creator of heaven and earth, who did not spare his only begotten Son, but offered him up for us all, will, with Jesus, give us everything necessary to be a part of the family of God (Rom 8:32). We can already experience peace and security here on earth. After the resurrection we will enjoy eternal life with Jesus and the other saints. Yes, we will not simply be placed back into the old status that humans had before Adam's sin. We will be like Jesus, as he is. That is more than just being a pardoned sinner who has just been released from prison, much more. We have been called to be kings and priests (see Rev 1:5–6, 20:6). Furthermore, Paul writes in 1 Cor 6:2: "Or do you not know that the saints will judge the world? . . ." And in the following verse he writes that we will even judge angels. That is more than simply having fellowship with God and living under his guidance and direction.

In John 14:23 Jesus promised that he and God the Father will make their dwelling in us when we are reborn. In this fashion, according to Rom 5:5, we will receive the Holy Spirit, with whom, according to Eph 1:13, we will be sealed. That means that we have been selected from out of this world and separated from those who are without God for the purpose of a holy life with Jesus and with God. The holy Scriptures refer to this as "saints by calling" (see 1 Cor 1:2) or "holy and beloved" (Col 3:12). According to Eph 1:13, the sign of our sealing is the Holy Spirit. For the natural person this is invisible (John 14:14–17). He marks us and protects us from the attacks of Satan. An example that might help us understand this would be the branding of cattle and horses. Through the branding sign of their owner, cattle and horses are identified as his property. We are marked as property of Jesus, of God through the Holy Spirit. When that happens, we witness the fulfillment of the promise Jesus gives us in John 14:20: "In that day you shall know that I am in My Father, and you in Me, and I in you." This tells us of one of the major aspects of the gospel: we have become part of Jesus (his body) and are recognizable as such. What that means is clarified for us by the apostle Paul in 2 Cor 5:17: "Therefore if any man is in Christ, he is a new creature; the old things passed away; behold, new things have come."

THE CONSEQUENCES OF BEING A PART OF JESUS'S BODY

We discover the consequences of this fact when we read Rom 6:4–5: "Therefore we have been buried with Him through baptism into death, in order that as Christ was raised from the dead through the glory of the Father, so we too might walk in newness of life. For if we have become united with Him in the likeness of His death, certainly we shall be also in the likeness of His resurrection."

The next step is outlined for us in Col 3:3–4: "For you have died and your life is hidden with Christ in God. When Christ, who is our life, is revealed, then you also will be revealed with Him in glory." In other words, if I have become united with Jesus Christ into one body, that is, if I am part of God's family, then I am dead to the temporal things of this world (Rom 7:5–6). I have been securely placed (hidden; Col 3:3) into Christ, or as Paul expresses it in Rom 11, I have been grafted into the olive tree of the people of God. There, in Jesus, I am safe from and hidden from the crafty attacks of Satan; I am kept and protected in my loving Lord. All this I have to accept and remember by faith. A subsequent, appropriate walk in faith and the continuous communion through prayer are signs of living in Jesus. However, as I stated at the beginning of this chapter, after I become a part of Jesus' body, I am more than just a forgiven sinner who belongs to God's people. I am quite concerned that this difference will not be obscured.

We need to remember that the Christian life begins with conversion and rebirth and is an ongoing process of growth. It is not a condition we obtain only after "a blessed departure," by which people mean after someone has died in the proper circumstances. There is no such thing as a "blessed departure." Either I am in Christ, or I am not. If I am in Christ, then death is only the end of life on earth in this body. My condition, "hidden" in Jesus will remain the same as I transition from this life into life eternal. I am kept in Jesus until the sound of the trumpet of God, which will raise me from the dead, to be raptured to meet the Lord in the clouds (1 Thess 4:13–17).

TRANSITORY WAITING PLACE FOR THE DEAD

In the original texts, the place where the dead will be kept is referred to as *hades*, which can be translated as "abode of the dead." The Scriptures do not say much about it. On the basis of Jesus' teaching of the parable of the rich man and poor Lazarus (Luke 16:19–31), as well as some other references in the New Testament, we can conclude that there is such a place in which we will await our final resurrection in Jesus. Earlier I alluded to Paul's comments in First Thessalonians, and I will now cite this passage in full (1 Thess 4:13–17):

> But we do not want you to be uninformed, brethren, about those who are asleep, that you may not grieve, as do the rest who have no hope. For if we believe that Jesus died and rose again, even so God will bring with Him those who have fallen asleep in Jesus. For this we say to you by the word of the Lord, that we who are alive, and remain until the coming of the Lord, shall not precede those who have fallen asleep. For the Lord Himself will descend from heaven with a shout, with the voice of the archangel, and with the trumpet of God; and the dead in Christ shall rise first. Then we who are alive and remain shall be caught up together with them in the clouds to meet the Lord in the air, and thus we shall always be with the Lord.

Another passage that we can look at in this context is Col 3:3–4: "For you have died and your life is hidden with Christ in God. When Christ, who is our life, is revealed, then you also will be revealed with Him in glory."

From these two just-quoted Bible references, we can clearly see that there is a special place in the abode of the dead where those who are part of Jesus are sheltered and kept. We will be called out of this abode of the dead, if we are hidden in Jesus, when Jesus calls us to himself through the trump of God. Let us remember, and this is critical, that only in this life can we become part of Jesus.

In order to prevent possible misunderstanding I want to reemphasize that there is such a temporary waiting place according to the Bible. The Bible, however, does not say that God and Jesus are obligated to send everybody to that location. Elijah and Enoch were called directly into God's presence. To the thief on the cross, Jesus said, "[T]oday you will be with Me in Paradise." From the Bible we learn a number of things that we can assert with reasonable confidence. We know that God keeps his promises, but sometimes there may be more than one way in which he can keep his word, and we must be careful not to try to dictate to God the exact way in which he must deal with individuals.

THE SECOND APPEARANCE OF JESUS CHRIST

Our apostolic confession (or creed) is good and correct. However, it does not contain all the details of our total Christian faith. It contains the statement that "Jesus is sitting at the right hand of the Father and will return to judge the living and the dead." Now let me ask this question: when Jesus returns for his second appearance, will he indeed come as judge of the earth? The Bible gives us a clear answer of "no." Initially Jesus will not come as judge, but as our salvation, to gather the members of his body into glory. The Bible says quite clearly in Heb 9:28: "[S]o Christ also, having been offered once to bear the sins of many, shall appear a second time for salvation without reference to sin, to those who eagerly await Him." Let us also recollect Jesus' statement in John 3:17: "For God did not send the Son into the world to judge the world, but that the world should be saved through Him."

The judging of the living and the dead will occur in a second act, namely when we are already with Jesus. This sequence corresponds directly to what Jesus says to Nicodemus in John 3:18: "He who believes in Him is not judged; he who does not believe has been judged already, because he has not believed in the name of the only begotten Son of God."

The Bible leaves no room for doubt: the one who is in Christ will not enter into the judgment! This we read in John 5:24, where Jesus says, "Truly, truly, I say to you, he who hears My word, and believes Him who sent Me, has eternal life, and does not come into judgment, but has passed out of death into life." Furthermore, it becomes clear from Rom 6 that in Christ we have already been judged, died, and resurrected.

Now we still have to account for the Apostle Paul's statement in 2 Cor 5:10: "For we must all appear before the judgment seat of Christ, that each one may be recompensed for his deeds in the body, according to what he has done, whether good or bad." This passage has enticed many theologians to connect this statement with the judgment of the world. But the context does not allow this interpretation. The Greek word *bēma* is most often translated in the New Testament with judgment seat. It's most basic meaning is "step," or "a step up," hence it can have the meaning of a dais or platform that required steps to ascend, such as a tribunal. A magistrate would address an assembly from a chair placed on the structure.[3] The idea here is that after the resurrection all the re-

---

3. W. Arndt, F. W. Danker, and W. Bauer, *A Greek-English Lexicon of the New Testament and Other Early Christian Literature*, 3rd ed. (Chicago: University of Chicago Press, 2000), 175.

deemed will stand before the throne of grace in glory. Here they will receive their new body and such dignities as the Lord Jesus appropriates to them. Under no circumstances does this refer to the world judgment day. Those who have been justified by faith have already been redeemed and will enter into glory with him. Even while still living here on earth they have already been set free by Jesus' sacrifice.

Due to this misunderstanding, many theologians draw an analogy to the parable of the talents in Matt 25 and talk about an awards ceremony for the disciples of Jesus. Additionally the passage in Second Corinthians talks about our appearance and revelation before our Lord. Nothing in the language suggests court proceedings or intimates that this is a time at which a separation of the lost from the redeemed occurs. As repeatedly stated above, our salvation has already been accomplished, and in Jesus we are his saints, who will, according to 1 Cor 6:2, judge the world.

I would like to clarify the concept of the so-called judgment day a little further, and hopefully that will make it clear in everyone's mind. When there is mention of Jesus' (second) coming in the New Testament, the word used in the original manuscripts is *parousia* (presence). An example of this is found in 1 Thess 4:15. Now, to us this Greek word does not mean much, but the people living in the Roman Empire understood it quite well. As we know, the New Testament was written in the days of the Roman Empire, sent to and read by the people living then. I want to illustrate the meaning of this Greek word by an example from the days of the Roman Empire.

The Roman general, and later caesar, Titus had received an assignment from Caesar Vespasian to quell the insurrection of the Jews in Jerusalem. He accomplished his task after a long and bitter campaign, in which the Jews suffered a horrible and bloody defeat. A messenger brought the news of the victory to Rome: Palestine was again under Roman control. The victorious general was still in Jerusalem. It took quite a long time for him to bring his victorious troops back to Rome, about one year. But then came the long-awaited moment. A herald announced: in three days Titus would enter Rome with his victorious troops. Then what happened?

Well, the entire city of Rome prepared for the arrival and welcoming of the victor and his army. On the day of his arrival they gave him an almost incredible reception. Two columns met, that of Titus and his victorious troops, and the column of the Roman citizens who had marched out to greet the victorious soldiers. Then both columns together marched into the city of Rome to celebrate the victory. People were beside themselves for joy. The entire event, the arrival of the victors, the marching out, the greeting and walking back of the citizens with the troops and the celebration that followed were called *parousia* or the "presence of the victor." The victors brought with them the conquered people as trophies. Then there followed a judgment and most of the vanquished were usually killed.

In the same manner Jesus will appear the next time he comes. It all will begin with the *parousia* of the Victor, who arrives with and for those who are part of his body. Then ensues for the entire world what we read in Rev 1:7: "BEHOLD, HE IS COMING WITH THE CLOUDS, and every eye will see Him, even those who pierced Him; and all the tribes of the earth will mourn over Him. Even so. Amen."

THE PLACE OF GOD'S CHILDREN IN THE JUDGMENT BY JESUS

From the foregoing example we can see without difficulty that the soldiers of the victorious general will be present at the judgment following the war. But obviously their function is different from that of the vanquished; they are there to judge, not to be judged.

This is the *parousia* of our Lord Jesus. First comes the great moment in which we will see the victorious Son of God in all his majesty and glory. It is described for us in 1 John 3:2: "Beloved, now we are children of God, and it has not appeared as yet what we shall be. We know that, when He appears, we shall be like Him, because we shall see Him just as He is."

Yes! When we shall see Jesus' *parousia*, we will become as he is. Then we will also be of heavenly nature. I cannot even imagine what that will be like. But the Bible says, "And Jesus said to them, 'Truly I say to you, that you who have followed Me, in the regeneration when the Son of Man will sit on His glorious throne, you also shall sit upon twelve thrones, judging the twelve tribes of Israel'" (Matt 19:28).

Initially this was said to the disciples who actually belonged to the people of Israel. But it is also said to us, "Or do you not know that the saints will judge the world? And if the world is judged by you, are you not competent to constitute the smallest law courts?" (1 Cor 6:2).

CONCLUDING STATEMENT

We will now bring our discussion to a conclusion, but not without first asking a very important question and providing the answer: What is the significance of this entire presentation for me, for you, for our walk of faith? Is it idle curiosity? No! When my faith rests on the firm foundation of the Bible, the word of God, then I know that in life and in death, especially in death, I am resting securely in my Lord Jesus. "I am convinced that neither death, nor life, nor angels, nor principalities, nor things present, nor things to come, nor powers, nor height, nor depth, nor any other created thing, shall be able to separate us from the love of God, which is in Christ Jesus our Lord." (Rom 8:38–39). These truths are very clear, when we stay on the foundation of the Bible, when we do not allow ourselves to be driven into the arms of idle speculators and their endless succession of books. Let me repeat, the Bible does not answer all of our questions in full. Especially, in regards to our Lord's return and most importantly as to the day and hour, it is silent. But the Bible assures us, we who have committed ourselves to his care, that he will call us in time to be present at the marriage supper of the Lamb (Rev 19: 6–9).

I would like to close with the promise that Jesus, our Lord, gave us in John 10:27–29:

> My sheep hear My voice, and I know them, and they follow Me; and I give eternal life to them, and they shall never perish; and no one shall snatch them out of My hand. My Father, who has given them to Me, is greater than all; and no one is able to snatch them out of the Father's hand.

Let me add: neither in life nor in death.

www.ingramcontent.com/pod-product-compliance
Lightning Source LLC
Chambersburg PA
CBHW062028220426
43662CB00010B/1516